J

School Library Media Centers
in the 21st Century

School Library Media Centers in the 21st Century
Changes and Challenges

KATHLEEN W. CRAVER

WITHDRAWN

Greenwood Professional Guides in School Librarianship
Harriet Selverstone, Series Adviser

GREENWOOD PRESS
Westport, Connecticut
London

Library of Congress Cataloging-in-Publication Data

Craver, Kathleen W.
    School library media centers in the 21st century : changes and
challenges / Kathleen W. Craver.
        p. cm.—(Greenwood professional guides in school
librarianship, ISSN 1074–150X)
    Includes bibliographical references and index.
    ISBN 0–313–29100–4 (alk. paper)
    1. School libraries—United States. I. Title. II. Series.
Z675.S3C76 1994
027.8′223′0973—dc20   94–5146

British Library Cataloguing in Publication Data is available.

Library of Congress Catalog Card Number: 94–5146
ISBN: 0–313–29100–4
ISSN: 1074–150X

First published in 1994

Greenwood Press, 88 Post Road West, Westport, CT 06881
An imprint of Greenwood Publishing Group, Inc.

Printed in the United States of America

The paper used in this book complies with the
Permanent Paper Standard issued by the National
Information Standards Organization (Z39.48–1984).

10 9 8 7 6 5 4 3 2

To the school library media specialists of the twenty-first century,
who will be asked to meet the challenges discussed in this book

Contents

Acknowledgments

I wish to thank Linda Payne, whose flawless word processing greatly facilitated the writing of this book. I would also like to thank my husband, Charlie, for his gentle encouragement and his thorough editorial assistance. I gratefully acknowledge the advice, enthusiasm, and support that my editors, Barbara Rader and Harriet Selverstone, gave me throughout this exciting project. I would finally like to express my appreciation to Production Editor Sasha Kintzler and Copy Editor Bayard Van Hecke for their highly professional assistance.

Introduction

You can't tell the future what to become.

Theodor Nelson

The few years between now and the year 2000 provide school library media specialists (SLMSs) with an unprecedented opportunity to contemplate the future and to forecast and propose how we might ready ourselves to begin the twenty-first century. Thousands of publications bombard us with admonitions that our century is passing and that we must prepare for the next one. Futurists issue dire warnings of time running out as if we were facing Armageddon by the year 2000. Most realists, however, know that events during the first week of the twenty-first century will probably not vary significantly from those of preceding weeks.[1] Even though change will occur at an increasingly accelerated pace, it will still be characterized by a certain constancy.

What these remaining years do grant school library media specialists is an interval of precious time to plan for change on the basis of current and future analyses of technological, economic, employment, social, and educational developments in our society. Extrapolating from these trends and other leading demographic indicators can assist us in discerning patterns, systems, and cycles of change that are likely to affect the future of school library media centers (SLMCs). Once these patterns are identified, they provide the means for effective future decision making.

Historians repeatedly remind us that our country has experienced three revolutions. We have evolved from an agrarian economy, whose products were foodstuffs, to an industrial one, whose products were manufactured goods, to a service economy, whose main product is information.[2] These changes have been rapid. "While the shift from an agricultural to an industrial society took 100 years, the present restructuring from an industrial to an information society took only two decades."[3] It is estimated that information workers now make up more than half of the U.S. labor force.[4]

The quantity of the product this new age generates is also expanding rapidly. Known information doubles about every eighteen months.[5] To place this growth in perspective, consider the fact that a weekly edition of the *New York Times* contains more information than the average person was likely to encounter in a lifetime in seventeenth-century England. In 1988, for example, Americans purchased 13.2 million tons of newspapers. Over 1 million books are published each year. The English language now contains 500,000 words, five times more than in Shakespeare's time. The impact on research libraries has been enormous. In the past fourteen years, the collections of large research libraries have doubled.[6]

Without a doubt, new technologies, such as personal computers, fiber-optic cabling, fax machines, CD-ROMs (compact disk–read-only memory), and videodiscs, are responsible for the increase in information and its faster distribution. They are affecting every aspect of our lives. Forty years ago, computers were housed in huge rooms.[7] Now, people use small, portable palmtop computers to accomplish tasks once thought to be executable only by mainframe systems.[8]

Technology has created an environment of unremitting change. Almost every day new developments occur in computer hardware, software, and, more importantly, in the ability to store, organize, and communicate more information. Storage technology, for example, has evolved from paper to microfilm to magnetic and optical media. Where a cubic inch previously stored only a few hundred characters, billions are stored today. Transmission operations have also advanced. Fiber optics has accelerated telecommunications from fifty words per minute to billions of words per minute. Processing has jumped from hundreds to billions of instructions per second, and parallel processing has become limitless.[9]

Technology has also altered the traditional concepts of time and place. Access to bibliographic records, for example, is no longer edifice- and time-bound. They are available simply by use of a computer, modem, and telephone line twenty-four hours per day. Document delivery no longer takes at least a day but occurs within minutes of a facsimile transmission.[10] Our sense of time has been compressed. With the release of each new generation of computers, processing speed increases, rendering our present computers slow and cumbersome. Our users have come to expect more materials from our collections. If we are fortunate enough to have an on-line catalog, they inquire about full-text searching. If we have pin printers attached to on-line terminals, they want high-speed laser printers.

For years, school library media specialists were insulated from the stress produced by the electronic revolution by technological and economic barriers. Large, expensive mainframe computers were initially required to automate libraries, followed by still-expensive minicomputers and finally, affordable microcomputers. At first, only research libraries were able to automate their collections, but, as the technology advanced and became less costly, public and school library media centers began to follow suit.[11]

Until the early 1980s, school library media specialists could attend professional meetings or workshops and return home confident that they had seen, learned, or acquired a finite amount of information. Librarians might not be able to incorporate everything that was demonstrated or discussed into their SLMC programs, but they could select and implement most of the new technologies and teaching units, and be assured that they had made cost-beneficial choices.[12]

The information age, accompanied by the previously described dramatic developments in technology, has shattered the complacency that school library media specialists once had regarding the growth and development of their libraries.[13] As school media specialists, we have arrived at the close of this century with more concerns and interests than our predecessors in the 1950s could have possibly imagined. Few of our colleagues were troubled by illiteracy, bibliographic access, multiculturalism, latchkey children, on-line catalogs and databases, CD-ROMs, networking, and massive budget cuts.

Many of the children we serve suffer from socioeconomic problems that were either nonexistent or unreported in previous decades. Now we know that there are 2.5 million reported cases of child abuse each year. We realize that thousands of children commit suicide annually, and that twelve-year-olds had a better chance of reaching the age of twenty-five in good health in 1935 than they do today.[14] While some of these problems do not affect us personally, they impact the educational goals and objectives that school library media specialists are trying to achieve.

Information illiteracy is a growing problem in America. Currently it is estimated that more than 23 million Americans cannot read above a fifth-grade level. Information illiteracy affects a school library media specialist's ability to disseminate information, transmit knowledge, and expose children to culture. The same children we are trying to help are usually in homes without the means to use advanced technologies that can improve their educational levels. Twenty-five percent of households below the poverty line, for example, have no telephone. As a result, school library media specialists are witnessing a widening gap between the information-rich and the information-poor that bodes ill for our country in the future.[15]

The technological changes that are transforming our school library media centers are also making us dependent upon new technologies not only for performance of daily tasks but also for educational enhancements and applications. Daily we are confronted with new advancements, a myriad of choices, and a growing realization of their ongoing maintenance costs. The future, with its predictions of virtual reality, speech synthesis and recognition, lightware, and artificial intelligence, has become something that many of us may wish to postpone until we can adjust to current technologies.

As software updates and faster computers arrive on the market, the ones we own are immediately rendered obsolete. With an obsolescence rate of three to five years for hardware and software, the term *state of the art* takes on a wholly ephemeral nature.[16] Despite the proliferation of information and its accompanying technology, school library media specialists have an appreciation of the amount of print and nonprint information available in America and a confidence that various technologies can assist us in locating and delivering it. We also have an abiding belief that teaching students how to access these technologies will make a positive difference in their lives.[17]

Because these advanced technologies are having a revolutionary impact on society, educational needs are quickly evolving. Proficiencies and skills once thought required for employability have become less important, while competency related to electronic technologies is deemed essential. Educators surmise that success in the information age will no longer be dependent upon rote memorization and mechanical skills, but on symbolic-analytic thinking and problem solving. If schools are to continue educating children to succeed in the next century, they will have to make major adjustments in all curricular areas. They will have to utilize various technologies to create a more productive learning environment.

Current use of computers in education includes drill and practice, word processing, simulation exercises, database management, and computer-based graphics. In general, they serve as a supplement to problem solving. Computers provide students with a sense of achievement, offer instant reinforcement, reduce the fear of failure, and permit a wider range of creativity and experimentation. Most students enjoy using computers in the school, library, or home.[18]

When the use of computers becomes more thoroughly integrated into classrooms, their presence will force many teachers to reevaluate their teaching styles and methods. Computers, by nature, lend themselves to individual work. With the addition of networked CD-ROMs, for example, thousands of books can be accessed simultaneously by students from their own workstations. The availability of a medium-sized library's collection on several disks renders a single-textbook approach to teaching superfluous.[19] It also paves the way for newer educational strategies such as resource-based teaching, collaboration, and on-line instruction.[20] All of these technology-driven educational changes will require a greater need for the SLMC and the services of a certified school library media specialist.

Although school library media specialists have experienced a changing instructional role vis-à-vis their media centers since the 1960s, only the computer has given us the opportunity to radically redefine it within the context of the teaching profession.[21] The omnipresence of computers, CD-ROMs, on-line databases, and networks in our classrooms and libraries obligates us to become partners in the educational process. Establishing access to the world of information via the on-line catalog and networks is necessary and exciting. Yet accepting that objective as the sole model for the role SLMCs are to play in the process limits us to a passive, external relationship to our institutions and users. School library media specialists who chose this path will place themselves in jeopardy of replacement by technicians who specialize in database selection and management.

If we are to continue to satisfy the needs of our users, we must understand the link between them and advanced technologies.[22] The connection between the ever-expanding world of information and the student requires an interpreter, consultant, and instructor as well as a gatherer of information. Equipped with various information systems and numerous databases, the SLMS of the future will need to become an essential guide through a maze of information.[23]

School library media specialists can never be content with showing students which keys to push and when. Our responsibilities require us to be active participants in the sharing of ideas and loaning of knowledge. Our students and faculty will depend on us to work with them rather than to merely acquire, process, retrieve, and borrow materials for them. We will only succeed in the next century to the extent that we are viewed as an indispensable link between an ever-expanding world of information and the minds of our students and teachers.[24]

PURPOSE

I have had the privilege of practicing my profession in a variety of geographic locations, socioeconomic environments, grade levels, and secondary and university institutions. During my eighteen years as a school library media specialist, I have coped easily with changes that have occurred in our field, such as the assimilation of nonprint materials, new courses, team teaching, individualized instruction, and resource-based learning. Nothing, however, has prepared me to adjust easily to the technological revolution that is just beginning to impact school library media centers. It has made me curious about where we are going so fast. How much will it cost to get there? Will it make a difference in the lives of our students? Can I keep up and how will I manage?

The main goal of this book is to examine and discuss some of the major forces for change confronting SLMCs and to analyze the general implications of these transformations as a guide for future decision making. For organizational purposes, these trends have been grouped within seven areas: (1) technological, (2) economic, (3) employment, (4) educational, (5)

social and behavioral, (6) instructional, and (7) organizational and managerial. A secondary goal is to provide school library media specialists with
current statistics and data that can be employed to formulate persuasive,
well-reasoned arguments for (1) the purchase of new technologies, (2)
instructional reform, and (3) full implementation of resource-based learning.

Throughout most of the chapters, readers will see references to the
influence of advanced technologies and the subsequent need for improved
student symbolic-analytic skills. Both trends are considered so powerful in
their potential to change school library media centers that they have been
emphasized in many aspects of the book.

School Library Media Centers in the 21st Century assumes that the majority
of media centers are in a transitional phase with regard to utilizing many
of the technologies discussed in the Scenario and Chapter 1. Some media
centers, for example, may already have access to on-line catalogs with
locally mounted CD-ROM databases, while others may have just purchased their first computer, modem, and fax machine. For this reason, the
discussion of electronic technologies has been confined to those either in
current use or projected to emerge within the next five to ten years.
Discussion of advanced technologies beyond this time frame would be
speculative and not particularly relevant to SLMCs.

Another assumption concerns the socioeconomic status of school library
media centers. Many of the issues and implications discussed are based
upon projected changes in the economy, employment sector, and society in
general. It is understood that these changes are somewhat dependent upon
the current economic and social status of particular SLMCs. The predicted
changes in technology and demography, for example, will affect some
media centers either negatively or positively more than others.

Differences among SLMCs are also assumed when readers approach the
challenges listed in Chapter 8. Given lack of support staff and substantial
budget cuts, many school media centers may find that the changes and
recommendations in Chapter 8 are impossible to achieve. What is important, however, is that they use these challenges as a foundation for future
measurement and evaluation of their school library media centers. Their
ultimate objective, however, should always be to integrate the existing
programs and services of the media center into the total life of the school.

OVERVIEW OF THE CONTENTS

Creating a scenario is a standard method researchers employ for predict-
ing and studying the future. It can assist one to visualize objects, events,
and their impact in alternative outcomes and to recognize the future
potential and consequences of specific trends in various professions.

The book opens with two scenarios reflective, respectively, of utopian and dystopian SLMC settings. The first scenario presents a picture of tomorrow that introduces current and new technologies such as artificial intelligence, voice-activated technologies, hypertext, interactive video, electronic networks, and advanced telecommunications in a plausible library environment. It combines technologies so that readers can vicariously experience their application in daily media center programs and services and grasp the promises and challenges they hold. All of the technologies discussed in Chapter 1 have been incorporated into the first scenario, so that readers can imagine their function in an electronic SLMC before they read about each one's potential and advantages.

The second scenario is designed to depict a less utopian view of a school library media center within the same time period. The school portrayed in this scenario suffers from a forecasted information rich-poor gap because of unequal educational opportunities. Social, educational, and economic problems abound in this vision of a poorly equipped urban school media center. Faculty and students have to make do with what they have in a building that resembles a prison rather than an educational institution.

Chapter 1, "Technological Trends," discusses the increasing digitalization of all media, regardless of format, and the convergence that is predicted to occur with various types of technology. Advances in telecommunications, particularly fiber optic cabling, are proposed as a means for school libraries to enter the electronic age. Uses of this improved technology to establish distance learning, instructional television services, and access to remote libraries' collections are suggested. New and future developments related to CD-ROM systems, hypertext, artificial intelligence, voice-activated technologies, interactive media, and virtual reality are also explored, together with their potential use in school library media centers.

The implications of this technological revolution on SLMCs are expected to be profound. Even the smallest and poorest school media centers can expect to benefit from increasingly powerful computers combined with sophisticated software. The presence of one computer, a modem, and a fax machine is predicted to expand every library's capabilities and enable it to provide better programs and services.

Chapter 2, "Economic Trends," considers the second major force to influence SLMCs in the future. The state of the economy is seen as a significant variable that can either accelerate or slow the technological progress of school media centers. America's constant problem with indebtedness at every level of the economy is forecast to be a permanent characteristic of the next two decades. A major change in demographics is also expected to impact SLMCs as the population ages and governments must decide how to allocate our dwindling resources. Should monies earned by current generations be used to pay for their medical and social services or be used to educate future generations who will continue to support them when they can no longer work? In an attempt to alleviate these two severe economic problems, government at every level has reduced spending, especially for SLMCs. School library media centers presently face rising costs for materials and new technologies at a time when their budgets are either stationary or declining.

To counteract these negative forces, school library media centers are expected to employ several economic strategies, such as creating school library/business initiatives; lobbying for mandated categorical funding at all government levels, citing recent national reports and research supportive of SLMCs; and building local, grassroots advocacy financial programs.

Chapter 3, "Employment Trends," outlines future trends in the general workforce and describes what types of jobs will be available in the next five to ten years. Patterns such as an increasingly competitive global economy, decline of routine production/service jobs, demographic workforce changes, and rising skill requirements are discussed. The earning potentials of employees with varying degrees of education are analyzed to demonstrate the growing need for education beyond high school.

As parents comprehend the diminished employment opportunities for their children, much of their discontent will be vented upon schools and their media centers. School library media specialists are expected to react by providing high-tech media centers designed to promote the types of learning experiences that many employers will require. These technologies will include expanded electronic access to other information systems and increased use of in-house CD-ROM databases and interactive media.

In response to increased company and corporate dissatisfaction with the work performance of recent graduates, school library media specialists will also acquire additional print and nonprint materials that encourage symbolic-analytic thinking skills necessary for future jobs. They will also have to alert students and their parents to current and future employment trends and to develop collections responsive to student career needs.

Chapter 4, "Educational Trends," charts the traumatic changes in the field of education by discussing the growing problem of illiteracy and declining scores on a variety of standardized achievement tests. These depressing educational trends have initiated a strong reform movement characterized by increased choice by parents and students and competition among schools. School districts, especially those in large urban areas, have created magnet schools, high-tech schools, college/high school partnerships, and open enrollment and self-governance plans as a means to solve problems of educational inequities and satisfy parents' concerns for their children's future.

School library media centers are also part of this reform movement. They are expected to provide materials, instruction, and information technologies that require higher-order thinking skills. They will also be under increasing pressure to develop effective instructional programs and services in order to remain competitive with other area schools.

Chapter 5, "Social and Behavioral Trends," discusses salient social and behavioral trends concerning children and how they will affect the activities of SLMCs. America is experiencing significant cultural changes as it evolves from a nation *with* minorities to a nation *of* minorities. Our economy is also now inextricably intertwined with those of other nations. School media centers must develop collections and furnish programs and services that are not only reflective of a more diverse society but also expose children to the cultures of nations with whom they will conduct business in the future.

The second major trend concerns the transformation of the American family. This part of the chapter discusses the impact of divorce, changing family relationships, working parents, and characteristics of the self-care generation. Expectations that SLMCs respond to children's needs in this area will range from pre- and after-school care programs to provision of self-help materials and how-to manuals. School library media centers are also expected to sponsor speakers and programs about at-risk activities and their consequences, such as AIDS, adolescent pregnancy, drug abuse, and violence. As more children use their unsupervised time after school to watch television, shop, or work part-time, school library media specialists will also supply educational videos, consumer research, and child labor information.

Chapter 6, "Instructional Trends," shows how the instructional role of the SLMS will change dramatically with the presence of advanced technologies. School library media specialists will become instructional technologists responsible for teaching faculty and students how to use and access on-line databases, interactive media, distance learning, and sophisticated software systems. Their instructional technologist role is also expected to extend to parents, who will be able to access the media center's on-site and remote collections from modems at home.

The methods and materials used to provide bibliographic instruction will also change to suit an on-line learning environment. School library media specialists will employ information literacy and symbolic-analytic skills to teach students how to determine their specific information needs, to select the correct information sources, to formulate search strategies, and to interpret and evaluate the results. Expanded access to networks and databases will change traditional classroom-textbook-lecture teaching. Media specialists will instruct faculty concerning the advantages of resource-based learning and design lessons and activities that relate to the subject areas of faculty members.

Chapter 7, "Organizational and Managerial Trends," addresses the role SLMSs will need to assume as the technological, economic, educational, and cultural changes affect the daily business of their media centers. In the future, schools are expected to assume many of the responsibilities once thought the province of parents and community organizations with respect to pre- and after-school care. School media specialists will be expected to organize and manage their facilities so that they can be used as supervised homework assistance centers, study sites, or recreational areas.

Installation of electronic technologies will require that SLMSs become managers of reference and information services. This new role will entail developing modern access protocols; updating, maintaining, and troubleshooting networks and databases; and simplifying access to complex software systems. Managing the collection will also involve new responsibilities because its definition, nature, and composition will change with expanded access to remote library collections and in-house CD-ROM databases.

Obtaining funds for various information technologies will result in increased demands on the part of administrators and parents for some type of performance measures to justify their investment. School library media specialists will have to concentrate and develop evaluative instruments that demonstrate student achievement and learning in an on-line environment. While other performance measures such as circulation and acquisitions statistics will be useful, evaluation of instruction with new information technologies will be emphasized.

Chapter 8, "Challenges," includes a series of challenges within several broad categories that school library media specialists will face in the next century. These challenges consist of: (1) acquiring and promoting new information technologies, (2) developing a performance-based model of programs and services, (3) creating a collection that reflects cultural, societal, and employment changes, (4) providing instructional programs and services that are competitive and reflective of student and faculty needs, (5) integrating symbolic-analytic skills into resource-based learning units, and (6) organizing and managing school media centers to meet the changing social and information needs of students and faculty.

Scenario

TWO VISIONS OF TOMORROW

A Utopian School

It is February 2000. You have been invited to visit a resource center for grades 7–12 in an independent, northeastern suburban school. The tuition, while considered high, is subsidized by a government-sponsored voucher program which permits parents to choose the public or private schools their children will attend. The majority of the students come from homes where one or both parents have at least one college degree and the family income is well into the top quartile.

The school is a notable one with a tradition of sending many students to the best colleges and universities. The curriculum is rigorous. Class size never exceeds twenty students. Disciplinary problems are minimal, permitting students, faculty, and administrators to focus on the principal goal, learning. Because of its excellent reputation, the school is able to accept only those students who score at the eighty-fifth percentile on the Educational Testing Service Secondary School Test. Since the test, according to Gardner's theory of multiple intelligences, measures mainly logical-mathematical intelligences, the students are already an academically homogeneous group.

The students continue to perform well throughout their years at the school, making the institution eligible for supplemental government funding based upon student yearly achievement scores. The additional funding has been used to create an electronic environment that is seamlessly integrated into all classroom activities. Faculty are required to design resource-based courses with a resource specialist, formerly called a school library media specialist.

The school has also been successful in forming coalitions between the business community, faculty, noted educators, and parents. Some of the nation's largest corporations donate employee personal time and company resources to ensure that the students have access to the latest technological and pedagogical advancements in their subjects. Students, faculty, and parents are well aware that by the year 2010 more than 90 percent of all jobs will be computer-dependent.

All students at the school are required to learn a foreign language beginning in seventh grade. Their teachers, parents, and peers are cognizant of an America that is changing demographically. They understand that by the year 2030, the Spanish-origin population will be four times its present size. For this reason, most students study Spanish as their principal foreign language.

The student outlook toward education is different from that of previous generations. Most of them do not visualize education as ending at a certain point in their lives. They view education as a lifelong task. Having seen so many of their parents and teachers change careers, they expect to have multiple careers during their lives.

They are technologically sophisticated and confident in their abilities to select, locate, and critically analyze information. Because they come from affluent homes, they have also been exposed to the theater, museums, films, and concerts. Most of their educational and personal material needs are easily accommodated. Almost all of them have a home reference collection and access to a personal computer. They have no pressing economic need to seek employment after graduating from high school.

All of these positive factors have combined to produce students who are capable of delaying many gratifications until they obtain a college degree. These students rarely succumb to the lure of after-school jobs that, while enabling them to buy clothes, a car or music videos, force them to neglect their studies. In short, the students attending this school are primed for success.

Their teachers have been educated in the latest pedagogical techniques. While the curriculum is demanding, with many required courses, instruction is tailored to the individual student. Students who are more gifted than others in particular subjects are permitted to advance as far as their own limitations.

The school is organized and managed differently. Since it is an electronic environment, teachers no longer present information, lecture, or issue instructions. Instead, their mission is to inspire, motivate, and moderate peer discussion on the basis of computer-assisted instruction. Teachers at this school serve primarily as subject experts in their respective fields.

The resource center is the hub of the school. The resource specialist is an expert at facilitating the connections between students, faculty, curriculum, and technology. This person also possesses expertise in innovative technologies and assists faculty to incorporate these resources into their curricula.

A visit to this resource center requires that you erase from your mind a picture of students curled up in futon chairs, surrounded by bookshelves crammed with books. In its place envision students seated in a room filled with computer workstations. Each workstation is electronically linked to other parts of the school, various CD-ROM databases, the library's on-line catalog, NREN (National Research and Education Network), and Internet. Print, as you recognize it in literature and textbook form, has almost disappeared.

A class enters the resource center. The students approach their workstations enthusiastically. Each one is carrying an electronic tutor. It is about the size of an average book and opens in the same way. One half of it contains a screen with a high-definition, full-color display. Similar to the school's workstations in function, it is capable of displaying three-dimensional, holographic images. The other half of the tutor consists of a keyboard equipped with a full alphabet, digits, mathematical functions, and one hundred function keys. Reading material is viewed on a fixed or scrolled screen. The reading rate is adjustable, and sound frequently accompanies text and imagery. When materials are delivered orally, the listening speed can be increased to four hundred words per minute.

The students are in the resource center to learn about additional reference materials that can be utilized for their reports, such as almanacs, encyclopedias, periodical indexes, specialized dictionaries, and various CD-ROM databases. All materials are current, because they are updated electronically. Reference and other library books are available in memory-capsule format and can be plugged into electronic tutors or networked onto student workstations when needed.

The unit students are working on relates to their reading of Harper Lee's *To Kill a Mockingbird*. While the entire class has been assigned the book as a text, each student has selected a teacher-prepared question designed to acquaint him with a particular issue, event, or person involved in the civil rights movement.

One student has chosen to study and present to her classmates an annotated, chronological history of significant events, dates, and laws leading up to the passage of the 1964 Civil Rights Act. To begin her research, she selects a multimedia electronic database. As we observe her using it, an astonishing array of options is presented to her. First of all, a copy of *To Kill a Mockingbird* is part of the database. Its presence enables her to locate by keyword searching all references to civil rights by any of the characters in the book. These references have been linked through hypertext to factual information concerning the people, places, and events that influenced the passage of the 1964 Civil Rights Act. The text that the student is reading concerning this part of American history goes well beyond those of traditional one-source print. A wall-mounted display screen features at least six full pages of text from one source, one page of text that combines eight different sources, and a bibliography of additional books, videos, maps, and appropriate selections from an American history database. The student selectively downloads the information she needs for her report to her electronic tutor, which contains one gigabyte of memory. Using her keyboard, she appends relevant typewritten notes to the margins of the text.

Her next decision concerns what media to use to present her report. After searching the media options, she chooses some video footage of various protests and marches as well as photographs of signs displayed at drinking fountains, restaurants, and swimming pools stating "Whites Only." She knows that the video sequences she is selecting from this multimedia database will enhance her peers' understanding of this critical period of American history.

The assignment requires students to cite at least one primary resource. While this student can rely upon the videos and newspaper articles from that time period to satisfy this objective, she is told by the resource specialist that arrangements can be made to interview Sheyann Webb, one of the authors of a book entitled *Selma, Lord Selma: Girlhood Memories of the Civil-Rights Days* (Tuskaloosa: University of Alabama Press, 1980). The author was eight years old when her hometown of Selma, Alabama, became the site of a huge SCLC (Southern Christian Leadership Conference) march sponsored to protest voter discrimination. The author, now in her forties, has agreed as part of an oral history project to be interviewed regarding her experiences as a young black growing up in such a volatile time in Selma, Alabama.

The resource specialist notifies the student that a holographic transmission will occur in twenty minutes. Meanwhile, she spends the time preparing for the interview by reviewing her questions. At the agreed-upon time, the hologram of the author appears. As the student interviews her about her experiences, fears, and reactions during that turbulent time in Selma, it is clear that Ms. Webb's memories of the events, people, and political climate in Selma during the 1960s, coupled with her writing on the subject, provides the student with a wealth of information concerning the civil rights movement.

The teacher has allocated only two class periods in the resource center for assisted research on each student's topic. The amount of time is sufficient, however, because the resource center is accessible from remote locations via fiber-optic cabling. It is "open" twenty-four hours a day, 365 days a year. All of the materials in the resource center are searchable electronically. No item is ever in use by anyone else, lost, stolen, or vandalized.

Students may dial in from their homes and access all of the materials they were using during the class period.

On the second day, the student asks the resource specialist if there are any VR (virtual reality) materials available on the civil rights movement. A search of the center's on-line catalog reveals that there is a virtual reality trip in the collection concerning a protest march in Birmingham, Alabama. Even though the student understands that virtual reality is a computer-created world where she can enter and move through computer-generated three-dimensional images, she is apprehensive about how she will react to being in such a potentially violent and dangerous setting. Despite her misgivings, she adjusts the glove on her left hand. It is connected to delicate sensors designed to detect the head's orientation and transmit it back to the computer. The eye goggles simulate a full-motion, three-dimensional scene to her eyes and senses.

Suddenly, it is May 1963 and the student is walking down a street in Birmingham, Alabama. Martin Luther King, Jr., has announced a goal to integrate Birmingham's public facilities and department stores. A group of young blacks have joined hands and in trembling voices are singing the chorus from "We Shall Overcome" as local policemen shout for them to disperse and prepare to loose snarling German shepherds and water cannon on them. The sights, sounds, smells, and perhaps the sensation of the sticky, humid air against her skin combine to produce an indelible impression on the student. For a short period of time she is able to experience what it was like to be involved in the civil rights movement.

After this experience, she finishes preparing her chronology of events, issues, and laws that she considers significant to this historical period. Before she electronically transfers the report to her teacher's computer for evaluation, the resource specialist insists that she interrogate the knowledge navigator. Even though the student is confident of the veracity, logic, and organizational structure of her report, she agrees to consult an expert system as a final check. This particular knowledge navigator is an expert system on American history. It is considered an incipient form of artificial intelligence. It is able to answer questions that would require faculty members to have doctoral degrees in at least three areas of American history. A special advantage of this system is its nonhuman form. Students, especially adolescents, are not intimidated by it as they frequently are by their teachers.

The student begins by downloading her report into the knowledge navigator and querying it by voice, asking questions such as "Have I left any major event out of my timetable?" The computer answers "Yes." "What have I omitted?" asks the student. The computer replies that the student has failed to mention and discuss *Brown v. Board of Education of Topeka* (1954)—a major event in the history of the civil rights movement. The student saves the additional information provided by the knowledge navigator on her electronic tutor so that she can incorporate it into her report at home. She then asks the expert system if her report is organized logically. "No," replies the knowledge navigator. "Where should I make adjustments?" queries the student. The expert system recommends that she discuss the Civil Rights Act of 1957 before mentioning the crisis in the Little Rock schools. In this way, the events follow one another not only chronologically but also logically. The final check that the student requests is for spelling, grammar, and paragraph development. For these tasks, she leaves the knowledge navigator and logs into a sophisticated software package called Prowrite. The system alerts her to two one-sentence paragraphs and asks her to repair several split infinitives. After making the necessary corrections, the student downloads the assignment to her teacher's computer before presenting it to her classmates.

Before grading the project, her teacher consults with the resource specialist to confirm that this student has indeed used all of the available multimedia packages, databases, and so forth. A percentage of every student's grade is allocated to her ability to select materials appropriate to the assignment and to use them effectively. Another percentage of the grade is assigned to the student's ability to present the material using a variety of media so as to stimulate and motivate the multiple intelligences of her peers. The entire class will be tested by a computer-assisted instructional program after all the presentations are made. Therefore, it is incumbent upon each student to present her material in the most organized and engaging manner to facilitate her peers' comprehension of it.

Once the presentations have been given, they are downloaded into each student's workstation. A computer program formulates questions designed to measure students' knowledge of the material. The computer reinforces correct answers with a first-name acknowledgment and complement. When students answer incorrectly, it provides a gentle admonishment and the correct answer, accompanied by an explanation.

A Dystopian School

Now let us travel to another resource center within the same month and year. You have also been invited to visit a second resource center in a public, northeastern urban school. As you drive to it, you pass blocks of rusting, abandoned, gaping factories. You see groups of adults, mainly young males, standing idly on street corners. You begin to wish for a series of green lights so that you can speed to your destination, because you are afraid for your personal safety.

When you arrive at the school, your impression is that of a prison. All of the windows are covered with wire mesh to protect against breakage. When you open the front door, a guard greets you and asks to search your handbag. As he searches, you are told to pass through a metal detector. A bell sounds as you walk toward the resource center, and students pour into the halls. Their demeanor reflects boredom and a certain wariness of their peers. Glancing into the classrooms, you are struck by the absence of computers, the large numbers of desks and the security telephones on the wall. The students do not linger outside the classrooms. A disembodied voice over the public address system reminds them of the physical danger and subsequent punishment they face if they are not in their assigned classes by the time the bell rings. Within seconds of the bell's sounding, all teachers lock their doors. Guards begin sweeping the halls searching for trespassers or students who belong in class.

Unlike the independent school you just visited, this institution has to devote a substantial portion of its budget to security rather than to acquiring equipment that enables students to become productive learners. In general, faculty members are demoralized. Teaching at this school is clearly an early-entry and early-exit profession. While the majority of teachers have been trained in the latest pedagogical techniques, most of their teaching time is spent on discipline and the clerical aspects of preparing for class.

The majority of the students are from single-parent homes with incomes at or below the poverty level. Few of the children have computers at home or reference books. Many drop out before graduation. More than 20 percent are functionally illiterate when they graduate. By the age of fourteen, many of them are employed in part-time service-sector jobs. Because they have so little in the way of material goods, these students neglect their studies in favor of earning money to purchase the clothes, cars, and electronic entertainment equipment that their peer group values. Their inability to delay gratification, coupled with a myopic view of tomorrow, dooms most of them to an uncertain future. They view education as a final rather than as a lifelong activity.

Although their parent(s) may use the voucher system and choose any area school, they must pay additional tuition and transportation costs to any school they select outside their neighborhood. Since so many parents are receiving some form of public assistance, the voucher system is not an option for them because of the increased costs.

The curriculum is not rigorous. Students have only to satisfy the minimum requirements on state proficiency exams to pass from grade to grade. Achievement test scores are so low that the school cannot qualify for supplemental funding. Despite these conditions, the school has tried on numerous occasions to form a coalition between noted educators, corporations, faculty, and parents. The programs that are successfully funded, however, are mainly designed to reduce the number of dropouts, teenage pregnancies, or gang clashes. Few programs are funded that might increase academic achievement or learning.

The resource center looks like a museum exhibit reminiscent of a SLMC from the 1980s. It is only euphemistically called a resource center. There are three computers in it. One is dedicated to administrative and clerical tasks such as printing acquisition lists. The other two are linked to an outdated CD-ROM encyclopedia and a local area network. The resource specialist is busy unpacking several boxes of used books. Independent schools regularly donate books to urban public schools as part of their community service projects.

A class enters the resource center. They too have been assigned a report/presentation related to civil rights. They are also reading Harper Lee's *To Kill a Mockingbird.* As thirty students take their seats in the resource center, the specialist wheels a book cart out to them which is stacked with books about the civil rights movement. Some of them are high-interest/low-level for students who read below grade level. Unfortunately, she does not have any books on civil rights in Spanish. Students for whom English is a second language look disappointed.

Several of the students approach the resources with eagerness. The resource specialist and teacher know that this topic is of particular interest to the many minority students in the class. The resource specialist begins the unit by showing a short video which highlights some of the important events in the civil rights movement. After passing out a bibliographical pathfinder to each student and explaining it, she tells the students to begin their research. As students search for materials on the reserve cart, it is readily apparent that there are not enough books on each student's topic. Students are fortunate if they are able to find one book that contains information about their subject.

The students' attitude toward this problem is one of acceptance. Most of them are unaware of the on-line catalog, CD-ROM databases, modems, holograms, and virtual reality programs that their suburban counterparts may readily access. While they have seen the excellent facilities when attending sporting events at more affluent schools, they do not comprehend the impact of such technological advancements on future educational and employment outcomes.

One student has signed up to complete a brief, chronological history of the civil rights movement. She is enthusiastic and eager to begin her search for print and nonprint materials. Unlike some students who quickly discern that there are an insufficient number of materials on their topics, she discovers that Patricia and Frederick McKissack's book *The Civil Rights Movement in America from 1865 to the Present* (Chicago: Childrens Press, 1991) and Ellen Levine's *Freedom's Children: Young Civil Rights Activists Tell Their Own Stories* (New York: G. P. Putnam's Sons, 1993) have a great deal of information pertaining to her topic. She is also grateful because both books contain black and white photographs of various people and events. Since all of the students are required to present a visual relating to their topic, this student intends to enlarge an appropriate photograph on a photocopier and pass it around to her classmates while delivering her report orally. She is also pleased with her second book, *Freedom's Children*, because it contains interviews of various civil rights activists. Citing from this source will enable her to satisfy an optional primary source requirement. The teacher and resource specialist did not make this a mandatory part of the assignment because both realized that the resource center did not have enough primary materials on civil rights.

The student works swiftly to create a bibliography card for the McKissack book and then begins writing note cards as she reads. Needless to say, students do not have electronic tutors that enable them to scan and save text to read, edit, and cite as they find appropriate materials. Instead, they must queue to use the photocopier to copy relevant passages so that other students may have access as soon as possible to the same materials.

The teacher and the resource specialist stop the class midway to introduce students to an on-line local area network containing the catalogs of the public library system and a public university system. Since there is only one terminal available for searching, most of the students must schedule appointments to search after school. The teacher and resource specialist are not surprised at the small number of students who schedule appointments. They realize that most of the students work after school or are baby-sitting younger siblings. The majority will not have the time or the transportation to retrieve books located at various branch libraries. Two years ago, they could have walked to a nearby branch library on their way to a job or home. Budget cuts, however, necessitated its closure. The nearest branch library to students at this school requires a fairly long bus ride across town.

The student who has located two books directly relevant to her topic is very satisfied. She is only disappointed with one aspect of the assignment. She would like to take the books home and continue working on her report that evening. She already knows that it is impossible because so many classes will need the books during the following days. The teacher and resource specialist have placed them on closed reserve. No materials on the reserve cart may circulate outside the resource center. When the class ends, the student finishes writing a last note card, packs up her book bag and passes through an antitheft detector across the resource center's only door.

This student was one of the fortunate few who found material on her topic in the resource center. The ones who did not spent their time joking with their peers or searching superseded sets of encyclopedias hoping to locate enough general information on their topics to satisfy their teacher's minimal requirements and receive a passing grade on the assignment.

After seeing two extremely different resource centers, the visitor is struck by their similarities and dissimilarities. She realizes in a perverse way that there are several similarities. The first is their physical size. With the exception of the reformatory atmosphere that is almost palpable in the urban resource center, the visitor is shocked to find that both centers are almost identical in square footage. While the urban center is filled with books, most of them out-of-date, the suburban resource center is filled with computers and wall-mounted screens. In fact, print materials are not plentiful in the suburban resource center. The most circulated print items are recreational paperbacks purchased for their current interest and portability.

A second similarity concerns the attitudes of the two resource specialists. The visitor recalls that both seemed especially eager, and dedicated to ensuring that their students make maximum use of their respective resource centers' time, on-line facilities, and materials. The visitor is also impressed with the pleasure that students in both schools expressed when they located information on their topics. There was an eagerness on their faces that was universal to youngsters when they experience success. Their desire to meet the expectations of their teachers is another similarity that the visitor remembers. Initially, the majority of students at both schools genuinely attempted to complete their assignments. Only lack of materials and technology prevented the students in the urban setting from experiencing a success similar to that enjoyed by students at the first school.

At this point, however, similarities cease. The many differences between the two schools are also imprinted in the visitor's mind. The first difference concerns technological advancement. The suburban resource center has dedicated all of its resources to acquiring electronic access to such things as full-text on-line databases, catalogs, multimedia packages, expert systems, and virtual reality. Its connection is to the future, while that of the urban center is to the past. Security is not a problem in the suburban center, so its finances are targeted toward providing students with the most recent technologies rather than securing their safety within the building.

The visitor also recalls that the levels and styles of activity in the centers were different. At the suburban site, students had access to their own portable computers and workstations. Students appeared more focused and organized in their approach to the assignment. In contrast, the urban resource center exuded an air of barely controlled chaos as students grabbed the books on the reserve cart, rifled through them for information, and disappointedly laid many aside.

The visitor was finally struck by the difference in student gratification time. It seemed that providing students in the suburban setting with electronic access to the very latest technologies made them unwilling to wait any significant interval of time for information. The technological advancements served to compress time for them, thus making students actually impatient for an article to scroll by or to be printed from a high-speed printer. Their impatience was also evidenced by their sighing and occasional looks of exasperation when a computer responded in more than a nanosecond to their search requests.

The students in the urban setting, on the other hand, seemed able to delay their educational gratification time. They quietly lined up to take a turn at using the local area network or the out-of-date CD-ROM encyclopedia. They took turns at using the small number of books available on their topics. They were even willing to postpone the pleasure of receiving a higher grade because their assigned topic lacked sufficient primary and secondary sources.

Seeing such differences and similarities in these two extreme settings has sharply focused the visitor's attention on the potential technological, educational, and cultural changes and challenges that school library media specialists will have to face in the next century. While most resource centers clearly lie between these obviously polarized exemplars, the visitor realizes that planning must begin now to provide the next generation with the knowledge and skills necessary to succeed in an information-based economy.

School Library Media Centers
in the 21st Century

Technological Trends

1

> Now, here, you see, it takes all the running you can do, to keep in the same place. If you want to get somewhere else, you must run at least twice as fast as that.
>
> Lewis Carroll

The Queen's concept of progress in *Through the Looking Glass* is probably an accurate reflection of school library media specialists' feelings as they attempt to cope with current and emerging technologies and their effects on SLMCs. Almost daily SLMSs are faced with expanding new technologies that help to promote library services and concomitant pressure to utilize these new technologies to enhance programs and services.[1] The speed with which they appear on the market makes predictions of dominant electronic developments rather difficult. Given this rapidly fluctuating situation, the subsequent discussion of technological trends is confined to those which most specialists believe will occur within the next five to ten years. Estimates beyond this point are too speculative. Moreover, this discussion is further complicated by the fact that some of these technologies are emerging at a faster pace than others. For example, the processing power of microcomputer systems doubles every year,[2] while activation and speech recognition technologies are developing more slowly. Despite these developmental differentials, it is important that we perceive their current and possible future use in our media centers.

TELEPOWER

In the previous utopian scenario, one could discern, within the description of various technologies, an overall communications infrastructure described by Seilor as a digital electronic medium (DEM).[3] Information previously available in individualized print and nonprint formats had been seamlessly integrated into student electronic tutors. The student in the utopian scenario no longer, for example, consulted books, periodicals, or videotapes separately to complete her assignment. Instead, she used an "electronic tutor" and other multimedia databases containing all of the relevant material. Their transparent integration and multistation access is an example of convergence that is soon to occur with several types of current and emerging technologies. DEM refers to information, regardless of its original format, that is stored as electrical charges in digital form. Once information is stored in this form it becomes machine-readable, inexpensive, and highly transmittable. Its overall effect is to permit the creation of an electronic database containing all of the materials in a particular library, regardless of whether they are books, recordings, or videos, plus providing access to other electronic libraries via wide area networks.

It is within this overall framework that the following advances in technology must be viewed. Although each development merits a separate understanding and evaluation of its contribution to the information systems depicted in the utopian scenario, the concept of integration is vitally important to anticipating future SLMC technological trends. DEM is not yet a reality but with the rapid advances occurring in the following technologies, it will be a salient characteristic of electronic systems by the year 2000.

TELECOMMUNICATIONS

Telecommunications is a term used to connote "communication over a distance."[4] Broadly defined, this encompasses transmission of information by such means as telephone, telefacsimile, television broadcasting, and computer systems. Currently most telecommunications are achieved by using existing telephone lines as the conduit for information delivery.[5] Since telephone lines use analog signals to transmit the human voice and computers require digital signals to achieve information delivery, modems (modulator-demodulators) and communications boards inside computers are used to convert analog signals into digital signals for information transfers.[6] While this system is a fairly cost-effective way to deliver and transmit digital information, it is still not the optimum means.

Until recently, the digitalization of various media has been impeded by a bandwidth limitation. That is, all the information necessary for a high-resolution picture and quality sound could not be transmitted via the copper wires of conventional telephone lines.[7] With the development of fiber-optic cabling (slender glass rods a fraction of the size of copper wire cables bundled together), there is no longer a limit on the amount of data a medium can transmit per second. Fiber-optic cabling permits the delivery of half a gigabyte (500 million bits per second) of noise-free and error-free digital information.[8] "A single strand, for example, can transmit the contents of the entire *Encyclopedia Britannica* every second."[9] This type of cabling provides a virtually limitless environment for information delivery and removes the last obstacle from further digitalization of various electronic media.

For years, the fiber-optic cabling of the country was considered to be a Herculean task costing $200 to $400 billion. This economic barrier was solved with the discovery that coaxial wire could easily carry fiber-optic cabling information for a quarter mile or more. This knowledge enables cable and phone companies to discard sometimes ineffective amplifiers and receive "two-way interactivity" with almost no cost.[10] It also paves the way for an information highway that will fundamentally alter the current programs, curricula, and services of even the smallest school media center.

CABLE RESOURCES

Many major cable companies install cabling in schools as a public service. Columbine Cablevision, for example, provides Fort Collins, Poudre, and Rocky Mountain High Schools (CO) and their district media center with a two-way video and audio network. Termed an interactive educational network, the system permits students and faculty in remote locations to listen to and view one another and to respond to each other in various educational programs.[11]

Prince Georges County (MD) has a similar system in place, but has extended interactive distance learning further. The county's educational access channel transmits to 130,000 homes and 169 schools. Viewers receive access to school-produced programs, remedial mathematics courses, and, in schools with insufficient enrollment, advanced placement courses.[12]

In the past, most interactive cable systems have been limited to large school districts with the resources to afford them. These schools have also been confined to selecting from relatively few cable-supplied educational television programs and channels such as Newsroom, the Discovery Channel, the Learning Channel, and C-Span.[13] With the coming of telepower, choices will increase geometrically. The approximately 57 channels currently available are expected to mushroom to 500. TCI (Tele-Communications, Inc.), for example, the world's largest cable TV operator, is expected to create spin-offs or further subdivide into subject specialties such as news and community information channels.[14] The potential for the proliferation of educational channels is substantial. School library media centers will soon have greater selections at more competitive costs.

SATELLITE RESOURCES

For SLMCs without access to fiber-optic and coaxial cabling, satellite technology will expand and improve. Hughes Communications, for example, is expected to introduce "Direc TV," which "can transmit 150 television channels through a $700 rooftop disk the size of a large pizza pie."[15] Currently, schools using satellite technology have access to such channels carrying PBS programs, Star Schools, and the Whittle Communications Educational Network. With the predicted increase in programs and channels, various companies will specialize in educational programming. School library media centers will become the beneficiaries of this expansion.

INTEGRATED SERVICES DIGITAL NETWORK

The blurring that is expected to occur between various forms of hardware will happen primarily because all information will become digitalized. One of the programs accelerating this process is ISDN (Integrated Services Digital Network). Using the combined creative resources of AT&T, NCR, Siemens, Hitachi, Telecom, and all of the U.S. regional Bell operating companies, the ISDN program enables non-fiber-optic telephone circuitry to convert analog signals to digital signals. Users can then connect their personal computers or any digital hardware to a data wall outlet. ISDN is designed to facilitate the networking of computers and, more importantly, to further their electronic connection to larger computer systems such as minis and mainframes. ISDN is already available in Chicago, Houston, Atlanta, and Washington, DC. The ability of SLMCs to utilize existing telephone circuitry to access databases, electronic mail, and the collections of other libraries is unprecedented.[16] Advances in this area mean that school media centers will no longer be excluded from the world of information because they lack the funds to pay for all of the hardware once required for electronic access.

TELECOMPUTER TECHNOLOGIES

Although the telepower revolution is going to blur the distinction between televisions, computers, CD-ROMS, videodiscs, and other forms of technological hardware, improvements, enhancements, and discoveries are also occurring separately within these areas. It is important that SLMCs stay abreast of the latest technological developments, especially with regard to a variety of hardware, software, and their likely connections.

Computer Hardware

The capabilities of computers continue to expand almost exponentially each year. The number of components, for example, on a silicon chip continues to double approximately every eighteen months. A second gauge of microelectronic power—processing speed—doubles every year.[17] The advancements in storage and processing speed create exciting new vistas for computers in terms of physical form and access. The machine that was designed to manipulate numbers, then text, symbols, and graphics, has finally evolved into an "information integrator."[18]

Since the power of a computer is dependent upon its ability to store and process information, computer hardware specialists are competing to increase machine proficiencies in these two areas.[19] The result of these achievements is the marketing of desktop microcomputers that are as powerful as mainframes. The most recent advancement is the development by Intel of the Pentium chip. Described as "almost as fast as a supercomputer," the Pentium chip is available in PCs priced as low as $4,500.[20] The Pentium chip, which is silicon, is just a step in the continued increase in the storage and processing capacity of computers. Currently researchers are working on gallium-arsenide chips that process information five to six times faster than silicon chips.[21]

The previously described technological advancements complete another stage in the evolution of the computer. They make possible dramatic changes in the form and function of computers. These structural and functional alterations will have a major impact upon educational institutions. The first change caused by more efficient chips is to permit computers to shrink in size so that they are truly portable. As such, they will replace the ubiquitous pencil and notebooks seen on all classroom desks.[22] Students will be using something similar to Apple's Newton PDA (personal digital assistant) or Tandy's Zoomer. Both devices are digital notepads that employ a stylus for handwriting on a screen. The PDA then converts the handwritten notes into computer files, which in turn can be transferred to networks, fax machines, or cellular connections.[23]

Another portable advancement that will be in widespread use by the year 2000 is the notebook computer. Currently the best-selling notebook computer is Apple's, Powerbook. It contains an 85-megabyte hard-disk drive, a 386 SL microprocessor, and a color display, and it weighs only one pound. Through a grant, Apple Computing, Inc., has provided Ward Chapel Primary (Middlesboro, KY) students in grades 1–3 with five Powerbooks. Working in groups, the students used them to complete a project on transportation that required off-school-site learning. The Powerbooks were also connected to desktop Macintosh computers to permit students to integrate their findings and obtain related transportation information from their main computer.[24]

Mobility and round-the-clock availability are not the only benefits to be derived from the increasing portability of computers. The second enhancement involves connectivity. The large storage and processing power contained in portable computers means that students may use them to access the SLMC's on-line catalog, other networks, CD-ROM files, and even commercial databases. While in the school media center, they can download research from a selected database directly into their portable computers, slip them into their backpacks, and complete the rest of the assignment at home.[25]

It is this combination of portability in computers, coupled with advancements in telecommunications linkups, that will produce what Perelman terms the telecomputer.[26] This device will possess the attributes of a powerful palmtop computer and a cellular telephone in one. Recently the Federal Communications Commission approved experimental trial applications from three cable TV companies to test a wireless communications local area network. One of them, termed Altair, permits laptop and other portable computers independent movement within a building while they access information from a central network. Portable computers with internal cellular telephones are also being marketed. Hewlett-Packard's recent palmtop portable 95 LX computer is constructed to share information with similar 95 LX terminals by infrared beam. It too can work with cellular telephones and wireless networks.

Most of the hardware discussed in this section is prohibitively expensive for the majority of SLMCs at the present time. What is important to note, however, are the trends of increased storage and processing capability of computers and their direct relationship to increasing portability and connectivity. School library media centers will benefit sooner than ever before from these advancements.

SCANNERS

Optical character readers (OCRs) are another form of hardware that will alter information search and retrieval and aid in the creation of full-text databases in libraries. Although scanners have been employed in academic/research institutions for many years, the decline in hardware prices and improvements in scanner software now make them viable options for SLMCs. In 1990, for example, the majority of 24-bit, 300-dots-per-inch color scanners cost from $7,000 to $9,000. At the present time, a 24-bit, 600-dpi color flatbed scanner sells for about $900.[27]

Scanners are not difficult to use once software setups are selected. Basically, the machine reads in pages of hard copy and converts a document into either ASCII files (American Standard Code for Information Interchange) or into a file format used by word processors or spreadsheets.[28]

Once the text is in machine-readable form, it can be incorporated into a research assignment or added to a full-text database.

In addition to a reduction in the cost of scanners, there have been major improvements pertaining to installation and quality of software. For years scanner software was difficult to set up because it did not recognize that it was part of an overall computer operating system. Scanner programs can now use the scanner's driver, thus enabling the computer to communicate with the scanner.

In the past, scanner results also required extensive amounts of editing and proofreading because the software incorrectly interpreted characters, omitted characters, or omitted or inserted spaces. Scanners also had difficulty reading images or pictures with a high degree of resolution. Current advancements in the scanner and the software permit users to scan color images. Specialists in this field are also working toward a true union between scanning hardware and software. One product, called TWAIN (developed by Hewlett-Packard, Caere, Aldus, Logitech, and Eastman Kodak), is designed to permit an image to be inserted directly into any DOS or Mac application, given TWAIN's compatibility with the program and hardware.[29]

So many problems indigenous to OCRs have been solved to such a degree that they are now cost-effective and beneficial for SLMCs to purchase. As a means to construct specialized in-house, full-text databases or provide students with increased capabilities for research and report presentation, they are a computer-related technology that will have important future applications.

CD-ROM TECHNOLOGIES

Of all the recent computer-related technologies to appear on the market, none has affected school libraries as much as CD-ROMs (compact disk–read only memory). CD-ROM is a computer storage medium that employs a technology similar to that used for storing audio in digital form on compact disks. Information is transferred by imprinting minuscule pits and bumps on a metal-coated plastic disk. It is read by interpreting the reflections of a laser beam from the surface.[30] One disk can store approximately "250,000 pages of text, the equivalent of 500 books—a truckload—instantly computer-searchable and publishable at one-fiftieth the cost of printing on paper."[31] Since the cost of a disk is about $3.00, CD-ROMs are an "extremely inexpensive storage and distribution medium for large quantities of information that do not require constant editing or updating."[32]

The most recent study of CD-ROM use in school media centers supports their fast adoption. In a descriptive survey questionnaire of 379 secondary SLMCs in Maine and Pennsylvania, 80 percent of the school media specialists reported using CD-ROM technology for reference. Seventy-five percent of the group intended to acquire additional CD-ROM workstations. Thirty-three percent of those who were not using CD-ROM technology planned to by 1992.[33] A second survey conducted by University Microfilms, Inc., found that the employment of CD-ROMs is predicted to increase "dramatically" in high schools by 1994.[34]

The uses of CD-ROMs are myriad considering the fact that most CD-ROMs are read-only. The first use is the service of a CD-ROM as a bibliographic utility. School library media specialists can purchase access to MARC record CD-ROM databases such as Bibliofile and Laserquest. The latter database, for example, contains 7.3 million MARC records searchable by title, ISBN, or LC number via a CD-ROM player and computer. All MARC fields are editable so that local library information can be included and unwanted information deleted. Access to such an extensive database provides SLMCs with means to convert current card catalogs and input new materials into a variety of on-line software systems.

These same bibliographic utilities using CD-ROM-based technology also provide on-line catalog software that permits SLMCs with no existing on-line catalog to create their own CD-based union catalog. While not interactive for such purposes as original cataloging and circulation, these systems are a vast improvement over print and microform catalogs. The most utilized CD-ROM databases in Mendrinos' study were MaineCat and Access Pennsylvania. Both are statewide CD-ROM union catalogs that provide more than 2 million volumes to users in Maine and over 12 million volumes to users in Pennsylvania.[35]

A third use of CD-ROMs continues to be the manufacture of commercial databases ranging from general reference tools, such as *Grolier's Electronic Encyclopedia* and *Compton's Multi-Media Encyclopedia*, to more specialized products such as OCLC's DISCLIT (British and American Twayne author series on two disks). Large suburban schools, such as Olathe South High School (Olathe, KS), have media centers containing numerous CD-ROM workstations, and several attached printers, providing students with access to *Grolier's Electronic Encyclopedia*, *Newsbank's Electronic Index*, *Facts on File News Digest*, *Infotrac's Magazine Index*, World Book's *Information Finder*, Microsoft's *Bookshelf*, and McGraw-Hill's *Science and Technology Reference Set*.[36] The list of these commercial databases continues to expand as scanners with more sophisticated software and information already in machine-readable form facilitate the CD-ROM conversion process.

A fourth use of CD-ROM technology pertains to remote on-line databases such as DIALOG's ERIC and Magazine Index. Prior to their availability on CD-ROM, school media centers were hesitant to make these databases widely available to students and faculty because they are fee-based. Now, through such companies as Silverplatter, they are available on CD-ROM. Although they are still fairly expensive in CD-ROM format, browsing them without a monetary charge feature makes them easily accessible by unskilled searchers. School library media specialists can afford to await a CD update because there is usually sufficient information to satisfy most student research assignments.

Future trends with regard to CD-ROM technologies are interesting to contemplate, because all of them will improve the programs and services of school media centers. The first concerns storage capacity. With the increased storage capacity created by more efficient computer chips, the space for locally mounted CD-ROM databases will increase and the costs for CD-ROMs as the market expands should decrease. Increased storage capacity makes larger full-text databases feasible. Software will also provide better methods for compressing the data, so that a larger database can be stored in the same amount of space. The faster computer processing speed expected with a new computer chip will facilitate the search and retrieval of lengthy articles on CD-ROMs.[37]

A second trend concerns the networking of CD-ROMs. At the time of Mendrinos' study, only 4.5 percent of the SLMCs had networked their CD-ROMs. The problems they encountered centered around response time on a network, lack of network software, and the need for printer access.[38] Within this short period of time, CD-ROMs had become networkable using various forms of new networking software, such as Novelle's version 3.11, and stackable CD-ROM network players.

A third trend concerns the increase in the number of databases and the demand that they be full-text. For SLMCs whose users require almost instant information gratification, these changes will be heartily welcomed. Many students in a structured situation such as school cannot always find the time or transportation to retrieve cited materials located in remote libraries. They need timely, local access to the information, which only full-text databases can provide.

The continued growth of networked, full-text CD-ROM databases will also mean a continued diminution in the need for many seldom-used series and infrequently cited reference materials in print. School library media specialists will be able to make cost-effective cancellations similar to those their academic counterparts have been making for the past eight years.

The last and most important trend regarding CD-ROM technology relates to its potential for interactivity. While read-only is truly necessary to enable some forms of information to retain their inviolability, CD-ROM is considered by most technologists to be an inexpensive multimedia medium. With the creation of CD-I (compact disk interactive) by Sony and Philips, a special-purpose player enables the user to access 1,000 video stills, six hours of high-quality sound, and 10,000 pages of text in conjunction with a computer software program that renders the system totally interactive with the user.[39] In the case of CD-I, new developments in software are directly related to developments in hardware. It is this combination that produces what is referred to as interactive media.

SOFTWARE DEVELOPMENTS

Before discussing interactive media, it is important to understand the changes and advancements taking place in software. This will help place current and emerging technologies that combine advanced hardware and software in a more comprehensive perspective.

Software can be defined as the systems that give life to tiny silicon chips inside computers.[40] It is considered "the glue that holds the other technologies together and makes them work in systems."[41] At the present time sophisticated software requires creation from scratch, with thousands of programmers laboring many years at costs reaching millions of dollars.[42] Microsoft, for example, has employed 220 programmers for four years to develop a new operating system at a cost of $150 million. They have written approximately 4 million lines of intricate code.[43] It is this labor-intensive quality and its correspondingly high cost that have previously been major hindrances to making rapid progress in computer technologies. This pattern, however, is beginning to change as software is affected by increased programmer productivity and as the opportunity arises to reuse previously designed and tested software packages.[44]

Software Operating Systems

The developmental lag that usually exists between software and hardware is swiftly being closed by the design of new software operating systems. As more mainframes are replaced with personal computers comparable in storage capacity and microprocessing speed, they require software operating systems equal to the hardware power. MS-DOS (the current software operating system for all IBM-based computers) and Apple Macintosh (the software operating system for Apple-based computers) are considered too primitive for the sensitive and complicated transactions of the financial and business markets. To solve these problems, several large technology companies such as Microsoft, IBM, Novell, and Apple are racing to create a software operating system that can turn personal computers into supercomputers.

Microsoft's creation, Windows NT, claims to be the solution to harnessing the hardware power resident in new desktop computers. With Windows NT, users can work with specialized software only available on mainframes and minicomputers and with the click of a mouse switch to writing a letter using WordPerfect. With another click, the user will access a spreadsheet from another Windows software program such as Quattro.

Windows NT is slated to sell for $300 to $500 and is thus affordable even for SLMCs facing financial constraints.[45] For Apple users, Taligent, an IBM-Apple cooperative project, is also working on a similar operating system which is presently under the codename "Pink."[46]

Specialized Software

The creation of new operating software systems for PCs or desktop computers, enabling them to function as mainframes, is an exciting development for school library media centers. They will become the heirs to new specialized software packages that permit greater individualization, easier access, and more options. Most PC-based on-line catalogs, for example, still require the user to search within a systematized format such as author, title, or subject. New software design will allow more idiosyncratic access that is more likely to mimic the way children seek information.[47] Currently, the majority of PC-based on-line catalogs are not full-text. Yet new on-line catalog software will probably permit access via table of contents or chapter headings.

Another form of specialized software called front-end software will also permit more options. For years, the memory and storage capacity of computers did not permit the additional loading of user-friendly interfaces to assist users to navigate through fairly complicated library software systems. The emergence of super PCs will allow for menu and help screens that are more user-friendly and that can be designed for an individual user or local library. Front-end software will be particularly helpful to SLMCs as they access remote fee-based or free commercial databases or libraries. Instructions, for example, can be simplified. Natural language queries could be translated into formal searches. Downloading commands would be readily available from a menu screen. Search strategies can be seamlessly modified if no items or too many items are identified. Finally, it could screen out information, such as repetitive commands written by the student, so as to streamline a search.[48]

The ability to load front-end software to interface with larger and more sophisticated software modules will make it possible to permanently integrate what are now termed user-selected software options into larger systems. Students, for example, will switch back and forth from accessing on-line databases to scanning and integrating paragraphs from reference books into their assigned projects in a WordPerfect format. At the same terminal, software such as PC-Proof will automatically search for missing articles, subject-verb disagreements, and even sexist terms in their final paper.[49]

HYPERTECHNOLOGIES

Striving to integrate multiple technologies is an ongoing goal in software as well as hardware development. The increasing number of hypertechnologies (Hypercard, hypertext, and hypermedia) in SLMCs can be compared to the hardware proliferation of CD-ROMs. Both will have a major impact on programs and services and will continue to do so in the coming years. Hypercard, created by Apple associate Bill Atkinson, empowers computer users to organize and manage material without having to be fluent in the cryptic syntax of a computer programming language. Hypercard's MS-DOS equivalents consist of Hyperpad, Guide, and Toolbook.[50]

The software system, Hypercard, permits the creation of hypertext. Hypertext (the term was coined by Ted Wilson in the 1960s to define "nonsequential" writing) permits users to connect pieces of information, to forge branches through a body of material, and to edit or add to existing texts. Users can trace trails of footnotes and cross-reference related information without losing their original place within the document.[51]

The potential use of hypertext in SLMCs is tremendous. School media specialists and businesses related to school libraries can design on-line systems and bibliographic instruction units that cater to a user's level of knowledge or experience. Students may select the topic and information level to request information. At any point, they may stop when they have acquired sufficient information or gone beyond their level of expertise.

Using hypertext, SLMCs can create miniprograms, such as tours of the media center, that provide students with the option of learning the borrowing procedures or the availability of commercial database searching. The programs can be downloaded onto floppy diskettes and loaned out to new students. "Knowledge maps" that move learners through a series of article and book citations until they understand a recent discovery can be designed in-house.[52] Students at Upland Junior High School (Upland, CA) used hypertext to design and test a solar house. By combining preexisting software supplied by the California Technology Education Resource Center with an optical disk called Living Textbook Physical Science, students were able to obtain enough information to construct and test actual solar houses. They also used DIALOG to find answers to additional research questions about the project. [53] The applications of hypertechnologies to SLMCs are limited only by the programmers' imaginations.

With the continued striving to integrate multiple technologies, the creation of hypermedia, which include links to nonprint items such as pictures, diagrams, and sounds, is a logical progression in software development. Some of the hypermedia on the market, such as Harvard University's Perseus program of the ancient Greek world, is already being used by students at the Dalton School (New York City). Students at Shrewsbury High School (Shrewsbury, MA) have produced their own hypermedia program by synchronizing pictures from the National Gallery of Art's videodisc with songs from the Beatles White Album compact disc.[54]

Future hypertechnology applications will be just as exciting for SLMCs as the currently emerging ones are. The first area concerns "published compilations of information" such as encyclopedias and other reference works. In this scenario, all links or connections are created by the author, and students use the marketed product as they would printed text. Candidates for this use of hypertext would be reference books with a great deal of indexing and cross-references.

A second application concerns the ability to create active hypermedia. At Brown University's Institute for Research in Information and Scholarship, for example, a series of networked stations is used to provide shareable access to two sets of course materials. In English literature and plant cell biology courses, students can contribute their own additions and personal links to the original programs. They thus become active participants in further developing the course materials by inputting their own ideas, findings, and knowledge. Instructors report improvement in student essays and class discussions through this type of hypertext access.

The last application relates to the power of Hypercard as a user-friendly programming language. School library media centers can use Hypercard to design interfaces to more complicated software systems such as large academic on-line systems or commercial databases. More importantly though, Hypercard can be used to retrieve text and pictures from large databases and systematically form them into suitable classroom units. For example, the Perseus database contains five to ten thousand pictures and 50 million characters of text and commentary. It is so large that it could not be entirely viewed or read in a semester course. Hypercard is used as a tool to permit the user to access specific pictures, maps, and commentary so that a cohesive presentation is available on a certain topic for use by students.[55]

In the next five years, the main thrust of this type of software will be to provide users with a higher degree of activity. School library media specialists will be able to design resource-based units that permit students to contribute their own knowledge, facts, and evaluations of course materials and specialized databases. Cooperative learning, a recent instructional method, will be employed more frequently as teachers realize the opportunities for students in groups to use hypermedia to actively participate in the learning process.

Hypermedia will also continue to enhance various on-line databases by permitting: (1) increased full-text searching, (2) highlighting of search terms in the text, (3) emendability of text, (4) viewing of tables of contents, (5) personalized menu screens, (6) multiple entry points to search text, (7) screen displays with links to select desired reading areas, and (8) editing functions that permit text movement to word processing programs.[56]

INTERACTIVE MEDIA

The previous discussions focused upon separate developments in hardware and software, but always with an emphasis on their eventual union into one "digital palette."[57] This process has already started and is called interactive media (IM). In most cases, but not all, IM means the blending of hypermedia, videodiscs, and/or CD-ROMs or CD-Is. This merging of broadcast telecommunications and data processing communications has been more aptly termed "compunications."[58] Combining specialized software (hypertext/hypermedia) with videodiscs or CD-ROMs has created an interactive system with potential for revolutionizing current educational programs and methods. The individualization of instruction with the use of interactive media will finally become a reality not only in students' classrooms but also in their homes.

Despite rapid progress in IM, it is still not synthesized into a seamlessly integrated technology. As such, it is somewhat defined by "levels of interactivity."[59] These levels relate to such things as the use of particular hardware, program software and design, and the information furnished to the user and instructor. The first level pertains to the accessing of video pictures/drawings on a videodisc by using the remote control device to play portions of the videodisc material. Another option at this level is to show still photos as an impetus for discussion or a writing aid for a research assignment. Use of this technology as a visual aid employs only the videodisc (containing thousands of pictures/images and millions of characters as text or commentary), a remote controller, and a video monitor. The level of interactivity is minimal.

The second level of interactivity entails using the computer (with its specialized hypermedia software) and the videodisc to create teaching units by accessing selected portions of commentary/text or individual images. Interactivity increases appreciably at this level because the user is actually engaged in interpreting, analyzing, comparing, synthesizing, and evaluating the information. A final step permits users to impose their own voices over the material and save their created programs onto floppy diskettes.[60]

The use of interactive media has increased substantially in schools as more educational videodiscs have been produced. As of 1989, there were seven hundred videodiscs listed in the Videodisc Compendium for Education and Training. Most of them relate to the physical sciences. Highest growth areas are in the humanities and social studies.[61]

The growing use of interactive media in schools is also positively evidenced by the number of articles that describe successful use in conjunction with library research. Middle schools in San Francisco, for example, have used GTV, a videodisc about U.S. history, in their eighth-grade social studies program. Teachers were trained and developed their own units, and selected students were taught the technology. Projects have ranged from faculty-designed chapter review sessions targeted to a variety of student learning styles to student-prepared reports on westward expansion that have been employed in other social studies classes. In one class, teams of students were assigned historical themes and required to combine their use of GTV with library research.[62]

Three art teachers at separate New York elementary and secondary schools used a National Gallery of Art videodisc to create an artistic style unit, to research Victorian period dress for a student costume design portfolio, and to instruct team members participating in an academic quiz program about art periods and styles.[63]

Most of these articles also testify to improved student learning. Unfortunately, they do not include any quantitative data to support their observations. Previous studies, however, indicate that the insertion of an interactive component in nonprint formats, coupled with student activity in the lesson, produces the best learning results.[64] In the majority of articles describing IM use, teachers viewed this technology as a stimulus for students to search the media center for additional materials on a subject. Use of interactive media also provides a means to create individualized instructional units designed to appeal to particular student learning styles, interests, and learning speeds.[65]

INTERACTIVE BOOKS

The use of the SLMC as a complementary adjunct to interactive media may be transitory, as multimedia enhance books and, in some cases, replace them. The arrival of paperback-sized computers coincides with a generation of students who have grown up reading from computer terminals.[66] Franklin Watts, for example, claims sales of 4 million hand-held encyclopedia and dictionary units. So far, most of these sales have been for home use. The digitized information is accessible on some type of compact disk similar to Sony's Data Discman. Reference books such as *The Dictionary of Cultural Literacy* and *Merriam-Webster's Dictionary of English Usage* are available in this format. With the increased use of CD-I these products can become truly interactive. CD-I players access disks containing text, graphics, and sound in machines the size of a VCR or a hardback book. In addition, they can be attached to a television to view material on a larger screen. Interactive book offerings presently comprise children's books, travel guides, how-to manuals, and music appreciation. These titles all include graphics and sound, and are keyword-searchable.

Current reviews of interactive media indicate that there are still problems requiring amelioration before use becomes widespread. Electronic bookware, for example, discussed in detail below, has placed an emphasis on visual, rather than intellectual, stimulation.[67] Multimedia packages, in an attempt to give users the maximum amount of information, are also producing user-challenging units that really require additional user-friendly interfaces.[68] Although many of the products are presently not appropriate for school libraries, they are rapidly becoming more user-friendly.

The application of properly designed, intellectually stimulating interactive media will be an exciting development. Interactivity in reference books will be a welcome addition. Keyword searching and Boolean logic in a reference book will ensure that students have not missed vital information concerning their topics. For students who are visual learners, supplementary graphics will be of great assistance.

Most SLMSs recognize that the introduction of multimedia elements into reference materials will enhance intellectual or bibliographic access. It is the incorporation of these elements into literature, which has previously exercised the imagination and thought processes without need of pictures and sound, that is less understandable. With the use of more powerful and portable computers, however, a new form of literature termed bookware is predicted to emerge. Unlike some forms of bookware which still use hypertext permitting different denouements to the same story, these new products attempt to provide each reader with a unique literary experience. Will Wright's *SimCity*, for example, has the reader become an urban planner and then presents the results of his or her planning. *Its Name Was Penelope* is a narrabase consisting of 400 records within six files. Users can access text by menu searching and random record generation. "Random record production causes screens of text to appear in a natural, nonsequential manner."[69] Files are structured on the basis of chapters from the *Odyssey*. One can enter the text through a file of childhood memories entitled "Dawn" and proceed to a main file called "At Sea." Throughout the work, readers can elect different files and within that file different records. Thus readers can interact with the text and each character in their unique manner.

For bibliophiles who access information in a classic, left-to-right, linear format, *Its Name Was Penelope* still sounds disorganized, foreign, and not very intellectually challenging. To a computer-literate generation, however, electronic books are expected to become another source of recreational reading as available as paperback books are in SLMCs. School media specialists will probably be ordering them along with hardback and paperback materials within the next decade.

DISTANCE LEARNING

In previous publications, distance learning was sure to be placed within the telecommunications section, because the level of interactivity was limited and the hardware consisted mainly of television sets and telephone connections. Spurred by rapid developments in telecomputers, however, distance learning is now considered an interactive medium. It has become a cost-effective means through which education is transmitted to learners who are unable to participate in the educational process in a traditional way.

For years, distance learning was seen only as a cost-saving alternative to provide students in geographically isolated or socioeconomically disadvantaged areas with education in critical subject areas such as foreign language, math, and science. With the development of advanced telecommunications systems and computers, distance learning is no longer viewed as a compensatory medium but one that all schools will be using in the future.

Through the 1988 funding of the Star Schools Project, four consortia (Midlands Consortium, Satellite Educational Resources Consortium (SERC), Technical Education Research Center (TERC), and TI-IN) were designed as instructional networks to provide courses to students in forty-five states. Three of the networks transmit courses via television and satellite systems. TERC transmits through computer networking. Each consortium has installed distance learning in many schools and states through satellite connections. A recent assessment of the scope of the Star Schools Project reported 2,962 schools in forty-five states participating in one or more program offerings, with 8,000 students and 720 teachers receiving academic credit for program course work. A total of 62,000 students and 22,000 faculty enrolled in enrichment and staff development activities.[70]

While these figures are extremely positive, the potential for SLMCs nationwide is vast. Prince Georges County Public Schools System (MD), for example, was given an educational access channel and access to two other channels via two cable TV systems. The results have been an astounding array of programs targeting not only traditionally disadvantaged populations but also populations eager for enrichment and advanced educational opportunities. In addition to providing commercially produced instructional programs, the county also produced (1) an in-house drug education series for elementary school students, (2) a middle school science series, (3) a live call-in homework assistance program for mathematics students, (4) a thirty-six part elementary art series, (5) an eight-part Prince George's County history series, (6) a "Jeopardy"-style science quiz program for elementary and secondary school students, and (8) a series of pre-algebra assistance programs for middle school teachers. In addition, they created numerous staff development programs ranging from critical thinking and multicultural education to AIDS awareness. They continue to host an excellent program called "School Showcase" featuring new programs and services at different county schools.

The county's distance learning program is truly interactive. Their ITV network is configured to permit five sites access to one teacher while simultaneously allowing all participants to see and hear one another. Instructors transmit data via a computer network that employs multi-modem dial-up access through a digital bridge. A writing pad functions as an electronic blackboard, allowing the instructor to illustrate problems. The writing is seen simultaneously at all sites. A scanner is used to send tests or handouts within seconds. Even an overhead and TV monitor can be employed for entire class viewing. The same methods are utilized to teach SAT preparation courses, to stage mock trials, to teach community college courses, and to host teleconferences.[71]

The degree of interactivity with this form of distance learning is high. When conducted in this manner, distance learning is no longer viewed as a compensatory tool but as a cost-effective, educationally sound way of providing learners with more convenient resources. Studies also demonstrate that distance learning is at least as productive as traditional classroom instruction, regardless of subject. The expense of distance learning is also declining steadily.[72] To join SERC, for example, an individual state pays $35,000 per year. Student fees are $150 per semester.[73] When compared to the costs of full-time instructors, transportation, and regular classroom maintenance, distance learning is a technology that will be employed with greater frequency nationwide.

Many distance learning experts perceive its current interactivity as a transitional stage as we move toward a "telelearning environment." In this setting, distance, location, and attendance become irrelevant elements in learning. Experts in this area envision schools that are not associated with a particular building but rather with a type of establishment that dispenses education via telecomputer channels. Although the eventual demise of site-based education is hard to envision given our conventional educational settings, large school districts such as Broward County, Florida, are linking all of their classrooms in a computer network so that they can expand curriculum offerings without hiring faculty for every classroom.[74]

School library media centers can be expected to play an active role in distance learning. Collections will have to be developed that reflect courses offered not only on-site but also via cable and satellite. Depending upon the size of the school, SLMSs may be expected to serve as coordinators of schedules and equipment. More importantly, school media specialists will be involved in providing access to this rapidly developing educational technology by alerting administrators at the local level to its current educational potential.

NATIONAL AND INTERNATIONAL NETWORKING

Historically, networking among SLMCs entailed cooperative efforts to locate, acquire, and physically share materials. Resource sharing comprised activities such as coordinated collection development, interlibrary loan, acquisitions agreements, and reference referral services. When, for example, a student or faculty member could not locate an item, an SLMS usually searched another bibliographic network or telephoned another school library and arranged to borrow it. The process usually took several days or longer. While faculty were usually able to accommodate this arrangement, most students facing relatively short deadlines for research assignments found this form of interlibrary loan not feasible.

The second hindrance to network participation by SLMCs has been lack of any telecommunications facilities. The most recent study of network participation, for example, revealed that fewer than 50 percent of SLMCs had telephones in their centers. Despite this deplorable statistic, however, more than 50 percent of the survey participants were involved in some form of networking. The presence of a telephone in an SLMC also had a direct correlation with a media center's more active involvement in policies and planning for facilities use, staff development, and curriculum.[75] Thus it is evident how critical the presence of a telephone in the SLMC is to improving the programs and services it can offer.

With the previously described advances in computer technologies and telecommunications, the installation of even one computer, a telephone, and a fax machine in an SLMC can significantly expand the means for achieving resource sharing. Through locally integrated on-line systems, school library media centers can access a wide array of nonbibliographic and bibliographic databases. Computer networking provides a wealth of opportunities for interfacing library on-line catalogs and networking to databases around the globe. Moreover, systems are becoming so simplified that students and faculty will be directly involved in the networking process. New electronic advances in networking will also reduce significantly the document delivery time vis-à-vis interlibrary loan, thus introducing new issues such as higher user expectations, more library use, and additional costs to SLMCs.

One of the most exciting new developments to occur in networking concerns the generational advancements of on-line public access catalogs (OPACs). First-generation OPACs are generally thought of as having an abbreviated MARC record accessible by author, title, and LC subject headings. Second-generation OPACs are characterized by access via a full MARC record, author, title, subject and keyword searching, and Boolean logic. Third-generation on-line catalogs feature, in addition to the previously described access points, help screens, menus, abstracts of materials, and limited full-text searching.[76] It is this generation of on-line catalog that also extends networking beyond local, state, and even national boundaries to include the globe. Improved networking software has enabled this generation of on-line catalogs to serve as a gateway to even more databases and networks.

Academic libraries are now loading commercial or proprietary databases such as ERIC, Psych Abstracts, and Infotrac onto their on-line catalogs. These databases become part of the library's on-line catalog through a menu screen. Arizona State University Libraries, for example, have loaded twenty databases onto their on-line system. Users can access the general on-line catalog (the ASU Libraries and OCLC cataloging system), six H. W. Wilson periodical indexes (Applied Science & Technology Index, Humanities Index, Social Sciences Index, General Science Index, Business Periodical Index, and the Education Index), *Grolier's Academic American Encyclopedia*, the Map Index (locally produced), the Solar Energy Index (locally produced), the Arizona and Southwest Index (locally produced), three Career Service databases, Arizona Statistics (statistical tables, locally produced), the Song Index (locally produced), Performance Tapes Index (locally produced), National Indian Education Clearinghouse Directory (locally produced), and a gateway to a database called UnCover.

UnCover database provides access to the tables of contents to more than ten thousand periodicals via the CARL/Denver Computer System. Users are transparently connected to UnCover, which is searchable through a leased line, when they select it from the menu screen. Once connected to CARL (Colorado Alliance of Research Libraries) users can avail themselves of more than seventy additional databases and library catalogs. In totality, the Arizona State University Libraries user has more than fifty library catalogs to select from. The ASU library system is just one example of the growing trend toward networking integrated library systems. Access through a local on-line catalog loaded with commercial databases and gateways to more remote databases creates a world of almost unlimited networking opportunities.[77]

Most of the technological advances predicted for electronic networks will be extremely advantageous for SLMCs. Overall they serve to increase access, streamline search commands, reduce the need for intermediary assistance, and facilitate use by secondary school students. The first development concerns an increasing trend by large library systems to use similar software. Libraries in large regions of the country are cooperating by purchasing common systems. These networks have the advantage of not only shared software costs but also similar search interfaces. Besides the CARL system, examples of these regional consortia include LUIS, the Florida consortium of libraries using NOTIS, the Illinois consortium of libraries using ILLINET, and the University of California system using Melvyl. Users of these systems have a much easier time searching because the search commands are the same regardless of what database or library they are accessing.[78]

A second trend relates to the development of on-line systems that can manage numeric data and text of variable length. SPIRES (Stanford Public Information Retrieval System), for example, has a component in its on-line catalog which supports a homework database consisting of lecture notes, answer sheets, and practice exams. Syracuse University provides access to COMPUSTAT, which contains twenty years of numerical data regarding 2,500 corporations. Through the use of COMPUSTAT, users can view and manipulate the data.

A third trend concerns the ability of networks to put images online. At MIT, the library has succeeded in developing a collection of slides that are used in conjunction with an architectural course. The database of 7,000 images of Boston includes photographs, maps, and drawings. Students can access this visual database through specialized workstations attached to the campus digital computing network.

A fourth trend, and one of the most important for SLMCs, deals with full-text on-line catalogs. Currently available full-text databases are not for general reading. Many of them have been created to support intricate linguistic and textual analyses of ancient literary works. Their new features, however, will provide the foundation for future enhancements that will create full-text on-line databases on a major scale. One of these, for example, is the Thesaurus Linguae Graecae (TLG), a Greek-text database available through the University of California's Irvine campus to scholars in the humanities. Access is provided by keyword and line number.

As more of these specialized databases are developed and made available to a broader population, features such as structural browsing will be introduced that permit users to view an outline of the topic, appropriate chapter headings, or paragraphs. OCLC has designed software called GraphText that supports this type of full-text searching. Other companies are expected to develop similar software.[79]

A fifth trend in networking is unrelated to future software enhancements or database contents but is vital for SLMC participation. This development focuses on the issue of access. Many school library media centers currently have access to the increasing number of on-line databases by membership in state multitype networks such as ACCESS Pennsylvania or ILLINET (Illinois Library Network). Once logged into such networks they can select from the menu screens and search other libraries and commercial databases. A second form of access that is beginning to develop offers entry by using different systems available through Internet or with direct leased lines via each SLMC's own on-line catalog. School media centers without formal connections to state or regional consortia may access other databases through a traditional connect time and match charge arrangement.

It is obvious from these trends that there have been significant developments in various types of electronic networks that link academic libraries throughout the United States and the world. One of the most important developments in this area has been the growth of Internet. Internet is a constantly growing and mutating combination of approximately 280 academic and research center networks that permits users to search the catalogs of more than 500 research institutions. More than half a dozen international connections have been established with networks in Canada, Europe, Mexico, and other parts of the world.

Local and regional library consortia, such as the CARL system in Colorado and the Melvyl system in California, make their catalogs and even special in-house databases available through Internet. Some systems, such as Melvyl, limit searching to their catalog and restrict searching of commercial databases such as Medline to University of California patrons. Even though Internet consists of various networks administered by different institutions, it appears as an integrated entity to the user. Internet supports an increasing variety of other services such as electronic mail, file transfers between member Internet computers, and linkage to remote computers that emulate direct connections. Full-text files may even be downloaded from Internet host computers. Examples include the Bible, the Koran, Shakespearean works, *Peter Pan*, and Hardy's *Far from the Madding Crowd*. Song lyrics, news articles, recent Supreme Court opinions, census data, the *CIA World Fact Book*, and a wealth of government information are searchable through Internet. The contents change regularly as more resources are added to the network. Equipment requirements are minimal. Users need simply a telephone line, a modem, a computer, and communications software.

Payment for Internet access is on an institutional basis rather than the usual dial-up access charge method. Access, however, is still a problem for users who are not sufficiently computer-literate. Connection instructions are fairly detailed, and once users are logged in they must quickly master the search protocols of various databases. Some systems are also fairly narrow in their support of terminal emulations and require users to change the settings on their communications software to correspond with the on-line catalog they wish to search. Work is currently under way to standardize networking protocols and introduce more compatibility into system searching. Despite these problems, more than five hundred SLMCs are using Internet with positive results.[80] A recent article in *Library Journal*, for example, described an Argentinean fifth-grade class querying their American counterparts via Internet about their dress code regarding blue jeans.[81] Internet users could even read eyewitness accounts via electronic mail of the 1991 Soviet coup.

NREN (NATIONAL RESEARCH AND EDUCATION NETWORK)

The availability of Internet to SLMCs is a significant step in linking them to an international database of information, but it is not the final one. As a response to the increasing flow of data over Internet, plans are under way to upgrade the major network Internet backbone to a 3-gigabit-per-second level by 1996. This communication upgrade is part of the implementation of an even larger network called the National Research and Education Network. NREN will establish fiber-optic cabling and digital communications links in every U.S. school, thus enabling rapid transfer of textual information as well as video and audio. Each school will have a computer that performs as a local file distributor of NREN information to other terminals within the school's local area network.

School library media centers are considered the inherent site for NREN file servers because of the location of additional research resources. Students and faculty will be able to use NREN to access and transmit research materials and programs on a scale never before contemplated. Separate communications links can be established between different or like schools for such purposes as foreign language and cultural exchanges. Collaborative teaching units can be designed between schools that permit them to share resources.[82] The school media center will serve as an electronic navigator linking students and faculty to a truly global information network.

School library media centers are already connecting internationally to other schools and databases either through Internet or various other networks and communications systems. Students at the Juan Morel Campos Intermediate School (Brooklyn, NY) initiated electronic conferencing through an AT&T Learning Network. The objective of the network was to connect classes globally and design a curriculum-based project related to such topics as "Energy and the Environment" and "Global Issues and Society's Problems." Half of the schools in the project were in foreign countries. Students in New York, for example, were able to listen to students in Tübingen, Germany, discuss the ramifications of removing the Berlin Wall. Students assigned to write imaginary autobiographies about teenagers from different cultures used materials gained from interviews with German and Australian students.[83] The research information had been downloaded and made available in the school library media center. The use of the SLMC as the central site for the network helps students and faculty associate the media center with new electronic technologies and, most importantly, strengthens its position as the academic center of the school.

In Tallahassee, Florida, eleven schools participated in a project called the Florida-England Connection. The project involved forming a telecommunications link with selected member schools of Campus 2000, Britain's educational network. Students exchanged geographical information about each other's areas for the purpose of creating travel brochures. Test results of the project indicated that culture awareness had a consistent tendency to increase as more interactive exchanges occurred with students from the other country.[84]

SMART TECHNOLOGIES

The application of smart technologies to information retrieval and learning has been a constant area of research for not only computer scientists but also physical scientists. Despite the remarkable increases in storage capacity and processing speed of computers, the complexity of creating a machine that replicates human intelligence has remained an abiding challenge. During the past decade, there have been continual predictions that "artificially intelligent systems" are only years from development. Yet progress has remained rather slow.

The operating definition of artificial intelligence (AI) is a machine which can pass the Turing test, first posited by Alan Turing in 1950. Turing's definition of AI "involves the ability of a computer to imitate human performance, particularly in the ability to engage in written dialog."[85] Although there have been a number of software programs that have passed narrow definitions of this test, none has succeeded in meeting the complete requirements established by Turing.

In other fields of computer intelligence, there has been sufficient progress to warrant discussion of SLMC-related emerging technologies and future trends in this area. Because these advances do not meet the qualifications established by Turing, they are referred to as "applied intelligence" or "smart technologies."[86]

Expert/Knowledge Systems

Expert or knowledge systems are computer programs created to perform like a human expert in a defined area of knowledge. Most expert systems have four components: the knowledge base, the inference engine, the knowledge-acquisition interface, and the user interface. Once designed, the program functions as a "highly-informed insider" within its area of expertise. Users then interact with the knowledge to reach a conclusion. Expert systems, in addition to requiring the knowledge base of a subject expert, need to follow a complex set of rules involving decision trees, flowcharts, and inferential reasoning. They are time-consuming to construct but when done properly have many useful applications to school libraries and education.[87]

Most library expert systems have been designed to help users navigate through fairly complicated databases such as the National Agriculture Library's on-line catalog. Their expert system, called Answerman, assists users to find information in various agricultural reference books and guides them to more specific information by searching CD-ROM databases and remote on-line systems. CITE, an expert system at the National Library of Medicine, serves as an interface to the on-line catalog, permitting the user to query the database in natural English.[88]

Both of these library-related expert systems improve the ability of a user to find information. The use of CITE, for example, which allows natural English to access the catalog, would be very helpful in school on-line catalogs. Most students experience difficulty searching databases that require Library of Congress or Sears subject headings. Students are also not as intimidated by a computerized system as they are by a human expert. As a result, they are more likely to use the on-line catalog.

While these types of knowledge systems are not yet available for SLMCs, these features will probably be incorporated into future generations of on-line catalogs. In the meantime, school library media specialists should become acquainted with other educational expert systems designed for various curriculum areas. Elementary school students in California are using an expert software program called Dr. Know (Ventura Educational Systems, Newbury Park, CA) to understand animal classifications. Initially they input a series of factual statements into the program, such as "A monkey is a primate," "A primate is a mammal," "A mammal is an animal." Students then pose a follow-up question: "Is a monkey an animal?"[89] In answering "yes," the computer has not just processed data, but has rendered a decision as a result of inferential programming and complicated programming employing the services of a knowledge database on animal classification.

Other successful knowledge base software programs include A.I.—An Experience with Artificial Intelligence (Scholastic). Through a series of logic games, students initiate their own game-playing strategies. Throughout the game, the AI program learns from student choices. As the game progresses, it becomes more difficult for students to plan successful strategies, because the program has "learned" from previous errors. World Builder (Silicon Beach Software) is a construction set program for building logic puzzles. Course Builder (TeleRobotics Informational) enables faculty to design computer-assisted instructional programs ranging from question-and-answer series to more advanced question, answer, remediation types.

A more highly developed program employing an expert system is called CLASS.LD2. Designed by Utah State University researchers, CLASS.LD2 employs an expert system based upon state and federal criteria to help educators identify learning disabled students. A confidence factor has been built into the program which informs users about the certainty of their decision. The success of CLASS.LD2 has lowered Utah's misclassification rate by 50 percent.[90]

Neural Networking

The expert system A.I.—An Experience with Artificial Intelligence, whereby the computer learns from student strategies, exemplifies a second type of smart technology called neural networking. Neural networks are considered another step in the development of artificial intelligence because they permit computers to solve problems rather than crunch information or data in the usual hierarchical way. Neural networks employ a series of processors functioning in a fluid, parallel networking architecture that simulates the networks of neurons forming the human brain. Similar to the brain in function, they can recognize patterns of information and delegate various functions to other network parts. They can also "learn" from failure in some aspects of the network.

The rapid development of neural networks has exciting applications not only for artificial intelligence research but also for increased use of expert systems, computer-assisted instruction, and simplifying software. All of these advances can be expected to affect the future programs and services of SLMCs. Nippon Electric, for example, is designing a four-processor neural network personal computer capable of solving problems, reading text and voice inputs, using expert systems, and learning from use patterns.[91] Researchers at Johns Hopkins University have constructed a neural network that learned to read English by decoding series of printed symbols into words and sentences. What is important to note in this example is that the computer was trained to read through a series of recognizable patterns and feedback, not programmed to read. The process is similar to the method a human would use to learn to read. Although neural networks are still considered somewhat on the technological cutting edge, software has already been produced that permits users to install a primitive neural network on a personal computer for less than $200.[92]

The promise that neural networks hold for capturing visual images and sound, and recognizing complex patterns, causes some computer experts to envision them as "smart" interfaces for other computers or complicated on-line systems. Termed "knowledge assistants" or "intellectual robots," they will be stored in portable student PCs and will learn student information-seeking behavior patterns. Once these patterns are learned, they will shortcut routine tasks, respond to queries, and search for information.[93]

Voice Technologies

Until the development of neural networks, expert systems, and faster computer processing, voice recognition systems were not expected to impact libraries or schools until the next decade. The advances in these fields, however, have helped remove some of the technological barriers to this exciting field of research.

At present, many libraries use voice mail systems and some may use Kurzweil reading machines for visually impaired patrons. Both of these voice technologies are examples of speech synthesis or computerized voice output. While the voice sounds rather disembodied, this type of voice technology is helpful in furnishing information over the telephone regardless of the location or time, providing text-to-speech information to the visually disabled, and confirming computer input.

A second type of speech technology is called voice recognition. A voice recognition system is much more complicated, because of the nuances of speech signals such as accents, manner of speaking, and sometimes even emotion. Most voice recognition systems can be classified into two developmental stages. Some, which are speaker-dependent, require a user to supply a voice recognition template of each spoken word. These systems have a vocabulary range of 50 to 1,000 words and can recognize the clearly enunciated words spoken only by the person who has supplied a voice template. Libraries using this system are still dependent upon a computer keyboard for most inputting, since the vocabulary is so limited. At most, short commands such as searching an on-line catalog by call number or ISBN number are possible.[94]

The desirable breakthrough in this field is to produce speaker-independent continuous speech recognition systems that are economically viable. The standard that most companies expect to meet within the next three to five years is a continuous natural speech system with a 5,000–10,000-word vocabulary in a $500 speech computer board.[95] Dragon Systems in Massachusetts is currently marketing a 30,000-word recognition system that is also capable of accepting more than 40 words per minute of dictation at a cost between $3,000 and $9,000.[96]

If this cost could be lowered to $500, there would be many applications of voice recognition systems for SLMCs and schools in general. One of the first applications would be the improved service that could be offered to the visually impaired and learning disabled. A second application would be as a software front-end type of general help system. A voice recognition system could be used to answer such questions as "How do I borrow this book?" or "When is this book due?" Acquisitions is another applicable area for a voice recognition system. Ordering and receiving media center materials could be handled by voice instead of inputting all of the information initially into the computer. Circulation aspects could be improved by having borrowers ascertain the shelf status of an item over the phone by talking to a computer that would indicate its availability. The last and most important application for SLMCs would be the use of voice recognition systems to access remote databases, which would remove a complex barrier to searching for information.[97]

The applications of voice technologies to schools are numerous and especially relevant to elementary schools. In language arts, for example, students would be able to generate their own stories and vocabulary as preparation for reading. Since voice recognition systems allow for dictation, student stories and poems could even become part of their reading assignment. In the area of writing, voice-to-text transcription is four to six times faster than handwriting. Speech is a much quicker way to express thoughts than with pen or pencil. With elementary children, handwriting is even more laborious, averaging four words per minute by second graders. Researchers suggest that children's rich, fluent, and complex vocabulary and active imagination would be enhanced by use of voice recognition systems.

Applications of voice recognition systems at the secondary level are somewhat impeded by the vocabulary limit of current voice recognition technologies. High school students, for example, have vocabularies greater than 30,000 words. This type of system, while not permitting interaction on that level, would allow for speech recognition for such activities as revising and editing texts.[98]

VIRTUAL REALITY

As researchers continue to search for the "Holy Grail" of artificial intelligence—namely, the ability to simulate the human brain in a computer—they discover other valid and exciting learning technologies that are relevant to SLMCs and the educational process. The most futuristic of these is virtual reality. *Websters New Universal Unabridged Dictionary* defines *virtual* as "being such in power, force, or effect, though not actually or expressly such" and *reality* as "the state or quality of being real." Therefore, virtual reality might be termed a state of reality that in essence is not real. The use of an oxymoron to describe an emerging technology makes it even more difficult for educators to grasp exactly what it is and its potential use in education.

Virtual reality is part of the continual trend toward the merging of telecommunications, video, and computers. It is a step in the continuum from interactive to active participation in computer programs and active versus passive art forms. It also represents a growing tendency to emphasize artificial experiences rather than real ones. The merging of the technologies used to create virtual reality moves us from the conceptual realms of visualizing to the perceptual realms. It provides participants with the opportunity to visualize things that in the past had to be represented through the use of one dimension, symbols, or mathematical formulas or equations. Its uses in education are widespread.[99]

From a technological standpoint, virtual reality involves one or more users experiencing a computer-generated simulation. Usually participants don a head-mounted display system that is equipped with stereo LCD video goggles and headphones. The system simulates a three-dimensional visual and aural sensory experience. A tiny transmitter attached to the headgear permits sensors to determine the location of the participant. These signals are relayed to the computer, which correspondingly alters the user's point of view. Looking in one direction, for example, participants might see a main street in Birmingham, Alabama, or in another direction see policemen moving toward them as the user did in the civil rights virtual reality experience depicted in the utopian scenario.

In place of a keyboard that interfaces with the computer, participants move throughout the space by using a data glove. The glove is attached through fiber-optic cable to the computer and is equipped with sensors that react to hand and finger manipulation. Using the glove, users can grasp objects, turn down streets, and by pointing the glove move forward within the computer-generated environment.[100]

Currently, virtual reality systems are in a developmental phase for technologies. Various governmental agencies such as NASA are researching its potential with such tasks as aerospace simulation and management of battlefield trauma units. Industry is experimenting with VR to practice laser surgery or to enable architects to "walk" inside a building they have just constructed. Finally, entertainment applications of VR are being researched to provide users with the opportunity to experience fantasy-adventure games. The MIT Media Lab, the Human Interface Technology Lab at the University of Washington, and the Computer Science Department at the University of North Carolina are the most frequently cited educational institutions conducting research in this area. AutoDesk and VPL Research, Inc., are two private companies also pursuing work in this field.[101]

Most school-aged users will be introduced to virtual reality through shopping mall video arcades. Virtuality, a VR game, has already been produced and is available in some shopping malls. AutoDesk has developed a "cyberspace" VR system which lets the user experience a simulated building filled with different objects. By pointing their data gloves upward, users can fly and with a downward motion land unceremoniously on a computer-generated imaginary floor.[102]

Virtual Reality and Education

Most of the contributions virtual reality will make to education are currently speculative. Nonetheless, it is evident that students in the future will experience simulated environments that will employ their minds and bodies in a new type of learning experience. Perhaps students will become more proficient at integrating and comprehending course materials when they have the opportunity to physically experience events in history, discoveries in science, or trips to different parts of the world.

Researchers in this area envision three main applications for virtual reality in education. The first is "visualization." Virtual reality enables a student to literally see "connections and relationships" that are difficult to picture either as concepts or in two dimensional representations. Users will be able to enter a predefined space or grasp and turn an object previously only visualized in their minds. Picture, for example, an architectural student walking through a poorly lighted hallway with a professor. With a flick of the student's data glove, the wall opens to shed light into the darkened hallway. To visualize the concept of light either from a blueprint or a computer screen requires a high degree of abstract symbolic intelligence. Virtual reality provides an instant perception of the problem.

A second application of virtual reality concerns its improved capacity as a simulator of processes, procedures, and environments. For years, in-flight simulators have been used to train pilots to fly before actually operating expensive airplanes. Virtual reality systems can improve on simulators by increasing sensation and dimensions through a more sophisticated technological approach. Students could similarly practice first aid in simulated emergencies that provide them with computer-generated patients plus the surrounding sights, sounds, and possibly even smells of accident scenes. Driver education programs could require that students sign up for a virtual reality program that simulates the effects of operating a motor vehicle while substance-impaired.

In some simulations, students will be able to assume the role of particular individuals for psychological identification purposes. Imagine experiencing the horrors of the Holocaust from the perspective of a victim such as Anne Frank. Simulation not only allows students to experience hostile environments but also brings a sense of immediacy to learning.

The third application of virtual reality lies with its constructive qualities. At this level, school libraries house virtual library workstations that enable users to move through a knowledge database composed of text, sound, diagrams, moving images, and three-dimensional data fields and objects. Using an electronic tutor or personal digital assistant device to select and save information from the workstations, students can construct their own virtual reality programs or use the information from the virtual library workstation to solve problems, finish homework, or complete research assignments.[103]

While this last application for virtual reality may seem totally irrelevant to today's SLMC environments, each of the technologies from computers and hypertext to head-mounted display systems and data gloves are beyond prototype and inching toward production. There remains a short time until they become further integrated into technologies that will easily pervade our media centers and lives.

TECHNOLOGICAL IMPLICATIONS

Telepower

School library media centers are about to undergo a radical restructuring of the programs and services they have traditionally delivered. By necessity, they will become part of an electronic revolution that will enable them to provide information to students on a scale never before imagined. The major thrust for this change will be precipitated by the nationwide installation of fiber-optic cabling. This telecommunications backbone will serve as the engine that will drive every type of information to become digitized, whether it be a book, recording, or video. Once digitized, information is really no longer bound by time or place. It can be quickly and inexpensively transmitted through fiber-optic networks to schools and homes.

As a result of the fiber-optic networking of the country, SLMCs will also be deluged with an increase in cabling and satellite resources. The opportunity to select from among five hundred cable and satellite channels is going to be a reality. The time frame for these advances is being shortened almost daily by discoveries by telecommunications companies that fiber-optic cable transmission can be boosted through the use of inexpensive coaxial cables and microwave signals over the final distance to existing facilities. Thus, the last costly barrier will be removed from establishing access to a global communications network in homes, schools, and businesses.

The impact of these telepower advancements will be dependent upon individual SLMC electronic development. For some school library media centers, fiber-optic cabling is already in place, their card catalogs have been electronically converted, and they are networked to a variety of local and national databases. They will simply await the promises of increased channel selections, access to additional databases, and the increased conversion of reading material into electronic form.

The majority of SLMCs in this country are not at this stage of development. For them, the technological implications of the telepower revolution are serious and perhaps threatening. The demand for access to books and periodicals in electronic form will probably come from outside the school, as parents and students begin to have such information available through fiber-optic cabling in their own homes. Their expectations will increase and they will not be satisfied with the meager resources contained in a single card catalog. There will be increasing pressure on school library media specialists to convert their own catalogs and to seek electronic access to additional sources of information. The installation of at least a modem, computer, and fax machine to tap into this superhighway of information will be an absolute necessity if SLMCs are to retain their positions as the academic hearts of their respective schools.

While telepower will undoubtedly dazzle us with electronic access never thought possible for SLMCs, it will also challenge us with many options. The thought of channel surfing on waves of five hundred channels accessible by cable or satellite is truly mind-boggling. School library media specialists will have to develop selection and subscription standards to assist them in making cost-effective and beneficial choices. Despite these criteria, they will probably never satisfy all of their clientele because so much will be available. Even the wealthiest of SLMCs will be forced to make Hobsonian choices concerning channel and database subscriptions.

Telepower is going to lay the electronic foundation for all SLMCs, regardless of size and economic level, to provide students and faculty with a wealth of information never thought possible. Administrators and boards of education will need to be alerted to the power of this technology to give their students an equal opportunity to partake of an electronic feast of information.

Telecomputers

The advances of increased computer storage capacity, processing speed, and portability, coupled with connectivity, have produced what is currently called a telecomputer. The implications of this improved form of hardware for school libraries are monumental. The arrival of telecomputers means that SLMCs will finally have the means to design and create in-house databases, access remote databases, and provide round-the-clock availability. School library media centers with telecomputers will become the nexus of all sources of information within and outside the school. Even the smallest SLMC should be able to provide its students and faculty with access to a wealth of information that should satisfy the majority of their research needs.

The increased access that telecomputers are predicted to provide will also have its negative aspects. As students and faculty are exposed to this cornucopia of information, their demands for more precise information will increase and their patience for document delivery will lessen. School library media specialists may find that they have opened Pandora's box by showing their users what is available but being unable to deliver it in an expeditious fashion. While the digitization of all types of materials is expected to continue at a fast pace, the majority of items that users will need will still exist in print form. School library media specialists will have to devise courier systems and use fax machines to ensure that the information so tantalizingly available actually gets into users' hands. The problem with document delivery will also force many SLMSs, especially those in geographically isolated or economically disadvantaged areas, to acquire full-text databases. In this way, they can build significant in-house libraries to satisfy most of their patron needs.

Increased access will also result in student and faculty demands for greater amounts of information. For years, SLMSs have usually attempted to satisfy a request for information by finding a chapter in a book, periodical articles, and perhaps a brief abstract in a specialized encyclopedia. With access to large databases through networking of telecomputers, users will realize just how much more is available on topics and will demand to have those physical sources. Students assigned to find information about snow leopards, for example, will no longer be satisfied with a chapter about them from a book on leopards when they can locate three or four books solely devoted to their specific assignment in a college or university on-line catalog.

Once school library catalogs are converted and networked to a variety of in-house CD-ROM databases and remote databases, students and faculty will wish to access them round-the-clock. School library media centers will need to establish policies and protocols for dial-in access after school, at night, and on weekends.

Interactive Media

Interactive media is especially relevant to SLMCs because of the needs and interests of the diverse populations they serve. Children require information to be in as many different formats as possible because of the differences in their preferred learning styles. Interactive media, with its use of sounds, pictures, and video, in addition to commentary and text, has the potential for improving various curricula and increasing SLMC use. Most interactive media programs, because of their interdisciplinary features and the equipment they require to use them, are made available through school libraries. The collections of SLMCs and their in-house access to various CD-ROM databases make this technology a natural partner for developing course-integrated bibliographic instruction units.

This form of technology will probably increase as software interfaces are developed that facilitate selection from what is currently an overwhelming amount of information on one disk. In the meantime, school library media specialists will probably need to offer workshops on interactive media so that its full potential at the interactive level can be realized. As the use of hypertext becomes ubiquitous, more CD-ROM databases will become interactive. School media specialists will find that students prefer interactive reference materials to hard copy, because of their user-friendly searching capabilities. This preference will have important implications for future budgeting and collection development.

As students of the computer generation increasingly depend upon interactive media for information and recreational use, school library media specialists will acquire electronic books. An entirely different set of acquisition criteria will need to be developed as librarians with perennial budgetary restrictions decide if a particular electronic title is more intellectually stimulating than its print counterpart.

Distance learning, a variant form of interactive media, will affect SLMCs of all sizes. Students taking courses via this medium will still require library materials to complete research assignments, homework, and term papers.

School library media specialists will have to develop their collections to serve the research requirements of both on-site and off-site curricula.

A second implication of distance learning will depend upon the size of the school system. The coordination and scheduling of distance learning in a small school system may fall under the purview of the SLMS. A large school district, however, may have a learning resources department that assumes responsibility for coordinating schedules, supplying equipment, and troubleshooting electronic problems.

National and International Networks

The continual technological advancements in computers and telecommunications have made SLMCs the fortunate beneficiaries of networking at a time when it is vitally important. The most important step a SLMC can take to improve its programs and services is to gain access to electronic networks either by membership, lease arrangement, or outright purchase. With expected network enhancements such as full-text searching, similar search commands, and natural language querying, plus the availability of additional commercial and locally produced databases, networking for SLMCs should be mandatory. The ability to provide additional materials beyond the four walls of a SLMC is probably one of the most powerful public relations tools a school library media center can use to demonstrate its need for existence.

While the implications of networking are extremely positive, school library media specialists will still need to weigh several alternatives to ensure cost-effective decisions. Databases will continue to proliferate and assimilate. It will be imperative that SLMSs join, lease access, or purchase databases that give the most information in the most expeditious fashion. Geographically isolated SLMCs or ones in socioeconomically disadvantaged areas should not subscribe to networks that have hierarchical interlibrary loan policies. Some libraries, for example, require a user to go through another library to request an item before the largest library in the network agrees to circulate the item. Instead, smaller SLMCs should try to access or buy databases with full-text capabilities. Small SLMCs should also evaluate the command structure of various networks. If the media center is understaffed, a network that requires little or no intermediary assistance is preferable.

Besides formulating networking membership criteria, all school library media specialists will have to consider how they will manage the growth and development of their collections. Resource sharing and networking are extremely efficacious measures for SLMCs to take, but they also change how in-house collections are used. School media centers facing financial restraints will need to develop policies and procedures for future acquisitions, for retaining the hard copy of specific indexes, and collecting in seldom-used subject areas.

Networking will also affect interlibrary loan services. What for many SLMCs was an almost nonexistent part of the job will probably increase, depending upon the type of databases users access. School library media specialists will have to arrange for courier services, fax delivery, and telephone requests much more frequently as user demands increase via their exposure to a network.

The expansion of global networks will provide SLMCs with an unprecedented opportunity to achieve multiculturalism. Networks will introduce students to the concept of the global village. Furnishing access to networks that offer video and teleconferencing with students from other countries will constitute a valuable educational tool at a time of increasing worldwide ethnic tensions.

Smart Technologies

There are a number of positive implications from employing smart technologies in SLMCs. Some are directly related to the functioning of the media center, while others are connected tangentially by way of the curriculum. The development of expert systems to help students navigate by themselves through complex but necessary databases will be of inestimable assistance to chronically understaffed SLMCs. Elementary students will find it particularly helpful to be able to query a database using natural language instead of prescribed subject headings. The successful use of this type of smart technology will be dependent upon the knowledge of the expert. School library media specialists are the only ones who understand the information-seeking methods students use. They will have to serve as consultants so that a successful interfacing expert system can be marketed.

The production of expert systems for various subject areas also has important implications for SLMCs. New software and evaluation criteria will need to be developed to ensure cost-effective acquisitions. School media specialists may need to introduce expert systems to faculty members first, because they may consider the systems threatening to their own subject expertise. Faculty members may view expert systems as teaching replacements rather than as additional information resources.

Smart speech technologies hold great promise for SLMCs, especially in educational institutions that have literacy problems. The ability to interrogate an on-line catalog orally and obtain results will reinforce the sadly diminished self-concepts of many disadvantaged students who are struggling with reading problems. Voice technologies will also be of benefit in elementary SLMCs where student keyboard skills are still at the beginner level. The use of speech recognition systems to aid in the revision and editing of writing should be helpful to secondary school students. It will free them from the mundane tasks of having to move or edit text with more complicated word processing systems.

The success of many smart technologies will be related to the ongoing design of neural networks which attempt to mimic some functions of the human brain. The speed at which they acquire patterns of use or "learn" will enable the creation of knowledge navigators or assistants for SLMSs. Imagine, for example, the time saved if a computer could learn individual approaches to various databases or word processing tasks, and program them permanently into a personalized interface. For students, instructional learning models could be employed that examine student instructional strategies, correct their mistakes, and provide entertaining and educational remedial examples.

Virtual Reality

While virtual reality implies a new world in computer interface design, present VR systems being tested in government and industry suggest that educational institutions will be involved with this medium within the decade. Many specialists predict that VR will be marketed as different forms of media such as cyberspace and interactive simulated media. Others view it as simply a natural developmental stage of various merging technologies. For SLMSs, there will be many pedagogical issues to contemplate as instructional methods evolve from text-based to multisensory-based.

One of the first concerns the differences between learning in a conventional educational environment and learning in a virtual environment. Will students learn more or less in a virtual reality program? To what types of learning is virtual reality most suited? Can learning truly be enhanced by the use of virtual reality? What are the best systems that simulate or permit the visualization of a design, concept, or historic event? Will virtual reality supplant text-dominated learning or augment it?

School library media specialists will be heavily involved in defining new acquisition criteria for virtual reality systems. Balancing costs of information in different formats will be a constant concern. What will a virtual reality program on civil rights, for example, cost as compared to a CD-ROM multimedia database on the same subject? Designing instructional units that complement or supplement virtual reality systems will be a challenge.

A second concern relates to guidelines for development and use. Initially, entertainment virtual reality programs will be available. While this frivolous use of the medium does not require a high degree of regulation, its educational use is fraught with opportunities for downright deception and propaganda. Because virtual reality is totally a visual medium with an increased capacity for simulating real worlds, the potential for distortion, increased subjectivity, and emotional manipulation is high. Recently, television networks have produced docudramas or reenactments of famous events, that have born only a faint resemblance to actual truth. School library media specialists who are already at the forefront with information technologies will have to review virtual reality programs from a factual and ethical as well as pedagogical perspective.

Current interactive media systems already demand a high degree of computer literacy on the part of users. Many SLMSs serve as intermediaries, showing and even designing instructional programs for faculty. Virtual reality will probably require similar assistance from a media specialist, because the software and hardware at first will be fairly sophisticated. Teachers will need not only instruction for using VR programs but also lessons in applying them to their curricula. Virtual reality is certain to create opportunities for SLMCs to explore and set evaluation standards for new media forms. Yet in its attempt to satisfy the users' sense of vision and hunger for information, it will dramatically challenge traditional forms of learning in the years to come.

Economic Trends

Not even the ingenuities of debt
Could save it from its losses being met.

Robert Frost

DEBT

The two major forces that will impact SLMCs are technological and economic. While technologies are not as dependent upon the economy for development and sales, economic forces significantly influence the degree to which school media centers incorporate such advancements. The state of the economy will either accelerate or impede the technological advancement of SLMCs in the next century. Although some economists have published plausible boom or bust scenarios for future American growth, most find it difficult to predict an all-or-nothing picture because of the size and complexity of the economy. Almost all, however, agree that our growing problem with debt on both international and domestic levels is of paramount concern.[1]

Indebtedness is a characteristic of the economy at every level. Internationally, the trade deficit rose from $12 billion in 1991 to $33 billion in 1992. Over the past decade, the country has run a $1 trillion international trade deficit.[2] Nationally, the federal deficit rose from $59.6 billion in 1980 to over $300 billion today. During that same period, the national debt, which represents accumulated government borrowing, increased from $914.3 billion (adjusted for inflation) (1960) to over $4 trillion. The latter figure does not include an additional $6 trillion obligated to various government agricultural crop guarantees, loans, and insurance programs.[3] The U.S. government has become so heavily indebted that sixty-two cents out of every dollar paid in personal income tax is used solely to pay interest on the national debt.[4] This continuing interest payment on the debt has placed an economic burden on America's children that will oppress them for the remainder of their working lives. The interest payment alone constitutes a budget item approximately ten times the budget of the federal Education Department and is almost equivalent to the total amount spent on K–12 education by federal, state, and local governments.[5]

As the national debt increases, federal funds to state and local governments have been cut. Voter outrage at tax increases has prevented state and local governments from raising revenues to compensate for lost federal funding. In 1991, for example, state and local taxes grew only 4.7 percent, reflecting the smallest increase since 1952.[6] Consumer debt, exacerbated by a steady fall in real earnings since 1973 and easy borrowing inducements, has burgeoned to $4 trillion. Repayment, with its crippling addition of interest, will further reduce future disposable income. The corporate debt picture is even worse. In the 1990s, approximately 90 percent of after-tax profits of U.S. corporations is being devoted to paying interest on their debt. With production unable to compensate for this growing debt, the United States has been forced to borrow from foreign governments and corporations about $100 billion per year. In less than a decade, America has gone from being the largest creditor nation to being the largest debtor nation in the world.[7]

DEMOGRAPHIC TRENDS

Most economists agree that demographic trends will also affect the United States. The latest population projections suggest that the United States population will increase from 255 to 275 million, a 7.8 percent increase, by the year 2000.[8] While America's population is predicted to experience steady growth over the next several decades, critical changes are forecast within that population.

The first concerns the aging of America. In 1960, for example, only 16.6 million Americans were aged sixty-five and over. By 1990 this figure doubled to 31 million. By 2020 the number is predicted to rise to 52 million, and then climb to 65.5 million by 2030. Although many aging Americans will not fully require Social Security and Medicare programs until approximately 2020, the economic impact will begin within the next five to ten years. When Social Security legislation was passed in 1935, the worker-retiree ratio was forty-six to one. Currently there are three workers for every retiree, and by the year 2020, this proportion will have dwindled to two to one.

From 1936 to 1989, the maximum Social Security tax increased from $60 to $6,006. If current government projections are accurate, Medicare's hospital insurance will be totally depleted by 2003 and the Social Security pension trust will be bankrupt by the year 2010.[9] The fiscal crisis generated by the growing debt and the aging of America will have serious economic consequences for America's school-aged population.

Within ten years, there are projected to be 23 percent more secondary school students and 12 percent more elementary school students than in 1993. The number of preschoolers is forecast to peak at 20.2 million in 1994. This figure almost equals the 20.3 million preschoolers in 1960 that represented the height of the baby boom. Total K–12 enrollment is expected to rise to 51.6 million by 1996 and to 54.2 million by 2003. The latter figure represents a significant increase over the top level of 51.3 million attained in 1971.[10]

As a result of these two demographic trends, national, state, and local governments will be forced to make many Draconian decisions in the years ahead. One will be whether to allocate America's dwindling resources to future generations so that they can become economically productive. The other will be whether to divert funds to bolster social and health programs that current generations have already labored to provide. Legislators charged with this unpopular task will also find their decisions difficult to implement. If they decide to place needed monies toward creating educational and employment opportunities for future generations, they will encounter stiff opposition from well-organized voting blocs of retirees. Even the best of governmental intentions may be thwarted at the ballot box. An outbreak of age-based warfare is predicted by many economists as each generation fights for what it considers is its rightfully earned share of a shrinking economic pie.

SCHOOL LIBRARY ECONOMIC TRENDS

The general economic trends discussed in the previous section have been impacting SLMC programs and services for the last twenty years. Officially the decline in SLMC economic fortunes was ushered in when President Nixon proposed to reduce federal spending for libraries to zero. Although a significant amount was restored because of vigorously staged protests, the oil crisis and inflation of the 1970s, coupled with a severe recession, began an erosion of school media center collections, programs, and services that has made economic recovery difficult.[11]

A second blow struck at the economic heart of SLMCs when the Elementary and Secondary Education Act of 1965, Title II (ESEA II), was incorporated during the 1970s and 1980s into a series of block grants under the Education Consolidation and Improvement Act of 1981 (ECIA). School library media centers which had automatically been the recipients of these funds and used them to build core collections were forced to compete with other eligible departments. The combined result has been a slow constriction of library budgets as federal funds have diminished and schools have faced steadily escalating prices for materials.[12] While federal funds comprise only about 6 percent of all funds spent on elementary and secondary education, it still amounts to a sorely needed $13 billion a year. School library media centers desperately require the financial support they previously received.

The increased competition for federal funds also coincides with a diminution in state and local funding of SLMCs. State and local governments spend approximately $200 billion a year for education, but SLMCs are experiencing a decrease in expenditures from this sector as well. A 1992 survey of 1,560 school media centers covering all fifty states reported a significant decrease in median expenditures from local and state sources in FY 1991–92. Indeed, less money was spent for books, AV materials, and periodicals than in previously surveyed years. The disparity between elementary and secondary SLMC funding was even more dramatic, with elementary schools being allocated a significantly decreased percentage of local funding.[13]

School library media centers tend to reflect the conservative attitudes of their schools. The latter are slow to change even in prosperous economic times. The state of educational institutions has never been classified as a leading economic indicator. As a result, those entities tend to respond deliberately to economic and demographic changes that are themselves slow to develop. Unlike industry, where it is imperative to respond with new products, processes, or marketing ploys to maintain a competitive edge, schools adhere to centuries-old practices because there are no immediate economic consequences for failure.[14]

Evidence continues to build that SLMCs are experiencing a "silent crisis" as they compete for scarce resources. Former ALA president Patricia Glass Schuman terms it silent because "libraries have very few enemies."[15] Yearly surveys of voters continue to report that public education and libraries are top priorities. Yet the tax funds appropriated for schools continue to diminish.[16] Some educational analysts suggest that while the findings are clear that SLMCs are in jeopardy, parents are not convinced that their respective media centers are at risk. Voters seem to convince themselves that these grave economic problems are really worse in someone else's school district. Reformers find that their support wanes when parents realize that these problems necessitate greater economic expenditures in their own schools. The reform movement seems to lack the home-based sense of righteous indignation so necessary to effect change.[17]

All SLMCs, regardless of their position on the economic ladder, are expected to experience price increases in materials associated with the gradual loss of the dollar's purchasing power. School media centers that paid $13.98 on the average for a children's book in 1990 paid $14.73 in

1993.[18] This represents an inflation rate of over 5 percent. In 1990, the average cost of an adult hardcover novel was $20.01. In 1993, school library media specialists paid $20.34, or 1.6 percent more, for the same title. The situation with regard to periodicals has shown a similar, steady increase. The cost of general-interest periodicals increased by 3.4 percent from 1992 to 1993, and the cost of children's periodicals for the same period increased by 1.8 percent. Although this rate of inflation does not appear to be overwhelming, it is staggering when SLMC expenditures have declined 16 percent in public schools and 14 percent in independent schools since 1978–79.

In 1992, for example, the median per-pupil expenditure for books (averaging $16.64 per book) was $5.88. At this rate, an average elementary SLMS was able to purchase about one third of a book per child.[19] The average secondary SLMS was able to purchase one novel for every four students. If SLMC budgets continue to be reduced and the cost of books and periodicals continues to increase at a similar rate, the effects on collections and the instructional program will be devastating.

Collections are already reeling from the impact of reduced expenditures and increased materials costs. The average copyright date of a book in SLMCs is 1965. In Indiana, nearly 50 percent of the nonfiction books are over twenty years old, rendering much of the information on the Soviet Union, space exploration, and civil rights passé. Books related to the physical sciences, for example, do not contain information concerning recent genetic discoveries.[20] This problem can not be instantly remedied with additional funds. The average book remains in print for nine months. Therefore, many excellent titles, especially those pertaining to children's literature, are no longer in stock and available for purchase.

FUTURE ECONOMIC TRENDS

Given the current national economic situation, it is clearly evident that SLMSs will continue to grapple with reduced budgets and increasing costs for materials. In the past, however, concerns could safely center on books, periodicals, and traditional audiovisual materials. The cost of these materials, however, pales in comparison to the cost of computers and sophisticated software packages. Already, the last expenditures survey of SLMCs indicated that some SLMSs were spending more money for computer software per pupil than for books and audiovisual materials combined.[21] The pressure to acquire hardware and software to meet the instructional needs of users unfortunately may have to be satisfied at the expense of an adequate book collection unless other cost-effective measures are applied.

Last year's SLMC expenditures survey, for example, reported that the average media specialist spent $3,632 for books, $987 for periodicals, $800 for microforms, $500 on microcomputer software, and $983 for audiovisual resources.[22] While the cost of technology has declined dramatically—an IBM PC printer, for example, selling for $6,000 in 1982 now sells for less than $500—it is still going to require a substantial portion from the average SLMC's budget to purchase and maintain such items as CD-ROM reference databases. A second major economic trend relates to categorized funding. When ESEA II was merged into a Chapter 2 block grant, for example, it ceased targeting funds solely for the purchase of library materials. Perversely, it generated monetary competition among various educational departments, such as SLMCs and computer science labs, that should be natural partners.[23] The concept of mandated or organized funding also operates at state and local levels. The presence of allotted funds for SLMCs means that even though the state and local communities may reduce allocations as a whole, SLMCs are guaranteed a fair share. Unfortunately, as debt becomes even more burdensome to individual states, mandated funding is being abolished, with dire economic consequences for school media centers. A 1992 survey of state funding for SLMCs reported not only major state reductions in school media center allocations for personnel and funding per pupil but also an increase in the number of states that had discontinued mandated funding. If this trend continues, SLMCs will probably find it extremely difficult to obtain funds for new technologies at a time when they are an absolute necessity.[24]

SCHOOL LIBRARY MEDIA CENTER ECONOMIC STRATEGIES

Although the economic profile of the majority of SLMCs is presently bleak, these institutions represent a priceless resource for this nation's future economic health. There are currently 92,538 school media centers in the United States. Together they constitute an $80 billion investment. Just as corporations must report revenues and expenditures to their shareholders, school media specialists must employ such data as circulation statistics and positive library-related national research findings to garner additional funds for their students and faculty. Three of the most important studies to support continued investment in SLMCs are the Colorado Department of Education study, *The Impact of School Library Media Centers on Academic Achievement*, Stephen Krashen's report, *The Power of Reading*, and a service entitled SchoolMatch.

Combined, these studies form the basis for a powerful economic argument concerning the efficacy of additional SLMC funding. SchoolMatch is an educational information service company that uses priority-type questionnaires to search a database of fifteen school systems that come closest to meeting parents' needs. In compiling the database, researchers discovered that the strongest predictor of student test performance was not a school district's tax base or property values but the education level of the parents and the amount of money spent on library and media service. Of all expenditures that affect a school's performance, including funding for faculty, guidance services, and others, the level of expenditures for library and media services continues to have the highest correlation with student achievement and performance on standardized tests.

A second study of 221 comparable schools in Colorado further confirmed the SchoolMatch findings and delineated the positive correlation between SLMCs and academic success. In this research design, factor and correlation statistical tests were applied to determine the influence of the community, school, and library, respectively, on standardized test scores in reading, language, and information skills. The Iowa Tests of Basic Skills were used for grades 1, 2, 4, 5, and 7. Tests of achievement and proficiency were employed for grade 10.

The results of the Colorado study strongly reinforced the findings of SchoolMatch research. More importantly, it found that even among communities with similar economic conditions and where parents were not well educated, school library media funding promoted higher student achievement. A summary of results from the Colorado study concluded that (1) "the size of a library media center's staff and collection is the best school predictor of academic achievement; (2) the instructional role of the school media specialist determines collection development and, in turn, academic achievement; and (3) students who score higher on norm-referenced tests tend to come from schools which spend more on library media programs."[25]

Krashen's review and analysis of hundreds of voluntary reading studies in *The Power of Reading* found additional support for SLMCs and their positive influence on reading. While the benefits of voluntary reading have never been questioned, its positive relationship to the SLMC is considered a causal but unproven platitude usually attached to funding requests. Krashen's study results clearly demonstrate that (1) voluntary reading is the best predictor of reading comprehension, vocabulary growth, spelling ability, grammar usage, and writing style; (2) access to school media centers results in more voluntary reading by students; (3) the presence of a SLMS makes a discernible difference in the amount of reading done; and (4) larger SLMC collections and extended hours tend to increase both circulation and the amount read.[26] The citing of recent supportive SLMC research as a rationale for funding requests is just one economic strategy that school media specialists will need to employ in the coming century.

A second strategy requires using emerging technologies to extend capabilities by compensating, remediating, and amplifying existing SLMC programs, services, and collections.[27] As more SLMCs, regardless of their level of funding, access other collections remotely, they will have to decide whether to purchase titles or simply confirm their availability in other databases that they frequently use. For SLMCs with reduced funding, the purchase and use of computers, modems, and some inexpensive software can be a cost-effective means to compensate for an inadequate collection. On the other hand, affluent SLMCs will also find it cost-effective to coordinate collection development if they are members of on-line networks. The use of new technology, such as full-text CD-ROM databases, is also an extremely economical way to compensate for lack of space. Many SLMCs facing shelf overruns will find it far less expensive to purchase on-line databases on CD-ROMs rather than add a new wing or purchase more shelves.

As more school media centers become members of electronic networks, the opportunities for coordinated collection development and materials use studies will be greater. Both are cost-effective economic strategies that employ simple record keeping to help decide whether future acquisitions are either absolutely vital or only tangential to the collection. School library media specialists can also use the interlibrary loan and borrowing statistics generated by their networks to justify continued membership and future computer enhancements.

New technologies also possess a remediating function in cases where understanding and using various reference books may be too complicated. It may be good economic strategy to purchase a CD-ROM database of hard-to-access reference books that contain easy search strategies, keyword searching, and access to tables of contents and chapter headings than it is to purchase their hard copy equivalents. The decision to maintain parallel systems (i.e.,hard copy vs. computerized version) will be facilitated by improved computerized access.

CATEGORICAL FUNDING

Of all the economic strategies discussed, categorical funding at the federal, state, and local levels would have the most salutary effect on SLMCs. While library surveys continue to indicate continuing administrative, faculty, and parental support for school media centers, mandated funding would remove the option of administrators at various government levels not to comply with their public testimonies of support.

The economic havoc wreaked on SLMCs by the consolidation of ESEA Title II into a block grant has finally caused legislators to introduce a new bill entitled *The Elementary and Secondary School Library Media Act*. If passed, it would establish a division of school library media services within the Department of Education's Office of Educational Research and Improvement. The division would be charged with administering three grant programs. The first program would authorize $200 million for the purchase of materials. Each state's allocation would be distributed to local educational agencies. The second grant would foster collaborative curriculum instructional units between teachers and media specialists to access the full range of information resources. This grant would be competitive and would provide $20 million. The last grant, also competitive, would encourage SLMSs and teachers to expand the use of computers and computer networks in the curriculum. This grant would initially be funded at $40 million.[28]

While the distribution of categorized federal funds for SLMCs would provide some welcome economic relief, it could not compensate for the steady reductions in the largest source of funds, which is generated at the state and local levels. As more states experience budget crises, they are beginning to abolish categorical funding directed at school media centers. The declassification of these funds usually opens the door to eviscerating established SLMC programs, collections, and services. To employ categorical funding at the federal, state, and local levels requires careful accounting methods on the part of all SLMSs for such items as expenditures, personnel, collection development, services and programs, and technology. Even if these items were not submitted to a state database, school media specialists could use them at the local level (district or individual school) to influence the establishment of categorical funding.

Currently there are thirty-three states collecting school library media data ranging from expenditures to technology. The National Center for Education Statistics (NCES) has developed a SLMC questionnaire that will be tested on a national scale during the 1993–94 school year.[29] Once these data are collected on a regular basis in a standardized form, school library media specialists will begin to amass the information necessary to press for categorical funding for SLMCs. Nonetheless, categorical funding will not be an economic panacea for media centers. With the crisis involving the deficit, federal, state, and local budgets will probably continue their downward spiral. The institution of categorical funding, however, will ensure that SLMCs suffer a fair cut, rather than the unkindest cut of all—elimination.

SCHOOL/BUSINESS INITIATIVES

Characterized by unlimited access to information and instantaneous transmission via telepower systems, the shape of the information society is slowly becoming clear to parents and teachers alike. In addition to these two concerned groups, business has entered the fray. Spurred by realistic fears that America is losing its technological edge and that jobs will require information skills beyond what schools can provide, businesses are responding. A recent NCES survey, for example, showed that between 1984 and 1988, the number of business/education initiatives increased 234 percent from 42,200 to 140,800.[30]

Most SLMSs realize that business/education partnerships are not formed from altruistic or eleemosynary motives. They can be designed for such purposes as promoting corporation images, test-marketing products, and even reducing tax liabilities. While Corpus Christi (TX) public schools, for example, received $250,000 in business donations, they lost $900,000 because of business tax exemptions. Florida's public education system gained $32 million in charitable contributions but lost approximately $500 million from tax breaks to corporations.[31]

Despite these gross imbalances in corporate fiduciary responsibility, school librarians cannot afford to reject school/business initiatives as an economic strategy. It especially behooves SLMSs to pursue corporate partnerships, because many involve contributions of a technological nature. These types of gifts are exactly what SLMCs need to advance their media center programs and services.

Corporations are employing a variety of approaches in providing funds to schools. Some target specific problems in education such as drugs or adolescent pregnancy. Others fund teacher training, furnish management trainers, or donate in-kind services such as instructional materials and equipment. Most companies support schools in communities where the majority of their employees live and work. Many also encourage their employees to volunteer their expertise as instructors, tutors, and speakers.

Another trend in school/business initiatives involves the forming of coalitions between companies and schools. The Saturn School (St. Paul, MN), for example, is a $1.8 million model computerized school that includes $540,000 of new technologies donated by a coalition of partners from Control Data, Apple Computer, Pioneer, and Minnesota Educational Computer Corporations.[32] Roundtable is a New York–based coalition consisting of two hundred major corporations that have pledged a ten-year commitment to educational reform through corporate/school partnerships.

Although there are numerous local business/school initiatives successfully operating in America, several corporations stand out for their commitment to the improvement of SLMC programs and services. School library media centers may wish to investigate their applicability to various library needs. Apple Computer has been funding programs in schools since 1978. Their sponsorship of an Apple grant program called Crossroads resulted in $2.3 million being awarded to schools using computers as tools within the last year. The Paul Revere School (San Francisco), for example, received $51,000 in the form of six Apple Macintosh workstations and software to design a multimedia interdisciplinary literature program. One of the proposal's authors was a school library media specialist. The company has also spent $12 million to construct one hundred Apple Classrooms of Tomorrow (ACOT) in public schools throughout the country. West High

School (Columbus, OH), an urban school with a dropout rate of 30 percent, found that twenty-one randomly selected students in the ACOT program had a 100 percent graduation rate. In addition, 90 percent went to college, compared to only 15 percent of the non-ACOT students. The program is designed to individualize instruction rather than rely on rote drills.

A second program, Digital/STEPS (Maynard, MA), is a combination of corporate and school resources. The company promotes school/business initiatives where its facilities are located. Digital Equipment Corporation, as one of its community relations activities, sponsors book drives and educational television programming. Eastman Kodak (Rochester, NY) has developed the Kodak/21st Century Learning Challenge. In 1988, the company donated $10 million to education. This donation took the form of in-kind services, instructional materials, and equipment. While Eastman Kodak's main involvement has been with the Rochester Public School System, its Challenge program serves as a useful model for similar corporate/school initiatives. Another Rochester program is sponsored by Xerox. In this business/school partnership, Xerox is supplying the management expertise to help Rochester schools achieve their educational goals and objectives. In 1990, Westinghouse (Baltimore and Pittsburgh offices) spent more than one third of $4.3 million on K–12 educational initiatives. The company funded teacher enrichment and training programs. One of the most technologically helpful business/school initiatives involves IBM. In 1989 alone, IBM spent $20 million to support K–12 teacher-preparation grants, equipment, and technical assistance to schools nationwide. IBM's major focus is to promote the effective use of technology in the classroom. In 1990, IBM formed a partnership with the Austin Independent School District (TX) and their local facility that resulted in a $4.4 million donation in computer hardware and software to various classes. Their K–12 matching grants program, which increases an employee's in-kind contribution fourfold, resulted in National Cathedral School Library (independent 4–12 school in Washington, DC) receiving six computers, six laser printers, and several outstanding IBM software programs.[33]

The creation of the Public Education Fund Network began ten years ago with a grant from the Ford Foundation to help establish educational funds in schools nationwide. The fund assisted in the formation of business/school coalitions in fifty-eight communities. Its main contribution was to provide minigrant funds ranging from $500 to $1,000 to teachers and librarians for creative classroom instruction. By 1991, the program broadened its scope to furnish money through a Public Education Fund Network. In recognition of the beneficial impact of the network on educational change, the DeWitt Wallace–Reader's Digest Fund selected the Public Education Fund Network to administer National Library Power planning grants, which can go as high as $1.2 million for three years.

One of the most notable National Library Power projects features a resourceful collaboration between the New York Public Library and the city's public SLMCs. The $3.6 million grant, called CLASP (Connecting Libraries and Schools Project), is designed to foster increased cooperation among teachers, school and public libraries, and parents. Over a three-year period, the program will fund outreach activities, after-school and special children's programs, and teacher workshops. More than $1 million will be allocated for new books for various branch libraries. Recently, nine additional National Library Power grants of up to $20,000 each were awarded to school/business community coalitions in cities such as Chattanooga, TN, Lincoln, NE, and Washington, DC. All recipients are being challenged to develop further collaboration, increase collections, and provide places for children to learn.[34]

GRASSROOTS ADVOCACY

If SLMCs are going to become part of the information infrastructure, they will first have to form a strong local economic base of support. Some practitioners suggest that school media specialists should adopt the ecology movement slogan, "Think globally, act locally."[35] Many of the business/school initiatives described in the previous section were relatively local. While their company products have national name recognition, their donations centered mainly in the cities where most of their employees live and work. Most CEOs of even the smallest companies realize that their contribution to educate workforce participants is one of the best economic investments they can make. Many know that if they do not get involved, they will pay the price by having to furnish their own on-the-job training programs.

It is this type of reasoning that forms the basis for proposals that can be submitted to both local and national businesses. School library media specialists are ideally positioned to establish business/school partnerships. Their abandonment by federal and state governments makes them a sympathetic entity in an age of economic stringency.

Targeting local, small to mid-sized companies for contributions greatly improves one's chances of success because the competition will be less. These companies usually have deeper roots in a community, thus making it easier for them to forge connections with other businesses. Some school districts, for example, are creating wish lists of equipment that they would like donated. They include a description of proposed use, which is helpful to companies that need to justify their contributions. Partnerships formed and grants awarded at the local level can be used to establish a track record for applying for larger grants such as those offered by the National Library Power Program.

Local businesses also possess a great deal of expertise, especially in emerging technologies. While some may not be able to donate equipment, they may be willing to volunteer their time to help school media specialists draft an RFP (Request for Proposal), design a LAN (local area network), install a modem, and so forth. The level of corporate involvement can vary. What really matters is the forming of partnerships that have as their goal the improvement of SLMC resources.

School districts should have distinct grant officers who can help develop a plan to approach local businesses. In addition, SLMSs may wish to consult a new resource entitled *Education Interface Guide to Corporate Support* (Princeton, NJ: Information Interface Institute, 1993). It not only lists 450 corporations and their corresponding educational programs, but also explains how to write a request that will win corporate support.[36] Establishing a grassroots advocacy program for SLMCs based upon publication of supportive research findings and business/school initiatives helps ensure that SLMCs continue to be part of the information infrastructure.

IMPLICATIONS OF ECONOMIC TRENDS

The pattern of growing indebtedness at all levels of the economy has serious implications for SLMCs. Unless economic conditions improve dramatically, SLMSs will be under increasing pressure to accomplish more in the provision of new technologies, curriculum instruction, and collection development with less financial support.

Historically, Americans have willingly invested substantially in education. In 1989, for example, $350 billion was expended to support 45 million elementary and secondary school students and 13 million college and university students. Only Switzerland spent more money per pupil. In relative terms, the United States allocates 6.8 percent of its GNP to education, equaling the proportions spent by Canada and the Netherlands and surpassing Japan, France, and Germany. Yet this allocation is misleading with reference to elementary and secondary schools. A disproportionate share, 40 percent, is allocated for higher education. In reality, the United States spends 4.1 percent of GNP for elementary and secondary education and actually trails Switzerland (5.8 percent), Japan (4.8 percent), Germany (4.6 percent), and most other industrialized nations. If educational funding continues to diminish, the disparity between America and other developed countries will increase, with widespread implications for job training and employment.

Americans are also continuing to voice concerns regarding their children's mediocre performance on standardized tests and their achievement levels vis-à-vis children in European and Asian countries. Yet, the majority of citizens, even those with school-aged children, are rebelling at the thought of paying additional taxes.[37] Many Americans are not certain that increased expenditures are the solution to the problems that beset schools. In frustration at declining test scores and what they perceive to be sufficient educational allocations, they are demanding more accountability and productivity on the part of all educational institutions. Professor William Baumol of Princeton University argues that as increasing pressure is placed upon private sectors of the economy to produce, there will be an equal insistence that the public sector of the economy do likewise. Termed the "Baumol Crunch," the pressure is articulated by honest inquiries such as "Why can't they run the schools like a business?" and "We've developed more efficient ways of using resources; why can't the schools?"[38]

As the costs of materials, labor, and so forth continue to rise and the productivity of an educational institution remains the same, the Baumol Crunch operates by forcing schools to either increase public or private funding or decrease services.[39] Since the majority of public institutions have been unsuccessful at significantly raising public or private funds, they have been reducing services. Unfortunately, SLMCs have been and are more likely to become the victims of this steady erosion in school programs and services. Unless they can employ sound economic strategies based upon research findings and their own output measures, more of them may cease to exist.

BUSINESS IN EDUCATION

Because public schools are basically monopolies, they have the luxury of not responding to many of the technological changes that are revolutionizing our society. Yet monopolies do not exist in a vacuum. They can only function when bulwarked by promonopoly laws. Peter Drucker, the prolific author of management books, claims that without restrictive laws, competition will arise spontaneously.[40] The result may be a significant increase in private schools or the commercialization of public institutions. Both changes are already beginning to occur more frequently. More importantly, decisions to bypass public institutions are being made not just by parents but also by states. The state of Wisconsin, for example, paid for 1,000 low-income students to attend various private schools in Milwaukee.[41] Minnesota is providing tax breaks to parents who send their children to private, parochial, or public schools.[42]

The privatization or commercialization of public institutions is being experimented with not just for a small group of students but also on larger scales. Education Alternatives, Inc. (EAI—a for-profit company that operates private schools in Minnesota and Arizona) contracted with Miami-Dade school district to run South Pointe Elementary School. Although the financial arrangements involve the district running the school with EAI and no profits have yet been made, the project is still continuing. While the company does not employ media specialists in their Minnesota and Arizona schools, the school district has agreed to pay for one at South Pointe.

A third commercialization project, Ombudsman Educational Services (a private, for-profit company), provides special programs for potential dropouts. The company is presently servicing twenty-three school districts in Illinois, Minnesota and Arizona. OES was able to charge $2,000 per pupil less than the $5,500 per pupil it cost Chicago public schools to provide the same service because it eliminated study halls, lunch periods, and noninstructional time. The semiprivatization of Chelsea (MA) public schools by Boston University's School of Education, while encountering problems when the city of Chelsea declared bankruptcy, has resulted in improvement in standardized test scores and an increase in those going on to college.[43]

As schools continue to experience a dwindling tax base and abandonment by the federal government, they will have to look to the private sector for financial and perhaps even management assistance. The involvement of business in education poses problems for schools, especially their media centers. Applying a business model to managing educational institutions usually entails the development of a lean, cost-effective, profit-based system. School library media centers, like art and music departments, may be viewed as frills in a commercialized school.

The formation of business/SLMC initiatives for the purposes of garnering additional funds and applying for national grants is also fraught with potential conflict-of-interest problems. School library media specialists will have to decide what level of corporate involvement they are willing to permit in their media centers. Many manufacturers of tobacco products and alcoholic beverages, for example, are willing to contribute to educational programs. Yet taking funds from them may be tantamount to tacit approval of their products.

The incursion of business into education is likely to increase as SLMCs seek outside funding to maintain their collections, purchase new technologies, and provide quality programs and services against steady financial erosion. School library media specialists will need to develop policies and procedures to aid them in deciding what constitutes acceptable corporate involvement.

PRODUCTIVE/COST-EFFECTIVE USES OF EMERGING TECHNOLOGIES

The model of instruction as a business is expected to pervade many aspects of education, including SLMCs. As new technologies emerge, SLMSs will need to justify their acquisitions not only pedagogically, but also economically. This involves projecting technological cost-effectiveness and productivity. School library media specialists, for example, who propose that their schools purchase equipment for interactive television or distance learning will have to prove that the students will be able to learn as much or more with the use of these media. Membership in an electronic library network will have to be shown to increase student access to a variety of information resources. In turn, these additional resources must be demonstrated as helpful in completing research assignments, term papers, and so forth. The cost-effectiveness of network membership will need to be supported with data concerning such items as present collection size, level of development, and projected savings from coordinated collection management. The use of computerized acquisition software, for example, supports increased sharing and coordinated purchases, thus saving not only SLMC funds but also time so that SLMSs can devote themselves to instructional programs and thus be more productive.

Fostering cost-effectiveness and productivity through technology will probably become a permanent aspect of future school media center programs. Library media specialists, as a matter of course, will be expected to use technology as an effective economic strategy to counteract anticipated funding reductions.

OUTPUT MEASURES

The increasing demand for accountability from an economic perspective also has important implications for SLMSs. Parents, corporate sponsors, and administrators are going to require that all programs and services be economically justifiable. The result will probably be the development of output measures for SLMCs. In the past, output measures have been associated with public and academic libraries. Their primary use has been to assess the impact of various programs and services on users. In addition to collecting quantitative data, for example, patron attendance at author book signings, qualitative data are also gathered. Data collection might consist of a content analysis of positive and/or negative evaluations regarding a special library event or introduction of a new service. The majority of output measures have been used internally by libraries to aid interdepartmental evaluation and decision making.[44]

The adoption of output measures by SLMCs, however, may be necessary for external as well as internal use. Furthermore, school media center output measures will probably have to emphasize quantitative data because of the proliferation of education as a business management model. Most of the data, such as circulation statistics, use of the media center for bibliographic instruction by classes, and number of librarian consultations with faculty, are easily collected, maintained, and disseminated. School library media specialists will find these data useful for such things as discerning trends, comparing media centers, and justifying some expenditures.

What looms more darkly on the horizon are output measures that evaluate the efficacy of technology. Most technologies, even as they decline in cost, represent a substantial investment. It is expected that parents, business sponsors, and administrators will demand an accounting of how much their investment has produced. School media specialists will probably have to design research strategies for assessing the impact or influence of various technologies on learning. In many cases, the software will be designed to monitor or evaluate learning. All that SLMSs will need to do is collect, summarize, and distribute the results. In other instances, use of an on-line catalog versus a card catalog will require more sophisticated research techniques such as bibliographic citation analysis of research assignments in a pre-and post-test experimental mode.

While research and development is an integral component of most companies in America, it has not been for SLMCs. The scarcity of school media center data on the federal and state levels is lamentable. The last national survey of school library media was performed in 1985–86. A telephone survey of fifty states regarding such items as the current status of educational funding yielded responses from only thirty-eight states. Much of the information varied in quantity and quality, because reporting and collecting procedures were not standardized.

School media specialists, if they are to compete economically for their vital place within the information society, will require the assistance of the National Center for Educational Statistics, the National Information Standards Organization, and the American Association of School Librarians School Library Statistics Program Advisory Committee to supply them with much of the basic data regarding circulation, technology, expenditures, and so forth.[45] Many will also need assistance in designing research studies for measuring and evaluating the impact of new technologies. Local and state library associations may be able to find corporations and universities willing to donate their time and expertise to assist in this area.

Whether SLMCs are in affluent or poor communities, they are going to find themselves under increasing pressure to conform to a corporate style of educational administration. Indications are that they will have to employ a variety of economic strategies to survive a well-documented onslaught from financially strapped school districts, communities, and states that are desperately seeking to reduce costs.

Employment Trends

3

The only way to predict the future is to have the power to shape the future.

Eric Hoffer

In the United States, the world of work has evolved in stages from an agrarian society to a manufacturing-based economy to a technologically advanced, globally driven system. These waves of change have brought about significant shifts in the distribution of employment and the nature of work.[1] In 1920, agriculture employed over a quarter of American workers. By the 1980s, this number had dwindled to 4 percent of U.S. jobs and in the 1990s represents only 2.5 percent of the workforce. Manufacturing has followed a similar decline, furnishing one of every four American jobs in 1960 and one in five in 1980; it is expected to provide only one job in six throughout the 1990s. Fewer than 10 percent of American workers currently manufacture products, and this number is expected to drop to 5 percent by the end of the 1990s. From 1940 to 1990, service industries' share of total U.S. employment climbed from 45 percent to over 70 percent. Thus, it is readily apparent that occupations involved with the growing and making of things are fast yielding to jobs that involve doing things for other people.

The speed of change requires educational institutions charged with preparing the next generation for this type of work to ask themselves some questions. What are the general workforce trends? What will work and workers be characterized by in the coming decades? What kinds of jobs will be available within the next five to ten years? What skills and knowledge will be necessary to obtain remunerative jobs? Finally, what changes will schools and media centers have to make to ensure these opportunities for their students?

These questions are not easily answered by educators. Yet they must be. A recent study published by the World Economic Forum states that America now ranks fifth in the world's competing economies because of among other variables, its education base.[2] If we continue to ignore the warnings issued in these types of reports, we will put our most precious resource, our children, at risk for low-paying jobs, unemployment, and a depressing economic future.

GENERAL WORKFORCE TRENDS

Integration of the World Economy

One of the most important forces impacting America's workforce is the integration of the world economy. Fostered by gradual improvements in transportation and telecommunications, the economy of the United States is now inextricably intertwined with those of Japan, Germany, Great Britain, France, and other developed countries. World markets, not nations, decide the prices not only for commodities such as fuel but also for manufactured products.

Within the past decade, capital and labor markets have also become globally integrated. Multinational corporations borrow and invest in foreign markets, individual Americans regularly purchase stocks in the Japanese stock market, and the Japanese in turn invest in American companies and real estate.

Labor, once thought stationary, has become a fluid, global commodity with heads of corporations constantly seeking the cheapest source of it to produce their goods.[3] Workers in Mexico, for example, at *maquiladora* factories assemble American and Japanese car parts into finished automobiles which are shipped to the United States. A similar labor trail can be traced from AT&T's original employment of Louisiana assembly workers to cheaper labor sources in Singapore and finally in Thailand.

The information business is also not immune to this constantly shifting labor pool. Kansas City keypunch operators, for example, paid $6.50 an hour in 1990, are being replaced by Manila (Philippines) operators who earn less than $1.00 per hour. With the advances in telecomputer systems, data can be processed in any area or time zone of the globe. New York Life Insurance, for example, now routes insurance claims to Castleisland, Ireland, where data processors determine their status and transmit their computations back to the United States.[4]

As the world economy becomes further connected, the United States is losing control over its economic destiny. Our monetary markets, corporations, and banks are so intertwined with those of other countries that America's economic pulse can only be evaluated by that of the world economy. The fortunes of multinational companies and individual nations, unemployment patterns, and shifts in other countries' production must be planned for and monitored globally. Policies can no longer be arrived at unilaterally but must be negotiated with other countries.

Despite the formulation of international trade and monetary policies designed to equalize economical opportunity for all countries, the United States is experiencing increasing competition from other nations that are able to produce better products at lower prices. Where once multinational companies such as GM, Ford, and IBM reigned supreme, they are now being rivaled by more cost-efficient and productive corporate giants such as Toyota, Hitachi, and Matsushita.

The Shift from Manufacturing to Services

A second major economic force affecting employment is the move from a manufacturing-based to a services-related economy.[5] The problems associated with this trend are complex and have serious implications for every sector of the economy. When hundreds of thousands of agricultural workers were displaced by tractors and other labor-saving machinery, they poured into the factories to produce those machines. As assembly-line, mass-production industries downsized, millions of displaced workers found jobs in service industries. Services industries are burdened with two serious economic problems. First, productivity is hard to evaluate and to improve. Second, service industries historically offer a lower standard of living. The economic dilemma posed by lack of productivity in an industry that is becoming a main source of income for more Americans is difficult to solve. Unfortunately, we must if we are to settle the deficit and offer future generations their opportunity at the American dream—a decent standard of living and home ownership.

Since service industries are where the majority of future employment opportunities will be found, defining them may illuminate the future employment picture. The term *service industries* has been used since 1950 to broadly categorize workers such as sales clerks, hospital attendants, and waiters. It has also encompassed capital-and-technology-intensive industries involving health care, finance, and transportation. While the former classifications conjure up images of low-paying jobs in fast-food restaurants, the latter invoke visions of "the information age."[6]

When the economy was in a mass-producing, assembly-line mode, this set of classifications was a rational system for making equitable economic comparisons concerning similar standards of living. Today, too many occupations fall under the rubric of service industries, rendering this classification an obsolete one for understanding the economic forces at work in a global economy.

Within the category *services*, three classifications are taking shape. They permit economists to compare globally and nationally American employment and prosperity in services. The first one—called "routine-production services"—involves repetitive tasks usually performed by people in such occupations as clerks and data processors. These types of positions can also include tasks carried out by low- and mid-level managers who constantly monitor subordinates' work. Routine producers usually work with groups of other people who are engaged in similar work. In most cases, they must be able to read and to do simple math. By 1990, this type of work accounted for one quarter of the jobs performed by Americans, and this proportion is diminishing.

A second category—termed "in-person services"—involves simple and repetitive tasks furnished on a person-to-person basis. By nature, this service category is not globally mobile. Positions within this category include such occupations as sales clerks, janitors, hairdressers, and taxicab drivers. In-person service employees, like workers within the previous category, do not have much discretion over their terms and conditions of employment. Qualifications are minimal, with at most a high school diploma or some vocational training being required. About 30 percent of Americans worked in these jobs by 1990. In-person services, unlike routine-production services, are growing rapidly, because they must be performed in person and are not susceptible to global competition.

The third division covers "symbolic-analytic services." This category includes occupations that entail problem solving, problem identifying, and strategic-brokering functions. These types of services, in addition to routine-production services, can be exchanged globally and like their routinized counterparts have to compete in any location with foreign symbolic-analytic services. Their products are not tangible. Instead, they deal with the manipulation of data, words, and graphic representations. Occupations representing symbolic-analytic information services comprise, for example, software designers, engineers, lawyers, tax consultants, management information specialists, systems analysts, writers, and musicians. Unlike individuals employed in the two previous services categories, whose work is highly regulated and supervised, symbolic analysts usually have partners or associates. They often work alone or in teams that may be linked to larger organizations having further global connections. Qualifications for positions in this services area range from undergraduate degrees to graduate degrees in specialized fields. Workers engaged in symbolic-analytic services account for approximately 20 percent of American jobs. Unlike in-person services, this category is not predicted to grow appreciably.

It is important for school library media specialists to recognize that the "information industries" that have been ballyhooed as the answer to fewer manufacturing jobs will not be very challenging or remunerative for a significant percentage of the population. A look at the growth rate in these services categories also indicates that while unemployment may not be a factor in these occupations, job quality will definitely play a key role with respect to employee satisfaction and standard of living.[7]

Impact of Advanced Technologies

The role technology has played in shaping America's economy has always been dramatic, beginning with inventions such as the telephone, automobile, and airplane. All of these brought about significant changes in employment patterns but in a rather slow, manageable fashion. The invention of computers and advanced telecommunications systems has accelerated technological change, making it difficult to cope in the present, let alone the future. Advances with telecomputers are occurring so rapidly that change is occurring in almost every industry.

By 2010, 90 percent of all jobs will be computer-dependent. This forecast is confirmed daily by the proliferation of computers and modems in homes and businesses. In 1981, for example, there were only 750,000 personal computers in U.S. homes. Today, 30 million American homes have personal computers.[8] It is ironic that the one industry charged with the responsibility of preparing the next generation for work with these technologies is woefully behind. Educators have been remiss in not recognizing the need to instruct students in these technologies to ready them for the new challenges they will face. Already employers are indicating that the level of current employee technological literacy is too low to satisfactorily complete workplace demands. A survey of business executives indicates that they expect more than routine-production service work. They also desire analytical reasoning, logic, and communication skills to enable workers to adjust to increased workplace demands.[9] These are just the skills that characterize symbolic-analytic service workers who can be expected to remain competitive and well paid in the new global economy.

The situation in schools regarding technological literacy is not positive, but more disconcerting are the statistics concerning computer use. The Department of Education claims that schools have progressed in providing personal computers for primary and secondary schools during the 1980s and that more than 50 percent of all children in grades 1–8 use computers at school. The most dubious claim, however, concerns usage equivalencies among schools regardless of their ethnic composition, income level, and geographical location. Most national studies report that 98 percent of America's schools have at least one computer. These national studies cite a student-to-computer ratio of eighteen to one. According to Herb Lin of the National Academy of Sciences, "Even if there were one computer per classroom, that's less than two minutes per student for a one-hour class."[10]

The equitable distribution of computers in schools is a serious problem. In a report by QED entitled *Technology in Public Schools 1991–92*, states like Wyoming, classified in the top ten, had nearly ten students per computer, while Mississippi reported thirty students per computer. Census bureau figures indicate computer use nationwide to be deplorably low. While 52.3 percent of students in grades 1–8 reported using computers at school, only 39.2 percent of grades 9–12 students did so. Since the latter group will be in the workforce sooner than the grade 1–8 students, this figure is ominous indeed.

One of the most disturbing figures in the Census Bureau report concerns computer use by various ethnic groups. Only 35.7 percent of African-Americans in grades 1–8, compared to 58.4 percent of white students in grades 1–8, reported using computers at school. A similar proportion, 36 percent of African-Americans in grades 9–12, compared to 40.6 percent of white students in the same grade range, indicated that they used computers at school. Hispanic students fared no better. About 40 percent of Hispanics in grades 1–8 and 33.6 percent in grades 9–12 reported computer use in school. While the disparity between the proportions of white, black, and Hispanic computer users in grades 9–12 is less than it is between students in grades 1–8, the trend and its implications for minority student employment opportunities are disturbing.

There was no correlation between state per capita income and computer usage. While geography was somewhat of a factor (students in the South reported using computers less than did students in other regions), no strong correlation was found.[11] What did correspond, however, was the relationship between the nature of computer use and affluent schools. In inner-city and rural school districts, teachers are poorly trained and motivated to use computers for anything more than rote drill exercises or data processing. Statistics show that training in keyboarding and programming amount to 30 percent of computer use in U.S. high schools and 15 percent in elementary schools. In less affluent schools, however, this percentage climbs to 66 percent of all use. Poor schools tend to use the computer to teach routine production-type activities, such as data processing, while affluent schools use the computer for symbolic-analytic activities.

For example, students at Coral Gables High School (Coral Gables, FL), an affluent suburban school, can be found in a media center of 34,000 volumes with several CD-ROM newspaper, encyclopedia, and periodical databases, investigating the use of animals for cosmetics testing.[12] In contrast, students at Carol City High School (Miami, FL), an inner-city school, are in a building surrounded by a ten–foot, chain-linked, barbed-wire-topped fence. The SLMC contains eight Apple computers, two printers and a CD-ROM magazine database. Yet observers in five visits to the media center over two days did not report a single use of a computer by students. The media center was even referred to as "the mausoleum" by one of the teachers. Machine use in the computer lab consisted of playing Tetris or Joe Montana football games or in a nearby word processing class, copying text from books. In another comparison, of an inner-city East Palo Alto school (East Palo Alto, CA) with the Palo Alto Escondido School on the Stanford University campus, the differences were also disheartening. Grades K–5 at the latter elementary school were using a CD-ROM player with an overhead to view the story of Cinderella while others were finding books, typing papers on word processing systems, or using hypermedia programs for math or reading games. On the other hand, students in the East Palo Alto district were using the computer lab to learn touch typing.

Although the differential in use is consistent with research studies stating that students should master the basics before moving to higher-order skills, many less affluent schools never provide the opportunity for students to advance to the next level. As a result of this type of computer use or lack of it, students are doomed to low-wage jobs where they will enter endless streams of data in routine-production services positions. They will be as controlled by the computer as their forebears were by the assembly line and conveyor belt. Using computers only to teach students routinized production-type skills instead of symbolic-analytic tasks is fast creating a technological apartheid. Because members of the former group will learn skills that require minimal problem solving or decision making, they will become totally fungible commodities in an increasingly competitive global marketplace. For those who cannot master even routine-production skills on the computer, the employment situation will be even worse.

Increasing Competition

A fourth major trend affecting the workforce in general concerns increasing competition in product, service, and labor markets. This trend is considered an ongoing one because of "the integration of global markets, excess production capacity, the rapidly growing world labor force, the decline of labor unions and the general deregulation of industry by many Western governments."[13] The consequences of increasing global competition for the American workforce means a perpetual struggle on the part of companies and individual employees to create, change, and adapt to new markets and technologies. It also suggests that it will become increasingly arduous for employees to find secure, remunerative employment, and that companies will no longer be able to rely upon such things as a calculated market share or an advanced technological production technique to ensure their profits.

Demographic Forces

The last trend expected to dramatically change the complexion of the American workforce pertains to demographics.[14] Several demographic changes will impact the employment situation within the next decade. First, the population and the workforce are projected to grow more slowly than at any time in the past, with the exception of the 1930s. A second factor shows that as the population and workforce age, the number of young workers entering the workforce will decline. Third, more females will enter the workforce. Finally, minorities and immigrants will constitute a significantly larger share of the workforce.

The effects of a declining population and smaller labor force suggest that there will be decreased demand for population-sensitive products such as food, cars, housing, and even education. Growth of the economy is predicted to depend upon increased demand for income-sensitive products such as restaurant meals, tourism, and health care. The labor force expected to supply these items will be characterized by fewer well-educated workers. Their value is expected to increase as employers have even greater need of their services. On the other hand, the need for younger workers in a steadily shrinking labor pool may provide more opportunities at better wages because employers will need to replace older workers.

By the year 2000, approximately 47 percent of the workforce will be female and 61 percent of all women will be working. Although women are still concentrated in traditional female jobs, this pattern may change, particularly in fields requiring advanced education. The slow growth of the economy, coupled with a desire for a better lifestyle, has driven many women into the workforce. For those with children, however, this desire appears compromised by an equal pull to be at home raising their families. Results of a Gallup poll indicated that only 13 percent of working mothers with children wanted to work full-time. Six of ten working mothers desire some form of part-time employment and 16 percent indicated that they would prefer no work at all.

The fact that so many women will be in the workforce means that families may become less transportable because two jobs are needed instead of just one. It also creates a need for increased day care and preschool education to be funded by either government or business. Finally, the large influx of women into the workforce may help eliminate gender-based wage differentials as more women enter traditionally male-dominated occupations.

Within the decade, minorities will also constitute a larger share of the workforce. By the year 2000, nonwhites will represent more than 15 percent of the labor force. For this group, the employment picture is expected to be troublesome. Historically, these disadvantaged groups have been overly represented among vanishing occupations such as industrial assembly-line work and other routine-production jobs. As a population group, they are also heavily concentrated in many large urban areas already suffering from severe unemployment and corporate flight. While demographic trends such as slower population growth should force employers to hire a greater percentage of minorities, future jobs are not where they live and/or require a level of education that they do not possess.

The impact of immigration, viewed negatively by many American citizens, is actually expected to benefit the workforce. Studies of immigration and its connection to job losses and reduced wages show that service industry wages, where the majority of jobs will be available in the future, rose faster for citizens where there were influxes of immigrants. Immigration levels of 450,000 to 750,000 people per year are actually forecast to stimulate the economy by creating the need for additional products and services.

THE EDUCATION/INCOME CONNECTION

Throughout the discussion of workforce trends, there have been frequent references to the increased need for employees to possess higher-order thinking skills, symbolic-analytic abilities, and creative problem-solving techniques. All of these abilities are associated with education. The level of education workers attain is strongly related to their income level. In the next five to ten years, this equation will have a distressing impact upon those who are unable or unwilling to heed it. While the positive relationship between educational level and earnings has always been understood, it will have a gruesome reality in the years ahead because more than 50 percent of new jobs will require some education beyond high school and almost one third will be filled by college graduates. Only 22 percent of today's occupations require a college degree.[15]

While the employment picture will be grim for high school graduates, it will be even worse for the 30 percent a year who drop out or fail to graduate. A spring 1990 Census Bureau report shows that non–high school graduates earn an average of $492 a month compared to $1,077 for high school graduates. The likelihood that high school dropouts will need some form of governmental assistance, such as Aid to Families with Dependent Children, food stamps, or public housing, is 21 percent, whereas the probability that high school graduates will require such assistance is 7 percent.[16]

Although high school graduates fare better than their dropout counterparts, the earnings of both groups place them clearly in a category termed the working poor. This pattern of reduced earnings and opportunities will not lessen with an increasingly competitive global market and rising educational and skill requirements. The stark earnings gap between the dropout and the high school graduate is also projected to occur between high school graduates and college graduates. The earnings of male high school graduates, for example, fell from $24,482 in 1973 (in 1987 dollars) to $18,366 in 1987, a decline of 25 percent. The earnings of black males without a college education declined during the same period by 44 percent. On the other hand, male college graduates were slightly ahead, because their 1987 earnings were $50,115 compared to the $49,531 (in 1987 dollars) earned by 1973 college graduates.

While recent college degrees fail to provide a much higher income than previous degrees, the absence of a degree precludes any decent standard of living. In 1980, male college graduates earned about 80 percent more than their high school counterparts. By 1990, the gap had nearly doubled.[17] Several reasons are given for the growing divergence between male high school graduate and college graduate earnings. First, economists attribute some of it to the baby boom or too many job entrants for entry-level jobs. Therefore, employers could be more selective regarding entry requirements and wages. The collapse of the manufacturing base, which deprived many male high school graduates of relatively high-paying jobs, is another reason. The most relevant one to SLMCs, however, is a lack of education.

During the 1980s, when employers had the choice of replacing high school graduates with other high school graduates, they chose instead to replace them with college graduates. Economists believe that they were responding to increased competition and to changes in the way work was being performed. Some companies, for example, contracted high school–level work out to lower-wage countries and retained college graduates to complete marketing and financing tasks. In other instances, companies introduced advanced technologies that required better-educated workers to operate the machines. A frequently cited example relates to a textile mill that previously relied on minimal on-the-job training to teach mechanics to repair the shop's looms. Now the company looms contain microprocessors and other electronic parts. People repairing these machines had to read and understand complicated manuals and technical updates. The literacy skills needed for these new tasks necessitated that the company hire workers at the community college level as repair personnel.

RISING SKILL REQUIREMENTS

What are the skills that high school graduates need to increase their wages? One study cites the increasingly important role that reading and mathematics play in improving the earnings of recent high school graduates.[18] In 1972, for example, a difference of one standard deviation in the score on a multiple-choice mathematics skills test resulted in a 3-percent difference in male hourly wages six years later in 1978. For females graduating in 1972, it was 7 percent. Scores, however, from a similar test in 1980 were much stronger predictors of earnings for 1986 graduates than they were for 1972 graduates. A difference of one standard deviation on the mathematics test for male graduates in 1980 resulted in an 8-percent difference in hourly earnings in 1986. Female graduates, with similar scores, experienced an 11 percent difference. The results of this test do not negate other factors that are widening the gap between high school graduates and college graduates. What they do suggest rather strongly is that "basic literacy and mathematics skills and a facility to use these skills to solve problems matter more in today's workplaces than in the workplaces of the 1970's."[19]

The correlation between reading, mathematics, and reasoning skills and the fastest-growing jobs is direct. Natural scientists and lawyers, for example, whose skill requirements in these areas were rated highest by the U.S. Department of Labor, are among the two fastest-growing occupations.[20] Yet many labor economists are not confident that improving literacy and mathematics skills in a standardized, back-to-basics fashion is the answer to diminished employment opportunities. Reich, for example, in *The Work of Nations*, advocates that education should be centered around what will be "a lifetime of symbolic-analytic work." A symbolic analyst combines four skills: "abstraction, system thinking, experimentation, and collaboration."[21] To think abstractly requires more than a superficial glance at information. It involves the ability to discern patterns and meanings in information so that it can be equated, formulated, analyzed, or categorized. The abstract process of construing information into usable patterns is characteristic of occupations such as scientist, attorney, engineer, designer, and systems consultant. These are positions that, while susceptible to global competition, will be growth occupations accompanied by a decent standard of living.

System thinking is a more advanced stage of abstraction requiring that individuals be able to recognize patterns and meanings and how they may relate to something as a complete process or cycle. Problems are identified and then linked to other problems. The use of DDT as a pesticide and its deleterious connection to an entire ecosystem of animals and plants is illustrative of system thinking. Experimentation, rarely used as a teaching method in most disciplines with the occasional exception of science, is needed to establish cause and effect, similarities and differences, and possibilities and outcomes. It provides opportunities for students to use tools to structure their own learning situations.

Last is the ability to collaborate, to work in teams, and to share information and solutions. The means to do this can be provided through oral reports, designs, scripts, discussion groups, symposia, or focus groups. The emphasis on this form of learning, using reasoning skills instead of mere acquisition of unrelated facts, is to simulate the type of thinking that will be required to achieve success in a technologically advanced global marketplace. While routine-production service positions and in-person services will be available, the skills required to perform these jobs adequately will never be sufficiently in demand to achieve a decent remuneration. The skills of a symbolic analyst, however, are applicable to a variety of positions that will continue to grow and pay decently.[22]

FUTURE JOBS

As technology raises the skills level required to perform a job and countries compete for market shares and labor, it is difficult to predict the jobs of the future. If, for example, superconductivity were to be developed, the need for a variety of occupations connected to energy-related industries would be obsolete. Assuming steady technological advances without a breakthrough in an impact area such as cancer research or transportation, what are the kinds of jobs that will be available? According to *Workforce 2000* the fields that will grow two to three times as fast as the average occupational fields comprise lawyers, scientists, and health care professionals.[23] All of these positions, as noted before, need symbolic-analytic skills. Secondly, they all require education beyond high school. Conversely, what types of jobs are predicted to decline? Unfortunately these are occupations that entail only repetitive, routine-production work. They are handworkers, assemblers and fabricators, machine tenders, and agricultural, forestry, and fisheries workers. Even as these jobs decline, however, they will require some education beyond high school.

AUTOMATE OR INFORMATE

One of the most important employment trends concerns the decision by various industries to automate or informate the workplace. This decision will probably be dependent upon the overall educational level (literacy plus reasoning skills) of future employees. Companies are already finding it more difficult to find employees who are able to perform various tasks necessitated by increased automation. To compensate for these deficiencies, business has been spending an estimated $50 billion annually to train its own employees.[24]

With the powerful advances in information technologies, business now confronts the potential for two corporate designs. The first model structures various industrial processes, tasks, and decisions in a precisionlike mode. This strategy supports the decision "to automate" by removing as much as possible the human element from any or all processes of the business. The ultimate example would be the replacement of employees by robots. Steps in this direction that still involve humans would have them just pushing buttons and responding in some sequenced way to an electronic text that told them what to do next and simultaneously managed them. Airline representatives at work, for example, function in a demerit system monitored electronically. If employees spend more than 109 seconds talking to single customers, they receive one demerit. The demerit system is programmed to contact a supervisor when the employee has earned two demerits. The accumulation of six demerits results in a warning and thirty-six in dismissal.

As businesses, especially globally-sensitive ones, assess the costs of training employees, they will clearly contemplate this potentially cost-effective corporate design. It removes much of the burden of training employees who may or may not stay with a company for long. It also reduces the potential for production mistakes. Finally, it concentrates power in a clear and unquestioned fashion. The temptation to yield to this type of corporate design, where only several "experts do the thinking and workers execute prescribed tasks at command," is very real in light of the present levels of employee literacy and reasoning skills. The potential for abuse of employees and for creating mind-numbing environments is enormous.[25]

A second decision involves structuring electronic texts "to informate" the workforce.[26] This environment permits much more worker input, involves many more people in problem solving, and supports a more democratic work environment. A simple example of an informated work situation is the restructuring of grocery scanners. Currently they are automated so that they not only charge items to a customer but also generate data regarding inventory control, orders from warehouses, delivery schedules, and market analysis. Informating this device might give checkers the opportunity to decide themselves whether a specific item should be restocked or whether a delivery schedule should be altered because of an emergency. Informating the environment also involves using more than a few experts as designers of the electronic text. It requires collaboration of employees at various levels for troubleshooting and product improvement sessions.

Advances in computers and telecommunications can now create powerfully centralized work environments that employ the majority of workers in some robotic-like fashion, or they can create radically decentralized work environments that will tap the symbolic-analytic abilities of all their workers. The decision to informate, however, may ultimately rest with the skills and reasoning abilities that future employees have already developed in school.

IMPLICATIONS FOR SCHOOL LIBRARY MEDIA CENTERS

The trends in employment have political, technological, and pedagogical implications for SLMCs. For years, most school library media specialists have passively shared the economic fate of their schools. If budgets were reduced, they quietly bore their share of the cut in the interests of the whole school. If greater reductions were necessary, many closed their doors and departed, leaving future generations bereft of the most essential resource—information and knowledge. Now the employment evidence suggests that the availability of a technologically advanced SLMC is probably the best resource a school can have in its battle to improve the quality and quantity of jobs for its students. Convincing fiscally strapped school boards and state legislatures, however, will be a problem.

Political Implications

As the U.S. economy becomes more integrated with the world economy and jobs become increasingly mobile, it will be more difficult to protect American workers against competition from workers in other countries willing to perform the same job tasks for less money. Simultaneously, the jobs that are left will require increased education but will not necessarily pay better. Students, parents, and administrators will be puzzled at first by this trend and then, as it becomes permanent, will probably react negatively. While their anger and outrage will be directed at government in general for failing to insulate them from this vicious cycle, they will probably vent their frustration on their local schools. Teachers and administrators will be accused of not doing their jobs, especially in districts with significant numbers of dropouts and low standardized test scores. School library media specialists in these schools will be challenged to defend the expenditures for books when so many of their clientele cannot read them.

Increasingly the employment picture for students capable only of routine-production services work will be grimmer, as fewer of these jobs are available. In-person service jobs will be a last resort. But for those lacking in interpersonal skills, there will be no future employment. These students will continue to swell the rolls already on some form of public assistance. The creeping effect of social Darwinism will not be lost on the vast numbers of children who are doomed to chronic unemployment because of inadequate SLMCs. Their discontent with the economic status quo will be manifested in increased crime and other forms of social unrest.

On the other hand, students, parents, and administrators in affluent schools will already have prepared for these trends. They will continually voice their concerns over the employment future of their children. In the meantime, they will try desperately to make sure that their children have stimulating teachers that structure learning situations to increase higher-order thinking skills. They will continue to fund the SLMC budget, even if it entails raising outside funds, sponsoring book fairs, or vigorously protesting any reductions to their local school boards. This one fifth of the population will labor incessantly to ensure that their children get the 20 percent of American jobs in the symbolic-analytic category.

School library media specialists, regardless of the economic status of their respective districts, will be challenged to respond to this situation. There will be demands for materials that improve literacy and/or raise SAT scores. Career materials will be needed and, as a matter of course, will change frequently because the employment picture will be so fluid. Information that monitors the employment situation in local areas as well as globally will be requested, as schools try to halt a steady decline in employment opportunities for four fifths of the population. School media specialists will be involved in helping to raise the aspiration levels of many students through use of print and nonprint materials, speakers, and career programs. They will probably be asked to disseminate comparative data concerning the relationship between earnings and education to parents, teachers, and administrators.

Technological Implications

As jobs become increasingly computer-dependent, schools are going to have to invest more heavily in diverse information technologies to assist future generations to obtain employment. A dichotomy will probably emerge as schools in the top twentieth percentile try to secure their children's gainful employment by designing computerized activities that employ symbolic-analytic abilities rather than rote memory. Schools in nonaffluent districts will probably be supplied with equal numbers of computers. The discriminating factor will be that they will continue to be used for rote activities or data processing programs.

Library media specialists in either type of SLMC will be charged with developing high-tech environments to provide the types of learning experiences that employers will require of their employees. Electronic access to local and remote on-line networks, in-house use of CD-ROMs, and interactive media will be prevalent in both types of schools. Again, the critical operating variable will be how it is used. In schools without dedicated faculty and rigorous curricula, the SLMS may observe much of the material being used as entertainment or a plug-in drug until the period ends. In progressive school districts, the media specialist will need to design course-related units that require students to retrieve, organize, interpret, and evaluate the information they access.

Pedagogical Implications

Much of the employment trend information indicates that teaching higher-order thinking skills to students is an absolute necessity if the

United States is to have a highly productive and remunerative economy. Evidence further suggests that symbolic-analytic skills should not be limited to just 20 percent of the school-aged population. It should permeate every classroom. This mandate, however, may not be the case in most schools. The incorporation of symbolic-analytic activities would unfortunately entail a restructuring of many schools that are still producing graduates the way our factories, assembly-line-style, produced widgets. Most schools, until our present crisis, have been producing students already programmed to perform routine-production services work. While this was acceptable to many students and their parents during the heyday of manufacturing work, it is tantamount to negligence in light of today's employment trends. Since the 1980s, a host of national report cards have been published that have exhorted school districts to integrate critical thinking, higher-order thinking, or symbolic-analytic skills into their curricula, but mainly to no avail.

The present employment trends confirm the need for reasoning skills in almost all types of jobs. Employers seem to be coping with it by hiring workers with higher levels of education. A high school diploma is becoming worthless in light of increased hiring of college graduates to perform jobs only slightly more advanced than those previously held by high school graduates.

If more pressure is exerted on school boards by national and state departments of education, school library media specialists may be asked to acquire materials that require symbolic-analytic thinking (abstraction, system thinking, experimentation, and collaboration). If school boards, parents, and administrators demand it, expensive nonprint materials will be developed that require this type of reasoning. Library media specialists may also be required to incorporate symbolic-analytic thinking into course-integrated instructional units.

Educational Trends

It must be remembered that there is nothing more difficult to plan, more doubtful of success, nor more dangerous to manage than the creation of a new system. For the initiator has the enmity of all who would profit by the preservation of the old institution and merely lukewarm defenders in those who would gain by the new ones.

Machiavelli

By 1996, approximately 51.3 million children will be in school. Public schools alone are projected to spend $294 billion to educate these children, 42 percent more than they did in 1991–92.[1] As the problems of illiteracy and declining test scores continue, educators, parents, and school administrators hear the drumbeats for reform and listen to the demands for academic accountability. Everyone who pays taxes, has school-aged children, or has been educated in an American school will have an opinion on this multi-billion-dollar investment. More of them are expected not only to voice their opinions but also to exercise them locally and nationally at the ballot box.

Years ago education came to be viewed as a means to citizenship and a universal privilege. This philosophy of education, with its corresponding need to tax people to provide for all children, gradually replaced private schools and academies with public schools.[2] As America industrialized and waves of immigrants swept ashore, public schools reflected the factory assembly-line style of production. The curriculum was tidily divided into subjects, taught in a preset period of time, categorized by grade level, and measured by standardized tests designed to identify those suitable for routine-production work or higher education.[3]

This system served America well when companies such as GM, Westinghouse, and U.S. Steel employed millions of workers to perform monotonous assembly-line-style tasks. But, by the 1980s, many employers no longer needed this type of worker and the educational system had failed to produce ones with correspondingly higher skills. Unfortunately as demands for a more literate and skilled workforce increased, educational systems seemed to deteriorate creating a crisis that presently threatens the social, economic, and personal well-being of all Americans.

ILLITERACY

The severity of the problems afflicting American schools from the poorest to the most affluent centers around illiteracy and academic achievement. Educators will continue to be heavily involved in the process of determining the degree of illiteracy and halting the decline in academic achievement for years to come.

In a society as wealthy as the United States, the word *illiteracy* evokes feelings of defenselessness and anger. Witnessing adults placing Xs on the backs of their checks and implicitly entrusting bank tellers to correctly credit their bank accounts has a deep emotional impact. Worse still are the numbers of workers who must fearfully conceal their illiteracy from their employers, children, and peers.[4] Moreover, this problem still baffles many, because the 1980 census reported a literacy rate of almost 100 percent. Since then, studies have discerned between 17 and 21 million American adults who cannot read at all or can only read at the level of a nine-year-old. Among the 155 United Nations member countries, America ranks 49th in its rate of literacy. Almost 40 percent of school children read a novel once a year or never and only 27 percent read daily for pleasure. While 95 percent of the population supposedly can read the printed word, only a small percentage can understand complex material.[5]

The shift in jobs requiring enhanced literacy has led to a three-scale literacy test devised by the National Assessment of Educational Progress.[6] The survey measures (1) prose literacy, the ability to understand narrative texts; (2) document literacy, the ability to locate information in charts, tables, and graphs; and (3) quantitative literacy, the ability to use basic mathematics to solve everyday problems involved in making a bank deposit, dining in a restaurant, or reading and interpreting an advertisement. Administered to young adults (twenty-one to twenty-five years old) in 1985, the test yielded results further reinforcing bad news by finding that 80 percent of America's young adults could not read a bus schedule, 73 percent could not interpret a newspaper story, 63 percent could not follow written map directions, and 5 percent lacked the language and literacy skills of nine-year-olds.

To add to this educational misery index came tests reporting that many students could not identify the president of the United States or correctly state the location of New York City. Nearly one third of American seventeen-year-olds did not know the author of the Emancipation Proclamation, and nearly one half could not tell who Josef Stalin was.[7] The test results were almost simultaneously accompanied by Allan Bloom's *The Closing of the American Mind* (1987) and E. D. Hirsch, Jr.'s *Cultural Literacy*. Both, while considered somewhat Eurocentric in orientation, gave testimony that literacy involved more than being able to spell, define words, and pronounce them correctly. Literacy took on the connotation of specific background knowledge about particular subjects. Words and concepts could not be learned in isolation but required an understanding of their cultural context as well.

As Americans awaken to the changing qualifications for employment and the explosion of information generated by an array of CD-ROM databases, on-line catalogs and videodiscs, the concept of literacy encompasses these new information technologies and is referred to as information literacy.[8] This definition of literacy is considered more relevant to present employment conditions that require a higher level of education and thinking skills. Besides just the ability to read, information literacy involves the ability to find and evaluate needed information. Many of the skills necessary to become information-literate translate to those required for symbolic-analytic jobs. Students must be able to identify appropriate facts, knowledge, or data within a conceptual base, discern appropriate patterns for purposes of synthesis, and evaluate their usefulness in a learning situation. While all forms of illiteracy will need to be addressed by educators and school library media specialists in the future, an information literate population is considered to be a necessity in an increasingly competitive global economy.

DECLINING ACHIEVEMENT

Throughout the early 1980s, Americans were complacent about the illiteracy problem, because the vast extent of this phenomenon had not been documented and terms such as *illiterate* and *functionally illiterate* were not associated with economic disadvantage. The sudden revelation of millions of illiterates struck concerned educators and parents like a coronary. On the other hand, the general decline in educational achievement that began in the 1960s has been like a cancer, slowly eating away at the educational foundations of America. Unfortunately, it includes elementary and secondary levels. Not only have test scores declined on the Scholastic Aptitude Test (SAT) but also on the American College Testing Program (ACT) exams and the Iowa Test of Educational Development. Evidence of

SAT decline began after 1963 when the average composite verbal-and-quantitative score of 980 dropped steadily until it began to rise slightly in 1981.[9] Despite a rise during this period, the average combined verbal-math SAT score was 900 in 1990. This score was still 80 points below the score of 1963. In 1991, the average verbal SAT score dropped to a record low.

In trying to account for these dismal figures, educators such as Albert Shanker, president of the American Federation of Teachers, rationalized that many students normally unqualified to take the test had more recently done so, lowering the average. This assertion is contradicted by the fact that SAT scores even declined at the higher end of the spectrum. In 1972, for example, approximately 116,000 students scored above 600 on the verbal SAT, while in 1982 fewer than 71,000 scored that high. Between 1960 and the early 1980s, median SAT scores declined at the country's finest colleges and universities such as Princeton, Yale, Cal Tech, University of Chicago, Brandeis, and Reed. The composite score drop at the latter two schools was more than 100 points. Despite these contrary data, various educators continued to claim that America was providing an excellent education for students at the top. This belief, however, was quickly dashed when twelfth graders from the United States finished last on algebra and calculus tests administered to the top 5 percent of high school seniors from a dozen countries.

Another argument expressed to refute the decline in SAT scores concerns the number of minority students from academically disadvantaged backgrounds who have recently taken these college entrance tests. Since such individuals had not previously taken these examinations, it has been suggested that their belated addition to the test population has lowered overall scores. This explanation is also unpersuasive, because during the period of SAT decline, Hispanic and African-American scores have actually risen.

One of the most devastating findings that stripped the last vestiges of false arguments from educators relates to an international study of thirteen-year-olds which reported that Koreans placed first in mathematics and Americans ranked last. The educational establishment attempted to calm the nation's fears by stating that this type of test was only a measurement of rote memory, which is not emphasized in United States curricula. This rationale boomeranged when American students scored almost as well as Korean students (96 percent versus 100 percent, respectively) on scientific factual questions, but scored markedly lower on questions that demanded reasoning skills. Here the gap widened significantly. On questions requiring the application of simple tenets, Koreans responded correctly 93 percent of the time, while Americans were right only 78 percent of the time. At the next level, which required analyzing experiments, Korean students answered correctly 73 percent of the time, while Americans answered correctly only 42 percent of the time. The last level of analysis resulted in 33 percent of Koreans answering correctly, whereas only 12 percent of American students did so.

EDUCATIONAL INEQUALITIES

Demands for educational reform have been driven not only by growing illiteracy and lack of achievement but also by a growing realization of educational inequality. Parents are finally realizing that the quality of their children's education will have a decisive effect on their future standard of living. Although some of this inequality should probably be attributed to social and behavioral factors, most parents and educational reformers blame unequal school funding at local and state levels. The distribution of educational funds impacts every part of the school system from the hiring of quality teachers and purchasing of textbooks to the maintenance of quality facilities.

In East St. Louis (IL), for example, an economically ravaged area containing decaying, corrosive chemical plants, the science labs are 100 degrees Fahrenheit when the temperature is zero outside because the heating system has never functioned properly.[10] In 1989, two schools were awash, and subsequently evacuated, as raw sewage backed up and flowed into the basements, kitchens, and finally into student restrooms. Farther north, however, at New Trier High School (IL), suburban, economically advantaged students had access to advanced computer labs and, ironically, a chlorinated, olympic-sized swimming pool. The discrepancies between these two school systems still persist. East St. Louis school district spends an annual average of $5,216 per pupil from K–12, compared to New Trier High School, which spends $10,417 per pupil. Textbooks at the latter school can be replaced every year, while in East St. Louis the average wait is five to ten years. East St. Louis offers no college level or advanced placement courses; New Trier High School is able to offer eighteen.

Although this type of funding disparity substantially affects minority, urban students, race is not the sole factor. U.S. Department of Education survey data for 1987 indicate that only 5,576 (or 36 percent) of the nation's 15,667 secondary schools offered a physics course and that the majority of students had no science courses after the tenth grade.[11] Similar national data found that availability of math, science, and foreign language classes is worse among various subgroups of students and communities. Rural school students, for example, are at a distinct disadvantage regarding access to foreign language courses. Surveys report that 50 percent of rural school students are unable to take a third year of Spanish, 56 percent are unable to take a third year of French, and 83 percent are unable to take a third year of German.

The funding difference between the ten poorest school districts and ten wealthiest is stark. A Congressional Research Service report found that the ten poorest school districts spent an average of $2,004 per elementary school student, as opposed to $6,260 per student in the ten richest school districts. For secondary schools, the average was $3,179 for poor school districts versus $6,631 for wealthy ones. Accounting for these differences revolves around local property taxes, the main source of funding for most schools. The more economically advantaged the neighborhood, the more funds that are likely to be raised and allocated to schools. Even if poorer neighborhoods vote to tax themselves at a higher rate, their lower property values cannot equal the higher amounts generated by taxes in wealthier cities and towns. In the past, states such as Ohio have been under no obligation to explain why they spent $22,000 on one child and only $2,500 on another.

The gross unfairness of such systems and the realization of the subsequent disenfranchisement of millions of American children have resulted in twenty-five states being sued for operating unconstitutional school-financing systems. Eleven state supreme courts, including those of Montana, Kentucky, Texas, and New Jersey, have ruled that their school financial allocation systems violate equal-protection guarantees. Legal victories, however, have been rather Pyrrhic in nature. Wealthier school districts that are providing their children with all the necessary materials for a quality education rightfully wish to continue that course. Many are successfully countersuing under the grounds that shifting their hard-earned tax revenues to poorer school districts leads to taxation without representation.

The role of the federal government with regard to unequal funding has also been rather negligible. Their attempts at equalization of funds have been through passage of two congressional acts, entitled the Education for All Handicapped Children Act (PL 94–142) and the Elementary and Secondary Education Act (ESEA PL 89–10). The former, which granted all disabled children the right to an appropriate education, was slotted to pay 40 percent of children's expenses but is presently paying only 8 percent. ESEA, which was dedicated to supplement state funding to assist the poorest children with basics such as reading and math, is currently up for reauthorization by Congress.

As the battle for equal educational opportunity rages on against a backdrop of growing illiteracy and declining test scores, the formal education of 15 to 20 percent of the nation's children quietly progresses within America's elite private and high-quality suburban schools. Despite even their declining productivity in relation to students from other countries, these fortunate children continue to be well prepared for a future of symbolic-analytic work due to several critical factors.[12] First, they have parents who express a constant interest in their educational progress by becoming knowledgeable and involved in their chosen school's objectives and goals. Second, they have subject-oriented teachers who are dedicated to student learning. Third, they have access to advanced laboratories, computerized classrooms, language laboratories, and "high-tech school libraries." Fourth, class size is usually kept below eighteen, and their peers are intellectually motivated. Parents escort their offspring to museums and symphonies, arrange for travel abroad, and provide music, art, and dance lessons. Their homes are thoroughly equipped with learning tools such as books, educational toys, microscopes, telescopes, and personal computers. If any of these children waver academically in their march toward future success, private tutoring or remedial instruction is furnished. If any learning disability or other medical problem is diagnosed, these children receive excellent medical care.

The idea of economic progress for only one fifth of America's children with the concomitant loss for the other four fifths implies a form of social Darwinism, and, educationally, this may just be the case. In the past, economic progress and democracy were thought to be partners and this partnership implied "the democratization of affluence." Progress was associated with more labor-saving devices, greater options, and more comfort. It was usually related to a higher standard of living for all American children, not just the privileged, albeit hard-working, 20 percent.[13] Yet by the year 2020, this rising standard of living for the top fifth will mean that they will earn more than 60 percent of American income, with the bottom fifth dropping to 2 percent.[14]

EDUCATIONAL REFORM TRENDS

The dawning realization that a substantial portion of America's children will not enjoy the standard of living that their parents now experience is fueling the fires for educational reform. The risk of becoming a member of the working poor may just be the catalyst that is needed to spark a long-overdue educational revolution. In the past, reform has been characterized by a cycle of boom and bust. First there is a call to arms about the crisis, followed by a series of new policies, programs, and projects dedicated to a total overhaul of the system. This stage is followed by testimonials praising reformers, requests for time to change, increased funding demands, and "molasses-like inertia from the educational establishment." What ensues is gradual loss of progress, ennui, cynicism, and attention to other crises. Finally, in the name of cost-effectiveness during an economic recession there is a call for back to basics.[15] In the business world it takes approximately two years for a new idea to be incorporated into the business community. In education, with little fear of accountability and no profits to account for, it takes sixteen years.[16] Because of shrinking opportunities for economic advancement and new technologies, evidence suggests that change may occur more quickly. Unlike the 1980s, however, when efforts to improve schools rode in on a wave of prosperity, the next decade will be much more stressful. Schools will be under a great deal of pressure to achieve more, with less.

Choice, Competition, and Restructuring

The demand for better-educated students has created a concomitant demand for better schools. In response to a recent Gallup poll that reported 62 percent of the public was in favor of parental choice of schools, the educational establishment has been attempting to respond by providing a smorgasbord plan of schools and programs to satisfy disillusioned parents.[17] Proponents of choice plans argue that affluent families have a myriad of schools to select from either by paying increased school taxes in academically oriented communities or by sending their children to private institutions. In turn, why shouldn't less affluent parents be given a similar choice within their communities? A corresponding benefit would be overall improvement in the quality of education, because students and parents would choose only effective schools. Therefore, to maintain their student populations, all schools regardless of their location, economic status, or reputation would be forced to improve schooling.[18]

Opponents argue that school choice is not the issue. More productive learning can be achieved anywhere given the opportunity to permeate the curriculum with symbolic-analytic activities. Supporters of this view believe that it is only necessary to restructure schools with appropriate technologies and learning situations that foster higher-order thinking skills rather than offering limited choices.[19] Examples of this strategy include Sizer's Coalition of Essential Schools. In this plan, no two schools would be identical, yet all would share nine common principles. These consist of the following: (1) Every student should know how to learn and how to use his or her mind well; (2) each student should master a set of essential skills and be competent in certain areas of knowledge; (3) the means to achieve these goals should vary to accommodate different learning styles; (4) each faculty member should be responsible for the teaching of no more than eighty students; (5) instruction should feature the student as worker rather than the teacher as deliverer; (6) students should demonstrate a mastery of basic subjects such as language and mathematics via an "exhibition" administered jointly by faculty and higher authorities; (7) the school should exude a climate of unanxious expectation, incentives should be employed for students, and staff and parents should be heavily involved in the life of the school; (8) principals and faculty should deem themselves generalists first and subject specialists second; and (9) budgets should allow time for collective planning and competitive salaries for faculty and staff.[20] Sizer's Coalition of Essential Schools involved about two hundred schools in twenty-three states. Almost all were public institutions; only eighteen were private.

A second approach involves distilling in essence what constitutes good teaching and replicating it in other schools. George Wood in a book entitled *Schools That Work: America's Most Innovative Public Education Programs* (New York: Dutton, 1992) analyzed the elements necessary for an effective school program. Not surprisingly, Wood came to the conclusion that control of the structure of size, time, and governance were the most important concepts in reforming schools. Defining the mission of a school, in his view, should be a collaborative decision between administrators, faculty, and staff. Controlling the size of a school was directly related to establishing a sense of community. It also encouraged teachers to establish closer relationships with students.[21] Wood's concept of size is reinforced by a number of research studies that suggest size is a determinant factor in creating a healthy school environment. A 1987 study of 744 high schools nationwide found that the dropout rate at schools with more than 2,000 students was twice that of schools with 667 or fewer students. A year later, a similar study conducted with 4,450 students in 160 high schools indicated that discipline problems, student absenteeism, and dropout rates are greater in larger schools.[22]

The idea of governance, while clearly echoing Sizer's concepts, is an empowering factor. Wood noticed that in schools where the faculty were part of the governing structure, students received an excellent education regardless of their socioeconomic status. This idea of teachers as self-governing or even entrepreneurs is now being successfully tested within several large school districts. Since 1987, more than half the public schools in Dade County, Florida, have allowed faculty to assist in the hiring of principals, to draft budgets, and to structure curricula.

In 1991, Minnesota legislators furthered the process by allowing state-certified faculty to open and operate independent schools under three-year contracts with local school boards.[23] Empowering faculty with the "ownership" of their schools has resulted in reduced teacher absenteeism and has also given teachers new input in the educational process. Minnesota's schools are required to be nonprofit and nonsectarian. Teachers cannot charge tuition or selectively admit students but are otherwise free to design and create their own curricula. As a result of this enfranchisement, two St. Paul teachers opened a successful academy for dropouts that incorporates four days of interdisciplinary courses followed by a fifth day with some type of on-the-job training. Similarly empowered teachers at the 1,732-student Miami Springs Middle School (Miami, FL) substantially reorganized the school into eleven groups of about 160 students and four faculty. The teachers have used their recent autonomy and power to redesign the curriculum and select textbooks more appropriate for the largely Hispanic population.

Giving faculty autonomy is coupled with the movement toward smaller schools. Both are concepts that Wood witnessed in schools that work. Similar programs that involve teachers as entrepreneurs are being conducted at Fairedale High School Career Magnet Academy (Fairedale, KY), Greece Arcadia High School (Greece, NY), and Interlake High School (Bellevue, WA). The concepts that Wood and Sizer stress are in reality quite similar. Combined, they are innovations that would probably improve the effectiveness of the nation's schools without requiring a significant amount of additional funding.

Regional/Statewide Magnet Schools

One of the primary reasons for the expansion of free choice in public education has been the substantial increase in the number of magnet schools. Originally designed to help desegregate city schools in Boston, magnet schools now provide specialized curricula to children regardless of their school zone. These schools may include fine arts, computer science, technical trades, or advanced studies in the physical sciences or humanities. A 1982 U.S. Department of Education survey reported 1,090 magnet programs, but recent evidence indicates that magnet schools now number more than 10,000.[24]

Magnet schools have many different configurations. They can be schools within schools or entirely separate facilities. Some are created totally for higher-achieving students so that they will not opt for private schools. As such they are selective and thus offer better educations to only a specified group of students. Others are vocational schools, whose instruction is geared to gaining immediate employment. The latter in some cities, such as Washington, DC, are funded by corporations that are trying to improve the quality of the workforce.

In urban areas, magnet schools are increasingly able to offer students a wide number of curricula by also drawing on the resources of the city itself. Los Angeles city schools have developed eighty-five magnet programs offering, for example, a medical and health profession curriculum at King-Drew Medical Center High School, located next door to a hospital, and an Animal and Biological Sciences Center for tenth–twelfth graders that is situated by the Los Angeles Zoo. Approximately one third of Buffalo (NY) schools contain magnet programs featuring curricula in Native American studies, art, and bilingual education. Pittsburgh (PA) schools offer twenty-two magnet programs, including a classics curriculum that focuses upon Greece and Rome.

Open Enrollment

Magnet schools appear to be a developmental stage in the direction of open enrollment. Where magnet schools have been established, the marketing of the other schools in the system is a logical step. Many school systems have noted that when students and parents are provided with an opportunity to choose their schools, schools compete with one another for students. In turn, competition has a catalytic effect on schools to improve themselves.

In Omaha (NE), the options to choose are so varied that nearly one third of its 10,000 high school students selected a school outside their attendance zone. This new plan has created a buyer's market, since the majority of students are usually accepted by their first-choice school. On the other hand, it has turned many faculty who previously thought of themselves solely as educators into salespeople. Parents and staff meet regularly to plan marketing strategies. Videos of each school are sent to junior high and elementary schools. Two of the high schools are magnet schools. One offers a basic curriculum, while the other emphasizes technology and computer science. Omaha claims that it is not just selling options and that their curricula have truly improved. At one of the high schools, for example, which had experienced declining enrollment, the attendance has climbed from a low of 921 students to nearly 1,800. Omaha's parochial schools now are losing about one third of their students to the public schools.[25]

Where open enrollment is mandated and where there are real differences in schools, the opportunities for school improvement appear to be greatest. Smaller schools and increased teacher autonomy are also necessary to bring about change. The Cambridge plan (Cambridge, MA), for example, is mandated. As in Omaha's plan, students and parents must choose a school. Minnesota, by contrast, has a voluntary choice program that fewer than 2 percent of the state's students participate in. As a result, most schools have no incentive to improve the quality of their education.

The Cambridge model has been in effect for ten years.[26] Since that time, the dropout rate has declined from 9 percent to 2 percent, and daily attendance averages more than 90 percent. Faculty absences average 5 percent, which is considered low for an urban school district. The percentage of students attending Cambridge schools versus private institutions has also risen from 80 to 88 percent. The cost to the city in 1992 was $1.4 million out of a school budget totaling $71.5 million. Other model open enrollment plans include Community School Districts 2 and 4 in New York and Montclair Public Schools in New Jersey.

Cooperative College/High School Programs

Another approach to improving education for higher-achieving students is to affiliate secondary schools with local community colleges, colleges, and universities. Within the past decade, several states have high schools situated on local university campuses. In New York City, they are termed "middle colleges" and provide high school students with the opportunity to tap the variety of resources available at nearby colleges and to take courses for credit. One of the most successful divisions of Minnesota's open enrollment program is not school choice but the use of a "post-secondary option" permitting eleventh and twelfth graders to take courses at any college willing to accept them. State school funds pay their tuition. The postsecondary option was used by approximately 6.4 percent of all Minnesota juniors and seniors in 1990–91. This number was eight times greater than the number of eligible students who opted for school choice. Other models for this "microchoice" strategy can be found at the New World School of the Arts, a performing arts high school, which is located on the campus of Dade Community College (FL), and at a number of middle colleges on various campuses of the City University of New York.

While microchoice plans may not provide a sufficient incentive for schools to improve their own curricula, they can provide reform-minded administrators leverage with local school boards that may permit them to innovate or improve upon particular courses, especially in the areas of technology and computer science. States are in prime financial positions to develop joint college/high school programs, because many local colleges and universities are state-supported. In rural school districts that lack the capacity to form magnet schools with any increased advantages, this type of program can at least offer a relatively low-cost choice to students oriented toward higher achievement.[27]

High-Technology Schools

In addition to problems caused by illiteracy and declining test scores, another impetus for reform is the impact of technologies. Some schools have recognized the tremendous potential that technology has to improve learning and teaching by establishing super high schools with state-of-the art fiber-optic cabling, computers, satellite communications, and CD-ROM databases. For example, Westfield High School, a rural school in Indiana, purchased new technologies to give students national and international access to a variety of information sources and databases. Through the contribution of GTE, several other technology corporations, and nearby Ball State University, every classroom and office in the three-school, 1,919–student school district is in a local area fiber-optic network. Equipped with a TV monitor, each faculty member, at the press of a channel changer, can access and display newspaper articles, educational graphics, films, and live programs via satellite. Most of the material is housed in a technology distribution center that teachers use like a library. Teachers at the high school can even create their own multimedia materials. The satellite connection allows the middle school to offer, for the first time, courses in Japanese, Latin, French, and Spanish. The courses are being taught by teachers employed by TI-IN Network, a distance education programming company. The total cost of these courses is $2,000, a small percentage of the amount required to recruit and hire teachers locally.[28]

Realizing that school library media centers are predesigned for this type of technological change, Littleton High School (Littleton, CO) expanded its collection of 27,000 volumes to hundreds of thousands of volumes by establishing computerized access to the CARL (Colorado Alliance of Research Libraries) on-line system.[29] With access to CARL, students can search a bibliographic record database with 5 million items, taken from several public and academic libraries, browse a huge periodical index, and locate statistical information on Denver. Students can also access their school's on-line catalog from various classrooms throughout the school.

One of the most technologically advanced elementary schools is connected to the media laboratory at MIT.[30] The Hennigan School is located in Boston's inner city. The project, begun in 1985 by Seymour Papert, has been exploring the educational potential of what can only be termed a utopian situation—one computer per student. Papert has designed a computer language for children called LOGO which permits them to draw, write, do math, and create music. Visitors to the Hennigan School observe intense collaboration among students and different approaches to learning. The computer seems to have freed many of them who might not have been successful in a traditional classroom lecture mode to explore other means of learning. If enthusiasm is any measure of success, the Hennigan School definitely possesses it. All but three of Papert's forty-nine fifth-grade students voluntarily arrived on a Saturday morning to experiment with a new version of LOGO.

A second elementary school, referred to in Chapter 2, is called the Saturn School of Tomorrow (St. Paul, MN). In this high-technology environment students learn with computers and other technologies about a third of the day and then spend another third of their time in cooperative learning situations. Students are grouped by skill levels rather than grade levels. Other leaders in educational technology are Penn High School (Mishawaka, IN), Shorewood High School (Seattle, WA), and Watkins Mill High School (Gaithersburg, MO).[31]

For students raised in a technology-driven society, sitting in a desk and listening to endless lectures is probably the most archaic method for transmitting knowledge. High-technology schools offer opportunities to reduce teacher lecturing and provide for more active learning situations. New technologies hold the power to offer entire libraries of information to students and, through advances such as distance learning, to broaden their choices of study.

Self-Governance

A major bulwark to educational reform is unrelated to pedagogies or textbooks. Public school bureaucratic infrastructures are so entrenched that in many areas they are a major obstacle to education. Bureaucratic personnel in schools run the gamut from those who sweep floors to those who push paper. In any event, they effectively siphon off large sums that parents intended for the education of their children. Audits of the Milwaukee and New York City school systems report that less than half the money allocated per high school student in New York or per elementary school student in Milwaukee actually went to the school. Less than a third of the total allotment touched classroom services. Within the past twenty-five years, faculty salaries have been a declining percentage of school budgets, while bureaucratic and other noninstructional expenditures swallowed up the increasing sums of allocated funds. Redundancies in services produce grossly inefficient systems that can prevent improvement merely through byzantine chains of administrative excess. A Texas county was cited recently in a state audit for serving a total of 5,000 students through twelve school systems, twelve school boards and twelve superintendents.[32]

In the decade ahead, whose slogan will have to be "more for less," states may start allowing schools to declare themselves independent of these tentaclelike bureaucracies as a cost-savings device. Like colleges and universities, they would elect their own boards of trustees and fund their schools directly, thus limiting in effect the overhead function of education. Independent schools could save money by contracting out inadequate custodial and food services. They could purchase supplies and other instructional materials that they need without the endless requisition and delivery protocols that they presently encounter.

While self-governance is just being seriously discussed in the United States, it has been tried in Great Britain since 1988 with reported success.[33] As a component of the Education Reform Act a new category of "grant-maintained" schools was devised for purposes of emancipating schools from the fetters of local bureaucratic red tape. Communities wishing to have grant-maintained schools must have a majority vote of parents and trustees and then apply to the national government to "opt out" of their local school district. They automatically receive the same level of funding that they did when under local control. Grant-maintained schools suddenly receive their full share of allocations, not what remains after various administrative operations have extracted overhead costs. Reports of this system indicate that Britain's "grant-maintained" schools generally have more resources than regularly run schools. Opt-out schools had between 15 and 20 percent more money to spend. London's Hendon School, for example, was able to effect a 58-percent increase in expenditures for books and teaching materials, and a 400-percent increase in classroom equipment. At Bankfield High in Cheshire, opting out enabled the school to hire six additional teachers and increase per-student spending on books from $50 to $160.

Needless to say, the financial success of many grant-maintained schools has not been greeted enthusiastically by entrenched bureaucracies. In several instances school boards threatened to sell the school and its grounds rather than let the parents and trustees vote to opt out. Other schools banned grant-maintained school sports teams from competing within the school district. Yet grant-maintained schools achieved their goals. First, they freed up more resources to be spent for their children and second, they decided exactly what bureaucratic functions were really necessary for their particular schools.

FUTURE PEDAGOGIES

Unfortunately, curriculum reform has been characterized by the same boom-and-bust pattern that has typified educational restructuring. With few or no research findings, the nation's school districts embark upon the "latest" educational "ism" until it is no longer in vogue. Unlike the medical profession, which is required to conduct double-blind tests on significant numbers of human subjects before prescribing new drugs, educators are not held to this standard. As a result, they have been experimenting with the most precious capital America produces, its children. For years, the United States has countenanced the use of children in unstructured, poorly conceived and designed educational experiments ranging from new math to wall-less classrooms.[34]

Until now, many parents quietly acquiesced to the latest pedagogy, because they individually felt powerless to stop it and, more importantly, because it seemed irrelevant. Their progeny continued to obtain gainful employment and to enjoy decent living standards. But now there is a growing disparity between the quality of education received by the upper 20 percent of American children and the rest. This trend also mirrors a widening income disparity in society as a whole. While this deepening division can be partially attributed to the impact of technologies on work, it can also be ascribed to increased demand for higher-level reasoning skills and less demand for routine-production skills. Clearly, one of the components for balancing this unequal social equation is to provide all students with an education that is suffused with symbolic-analytic skills. Now the question is, will this become education's latest "ism" necessitating endless faculty workshops and more expenditures for new textbooks that incorporate these skills? Let us hope that the answer is no.[35]

SYMBOLIC-ANALYTIC SKILLS

Symbolic-analytic skills is a term coined by Reich in *The Work of Nations* to describe the types of abilities required of approximately 20 percent of the workforce in America. Other employment specialists reinforce Reich's forecast that a much larger percentage of workers will need these skills just to survive as more occupations become increasingly technologically advanced.

As a pedagogy, symbolic-analytic skills has been in existence since the first teacher-pupil relationship. More recently it went under the rubrics of critical thinking, higher-order thinking, and free inquiry. Basically all of them are age-old methods for teaching students to think rather than memorize facts. States such as California and Connecticut have precisely articulated and incorporated these skills into formal curriculum guides with less than notable results.[36] Most educators believe that their failure rests with the amount of time spent on developing symbolic-analytic skills. All too often it is easier for teachers, especially in unruly educational settings, not to engage students in any meaningful discussion of their subject. Sometimes the lack of student knowledge is so vast that discussions can only be conducted on emotionally based opinions rather than evidence-supported reasoning. Out of understandable exhaustion, teachers simply resort to rote drill exercises so that some achievement is reflected on yearly standardized exams. If this type of teaching persists, a huge percentage of the population will become a lost generation with little chance for any economic advance. Therefore, future curriculum reform must incorporate symbolic-analytic skills into all subject areas if we all are to prosper.

A day spent at any notable private (independent) or suburban school will vividly demonstrate how children acquire the four basic skills Reich lists as indigenous to symbolic-analytic thinkers. First of all, much of the factual information required as a standard foundation for symbolic analysts, such as multiplication tables, vocabulary lists, and memorization of chemical elements and atomic numbers, has been assigned and is completed by the students as homework. Lessons then proceed to use teacher and student time to discover, for example, a pattern of deductive reasoning in a Sherlock Holmes mystery or to discover the pattern of reverse logic in Lewis Carroll's *Alice in Wonderland*. The teacher acts as a stimulus, constantly probing and asking questions about the readings that develop students' capacity for abstraction. Students who mistakenly try to retell an incident in the story instead of extracting meaning from it are gently nudged in the right direction by the issuance of other probing questions calculated to elicit more than factual recitations. The teachers rarely refer to a textbook or teacher's manual for conducting these discussions, because they are too preoccupied with interacting with their students. There is an air of stimulation to this type of teaching that is unmistakably infectious.

A second skill is also being developed. This involves the capacity to see relationships within a system, or to use system thinking. Subjects are not isolated from one another but are more interdisciplinary. A unit, for example, about the discovery of the Americas involves studying botany, chemistry, geography, math, politics, history, literature, and art as students comprehend how the "seeds of change" were sown with the Columbian exchanges of corn, sugarcane, and horses. Students still need to know about Christopher Columbus and the date of 1492 but, more importantly, are forced to think of that time as a series of systems that over time became inextricably connected.

The use of experimentation, the third skill required of symbolic analysts, in elite schools is not solely the responsibility of the science department. Visitors would see history teachers conducting hypothetical discussions with students to test the premise of the stock market crash as a major cause of the Great Depression. Discussions would follow about whether it could be replicated given today's stock market situation. In other classes, students would be designing their own psychology experiments. Consulting a library book which lists a series of successful ones is frowned upon. Instead, students are given the tools to formulate their own hypotheses. They are only permitted to consult books and databases for a literature review of the project.

The last ability of a symbolic analyst involves the capacity for collaboration. Schools developing symbolic analysts regularly provide learning situations which call for working in teams. This type of activity is characteristic of much work performed by symbolic analysts. Group discovery of problems and solutions is preparation for working in a law firm, group medical practice, or business. A visit to schools that encourage collaboration would uncover groups of students engaged in such tasks as solving hypothetical economic problems and performing chemistry laboratory work. Their final assignments frequently entail an oral/written presentation to the class in which their peers serve as critics, reviewers, and editors. In many classes, students are given assignments requiring consensus before they can proceed to the next stage.[37]

The development of abstraction, system thinking, experimentation, and collaboration proficiencies is designed to prepare students for work that will require improved problem-solving skills. Educators will probably rename this pedagogy but that will not matter. What will be relevant is that educators in the poorest and most affluent schools teach their students that the facts that they are still required to accumulate are only peripheral to the central act of learning how to conceptualize problems and solutions.

IMPLICATIONS FOR SCHOOL LIBRARY MEDIA CENTERS

American schools and their media centers are at a critical juncture in deciding whether to provide access to education that emphasizes symbolic-analytic capabilities or routine-production skills. Responses to the future employment crisis throughout the nation's schools will probably vary in relation to the amount of parental pressure and economic status of particular schools.

Affluent schools will experience increased inquiries from parents about the curriculum, homework required, and test results to reinforce the demand that their children be on the right track toward securing rewarding jobs. School library media specialists in this type of school will be under increasing pressure to introduce students to the latest technologies, such as additional CD-ROM databases, on-line catalogs, and access to wide area networks like Internet and CARL. Parents in these schools will be concerned about declining test scores rather than illiteracy. They will already know the correlation between recreational reading and higher performance on standardized test scores. School media specialists will need to regularly furnish students with recommended reading lists and videos that focus upon the classics. At the elementary level, SLMCs will also be further technologically developed. Students will have access to encyclopedias and multimedia instruction on CD-ROM. School media specialists will read a great deal to their students and engage them in discussions that encourage critical thinking. They will continue to provide an enriched, stimulating environment in the SLMC that is conducive to learning.

In poor SLMCs, just the opposite will be the case. They will struggle to battle illiteracy with outdated books that for many poorly educated students are not on their interest level. School library media centers will be underfunded and may not be able to purchase necessary information technologies. They will probably have to seek corporate donations of equipment to provide students with additional information access. School librarians will have to be far more resourceful and dedicated in less affluent schools. There will be increased pressure to reform but less funding with which to achieve it.

The implications of growing illiteracy and declining test scores for SLMCs are realistically depicted in an increasingly bifurcated educational system. Unequalized funding at the local, state, and national levels foreshadows a bright future for some media centers and a dim one for others. If little is done in the future to rectify it, SLMCs in less affluent communities will serve as caretakers of a museum while their more fortunate counterparts preside over state-of-the-art facilities.

The issue of choice and its attending effect, increased competition, will probably impact all SLMCs regardless of their economic status. In an effort to assuage increasingly disillusioned students and parents, states will mandate that schools offer a variety of selections including magnet schools, college/high school combinations, supertechnology schools, and totally independent entities. At specified times of the year, SLMSs will probably have to describe their programs and services to consumer-oriented parents and students. For many, it will provide limitless opportunities to publicize their latest acquisitions (print or nonprint), justify budget requests, and demonstrate the success of various instructional programs. Finally, SLMSs may be able to show prospective students and their parents that they are indeed central to the curriculum of the school. For others who are serving simply as caretakers, choice plans will be threatening. Administrators will expect that all departments have strong instructional programs, advanced technologies, and well-developed teaching skills. School library media specialists who lack either the ability or desire to develop a more consumer-oriented approach to their media centers may find their future employment in jeopardy.

Many observers of education believe that the issue of economic advancement is the engine that is driving the educational reform movement. It demands that even poor schools produce symbolic analysts for the sake of the country's economic well-being. Library media specialists will find themselves at the center of this curricular reform movement because of their position as information specialists. Most of them will have sufficient tools to provide students with the opportunity to apply concepts like abstraction, system thinking, experimentation, and collaboration to various course-related units that they design. While it will be helpful for SLMCs to have access to the latest databases, cable programs, and multimedia packages, the skills necessary for increased economic opportunity will not be totally dependent upon access to the latest technology. What will be required is the integration of symbolic-analytic skills into every aspect of library curricula. School media specialists will have to resist the temptation to design instructional materials that merely call for finding the correct answer, fact, or picture. Instead, they will need to employ symbolic-analytic activities such as hypothetical situations in a drug abuse unit, simulations in a chemistry unit, class debates in a political science unit, or case studies in a sociology unit. All of these methods entail (1) defining a problem, (2) identifying its parameters, (3) deciding what kind of information is needed and searching for it, (4) exploring multiple solutions with their ensuing consequences, and (5) making a decision based upon the acquisition of subject knowledge.

There have been two scenarios operating in this discussion of educational trends. The first one strongly indicates that only a small percentage of the school-aged population is receiving an education that will give them opportunities for increased personal, social, and economic well-being. From the facts and figures supplied this scenario is not an exaggeration. America is fast becoming an educationally bifurcated society. If it continues on this course, we will sow the seeds for increasing hopelessness and despair among future generations.

More than ever before, school library media specialists will play a pivotal role in determining the direction their schools will go. For those in less affluent schools, their struggle will be to alert interested parents and administrators. In effect, they will have to sound the alarm for educational reform to let students know of the dangers they face if they neglect their educational opportunities. Their SLMCs can serve as the centers for change, but it will be a different battle with minimal financial assistance, except for various grants.

Affluent SLMCs, on the other hand, face danger from complacency. Declining test scores are now relative to those in other countries. Other nations are also busy producing their share of symbolic-analytic workers. Since these positions are sensitive to a global economy, it will behoove SLMSs to make certain that they are continuing to provide the optimum learning environment through new technologies and instructional units so that their students are really ahead relative to the world population and not just to each other.

Social and Behavioral Trends

5

> To exclude the majority of children from mainstream education and jobs would be a tragic waste of human resources.
>
> David A. Hamburg

Throughout the waves of academic reform that continuously sweep through schools, educational institutions have not modified their primary mission, which is to educate students. What has changed, however, is the culture of the United States. Some educators suggest that "the crisis is not in the schools but in us. The society we have constructed has given us the education we deserve."[1] Our values, beliefs, traditions, and thinking are acted upon and transmitted to our children. They in turn reflect the same social and behavioral characteristics in school. Basically, "Schools are microcosms of the expectations society has for its children. They are the institutions by which society creates the conditions for its perpetuation."[2]

In 1988, the graduating class of the year 2000 began its odyssey through the American educational system. They have less than a decade to be prepared for a world of work and a society that is undergoing fundamental cultural changes. The first cultural change affecting the class of 2000 is the transition of the United States from a nation *with* minorities to a nation *of* minorities.[3] How are we going to educate students in the years ahead to cope with increasingly diverse schools, neighborhoods, and work environments? A second change concerns the transformation of the American family from a traditional nuclear one into a blended one containing semirelated siblings and stepparents. Many times this restructuring is also accompanied by increased poverty and diminished opportunities for educational advancement. How are schools going to cope with the problems generated by family restructuring? A third change concerns children themselves. As our society becomes more violent and more entertainment- and consumer-oriented, what will future students be like? What programs and services will school library media centers have to provide to satisfy the social and emotional needs of the class of 2000 and beyond?

The questions posed do not have ready solutions. While many of the social trends such as divorce, working parents, and latchkey children have been forecast for years, schools and their media centers have been and still are reluctant to assume a greater parental role. Yet it is becoming increasingly difficult to fulfill education's primary mission without dealing with many of the grave social problems that beset children in even the most affluent school districts. The influence of the social and behavioral trends discussed in this chapter are considered a major cause in schools' failure to have all children learn.

A MULTICULTURAL SOCIETY

The ethnic composition of America is changing rapidly. According to the 1990 census, between 1985 and 1990, nearly one fourth of the 20 million foreign-born residents entered the country. This number has increased steadily from 1.5 million between 1960 and 1964 to a height of 5.6 million between 1985 and 1990. Approximately 7.9 percent of the United States population was foreign-born in 1990, the highest percentage in forty years.[4] The majority, even counting an estimated 500,000 illegals each year, are from Latin America, the Caribbean, and Asia.[5] Among these groups, Latin Americans constitute the largest influx. The number of U.S.-born Latinos and Latino immigrants to the United States doubled between 1980 and 1990. Hispanics living in the United States total 23 million people, almost 10 percent of the population, and are expected to become the largest minority by the year 2000. In addition, the median age for Hispanics is twenty-six, compared to thirty-two for other Americans, and the birthrate for Hispanics is 50 percent higher.

These factors coupled with continued immigration suggest that by the year 2050 almost 50 percent of the U.S. population will be Spanish-speaking. Los Angeles, for example, is already the second largest Spanish-speaking city in the world after Mexico City. San Antonio (TX) has been considered a bilingual city for the past 150 years.[6] Presently there are two successful Spanish-language television networks and numerous Hispanic radio stations in the United States.

The ethnic composition of the class of 2000 already reflects these demographic changes. About one third of these students are either African-American or Hispanics. These two groups presently constitute the majority of primary and secondary school students in twenty-three of the twenty-five largest American cities. By the year 2000, they will be the majority in fifty-three cities.[7]

Demographically, the "browning of America" is expected to continue. Population experts predict that as many as 15 million immigrants will arrive each decade for the next thirty years. The United States already accepts more immigrants than all other industrialized countries combined, and 80 percent of them are people of color.[8] Without the passage of extremely restrictive immigration laws, there is no reason to expect a cessation in this pattern. The consequences of a nation of many cultures are far-reaching for school media centers.

Social Consequences of Multiculturalism

During the past one hundred years, school library media specialists in urban areas most affected by the flood of immigrants responded by providing programs and services designed to assimilate immigrant children rapidly into the dominant society. These programs and services were characterized by citizenship study and dominant-language instruction. Then in the 1970s the Canadian Royal Commission introduced a concept termed "multiculturalism" which encompassed the enriching qualities that many cultures of the world brought to Canada. Australians embracing the same concept aptly defined it as "the willingness of the dominant groups to promote or even to encourage some degree of cultural and social variation within an overall concept of national unity."[9] This shift in immigration philosophy reflects an ethnic awareness that has resulted in the need for differing approaches to the provision of library programs and services not only to immigrant populations, but also to resident minority groups such as African-Americans.

In many schools, achieving this utopian goal is increasingly difficult. At Union Avenue Elementary School (Los Angeles), for example, the student population is 93 percent Hispanic. The next largest group is Filipino at 2.9 percent. Fewer than two thirds of the students were born in the United States, and more than 50 percent are not competent in English. More than half are thought to be the offspring of undocumented aliens. The Union Avenue School library contains books in Tagalog, Korean, Vietnamese, Spanish, and English. While the SLMC is valiantly attempting to provide immigrant students with access to their respective cultural heritages, the location of the school in the heart of a drug-infested and crime-ridden area means that the school media specialist has to wage an uphill battle against these elements to educate these students. Where there should be an influx of funds to assist states such as California, New York, Texas, New Jersey, Florida, and Illinois with the largest immigrant populations, there is only approximately $30 million a year from the federal government, or $42 per child, to assist them in providing specialized programs and materials to immigrant children. In 1993, California reported a shortage of 8,000 bilingual teachers.[10]

The price immigrant children will pay to belong to American society is going to be a costly one. Oscar Handlin, in his classic study of immigration, *The Uprooted*, wrote, "The history of immigration is the history of alienation and its consequences."[11] This statement is especially true for immigrant children. The cultural trauma of immigrant children is far more serious than that of their parents. Immigrant children are usually compelled to forget their past and, in some cases, to unlearn it. The conflict between their previous culture and the new culture pulls them in opposite directions. In many cases if they are to succeed, they must reject the past, which leaves them with feelings of guilt and betrayal.[12] Female immigrants, for example, whose original culture does not believe in educational opportunities for women, must run the risk of defying the family in order to receive an education and gain independence.

Parental academic expectations may also be confusing for immigrant children. In some cases they may be expected to go beyond the achievements of their parents in a new land, language, and culture. In other cases, their parents' academic aspirations for them may be minimal, because children are expected to leave school early and contribute to the family's income as soon as possible.

Learning the dominant language quickly is usually essential for survival. Immigrant children must often serve as translators for their parents with everyday domestic tasks, and also with employers, physicians, and businesses. The acquisition of the dominant language can be hastened with total immersion. For some immigrant children, however, the only time to acquire it may be at school, since it is not spoken at home.

Language acquisition is just the first hurdle immigrant children face. The second is cultural adjustment. In school, the methods of instruction may be entirely different from those of an immigrant student's previous educational experience. Jamaican schools, for example, have large classes where learning is done by rote and there is a strong oral tradition. Jamaican children operate from different temporal perceptions as well as from a different educational background. Their techniques for learning are considered inappropriate for classes in the United States.

Becoming a member of American society has its price. The lure of money and the dominant culture's concept of success, measured by wealth and occupational status, is ubiquitous. A chasm usually occurs between immigrant parents who possess less materialistic values and their children, who come to identify with America's definition of success.[13] The temptation to succumb to the "pathologies of the ghetto" with their quicksilver promise of easy money and belonging by means of gang membership are constant companions of this generation of immigrants.[14]

As immigrant children continue their education and associate with children whose only language is English, they may forget their native language. Despite their parents' attempts to maintain their children's bilingualism, the process of assimilation—total immersion into another cultural group—begins. The one experience that all immigrant children share is uprooting. After that, their socioeconomic and academic backgrounds may be extremely diverse. "An immigrant child's identity must be plotted on a number of axes—poor/rich, primitive, rural/megalopolis urban, nonliterate-oral/multilevel, academic."[15] The immigrants' country of origin may be very similar in culture, values, history, and language to the new country or it may be totally different. Many immigrant children, once they are attired in Western clothes, may resemble the majority population. Others, because of the color of their skin or the shape of their eyes, are "eternally visible."[16]

School library media specialists are ideally situated to assist immigrant students with the acculturation process by (1) correctly identifying the ethnic backgrounds of students, (2) assessing their educational needs, (3) acquiring appropriate print and nonprint materials for them, and (4) acquainting their classmates with the unique contribution their culture makes to America. Designing special projects to demonstrate the rich heritage of an ethnic community or group is also easily within the purview of the SLMC. At Carrillo Magnet School (Tucson, AZ), for example, a heritage center was created in the school media center. Students trained by a local folklorist were taught to tape and transcribe interviews with local residents of a barrio (Spanish-speaking community) concerning their lives and memories. The result was a sixty-two-page book, entitled *Tales Told in Our Barrio*, and a folklore series including a cookbook. With the assistance of the Arizona Historical Society, the SLMC developed a collection of books, audio- and videotapes, and photographs detailing the asset of a multicultural community.[17]

Future Trends of Multiculturalism

Presently the degree of participation in multiculturalism by a SLMC is usually dependent upon the ethnic composition of the community it serves. If there are significant numbers of African-Americans, Hispanic, or Asian students, the collection, author visits, speakers, literature courses, and bibliographic instruction units tend to reflect their needs and interests. Books of a more utilitarian nature, such as cookbooks, gardening books, and encyclopedias, may be available in Spanish. Periodicals that reflect the ethnic composition of the school community are also available. School media centers in areas with large concentrations of minorities may also serve as information centers regarding health care, career counseling, and community cultural events. On the other hand, SLMCs serving primarily Caucasian communities are introducing students to literature by Asian, African-American, Hispanic, and Native American authors. Their media center collections tend to reflect a truly multicultural approach to the curriculum. Because of their homogeneous populations, they have the luxury of designing relatively noncentric, multicultural curricula that will serve their students well as they enter a global workplace.

Although multiculturalism may be retermed "ethnic diversity" or "cultural pluralism" in the future, it will not be another educational "ism" on the road to academic reformation. The statistics concerning increased immigration and the changing employment picture previously described in Chapter 3 aptly demonstrate that America is fast becoming a nation of minorities. What is more important, however, is America's need for multicultural curriculum approaches in relation to the world. A single cultural approach, be it Afrocentrism, Eurocentrism, or Latinocentrism, will make little economic sense "in a world where, within twenty-five years, the combined gross national product of East Asia will likely be larger than Europe's and twice that of the United States."[18] Years ago, the term *globalized* conjured up an economy of plantations, reflective of the nineteenth century, or an economy in which companies established subsidiaries abroad but did not internationally integrate their operations. Then, identifying with a particular country made economic sense, because most of the market participants were Western in interests and location. Now, however, there are few companies that plan to develop their products with a national identity. As their industries become multinational, a multicultural approach to product development, planning, and marketing seems best.

For example, with the use of advanced telecommunications networks, companies may have headquarters in Los Angeles, strategic partners in Hamburg and Tokyo, factories in Ensenada and Trinidad, and a data processing operation in Thailand. Borders, as defined by nations, will cease to exist. The need for students to understand the values and beliefs of other cultures and how they relate to business practices will be imperative. Although the collapse of borders will not change time-honored ways of negotiating and completing business transactions within various countries, each nation's cultural habits, traditions, and customs will have to be respected by Americans, if the United States is going to prosper in a global economy.[19]

Historically, most recent immigrants and African-Americans have been at the bottom of the economic ladder with respect to job opportunities and access to education. Millions of these children have been relegated to a marginal existence in our society because of low levels of education and ethnic discrimination. Both groups have a dropout rate of approximately 40 percent from high school. Opportunities for decent-paying jobs for this group are almost nonexistent. Because these groups are faced with rapidly diminishing occupational opportunities in routine-production service jobs and increasing poverty, ethnic tensions have been exacerbated, especially between immigrants and African-Americans. In 1992, for example, when Los Angeles erupted in rioting, the tension between the African-American community and recent Korean immigrants resulted in more than 2,000 Korean-owned businesses being looted or burned.[20]

As various ethnic groups continue to be marooned on crime-infested and drug-ridden urban islands with even fewer opportunities for a decent standard of living, the concept of multiculturalism is perceived as a vehicle for empowerment or increasing self-esteem. As the idea of social injustice creeps into multiculturalism initiatives, the potential for polarization accompanies it. The writer Molefi Asante is quoted as saying, "There are only two positions; either you support multiculturalism in American education, or you support the maintenance of white supremacy."[21] In response to such a choice, Arthur Schlesinger, Jr., in *The Disuniting of America*, poses an interesting question. " 'Multiculturalism' arises as a reaction against Anglo- or Eurocentrism; but at what point does it pass over into an ethnocentrism of its own? . . . When does obsession with differences begin to threaten the idea of an overarching American nationality?"[22]

For years the arguments concerning the underlying goals of multiculturalism were mulled over in academic journals or debated in academic senates at various universities. Now, much to the detriment of students who desperately need a truly multicultural education, the battle is being fought in public schools across the nation. In 1987, for example, New York and California adopted new curricula for grades one through twelve. Both states increased the time and materials devoted to non-European cultures. New York State, however, under increasing pressure from minority interests, agreed to consider a revision of the history curriculum in 1989. Various consultants, representing their respective ethnic groups, demanded more pictures of Asian-Americans and references to the Spanish-American War changed to the ethnically correct American-Mexican War. Another consultant voiced opposition to the term *slaves*, because it "depersonalized the oppression of a people."[23] The Native American consultant demanded additional space for Native Americans and bilingual education in Iroquois.

Educational psychologist Asa Hilliard's Afrocentric curriculum, which, among other things, attributes the discovery of America, birth control, and steel to Africans, has had his African-American Baseline Essays adopted by the Portland (OR) schools. They have also served as the basis for Afrocentric curricula in Milwaukee, Indianapolis, Pittsburgh, Washington, DC, Richmond, Atlanta, Philadelphia, Detroit, Baltimore, and other cities.[24] If multiculturalism develops into ethnocentrism, the implications for school media centers evoke shades of McCarthyism and even Orwell's "big brother." If, however, multiculturalism is made a source of national identity and unity and a vehicle for competing successfully in a global economy, the picture for SLMCs will be much brighter.

THE TRANSFORMATION OF THE AMERICAN FAMILY

Most sociologists consider the isolated nuclear family of the 1950s an intriguing anomaly. Given the current decade of working mothers, single parents, and gay marriages, the term *nuclear family* seems antiquated at best. Families in the twenty-first century are predicted to be interracial, split by divorce, increased by remarriage, and reproduced through new genetic technologies. Single parents and working mothers will become typical and the number of out-of-wedlock children will increase. The nuclear family represented by a working father, housewife- mother, and two children will become an endangered species.[25]

The restructuring of the American family has not happened overnight. Mothers in the workforce have increased steadily since the 1960s. Divorce is not a recent phenomenon either. Approximately 50 percent of all marriages have been ending in divorce for the past decade. Yet the majority of schools, already burdened with the need for curriculum reform, have been reluctant to respond to the transformation of the American family in a major way. This pattern, however, is expected to change as schools realize that assistance to families is inextricably intertwined with academic achievement by children.[26]

Impact of Divorce

One of the major influences on the American family of the twenty-first century will still be the impact of divorce. Although divorce rates have stabilized in recent years, they are still accounting for the dissolution of roughly 50 percent of all marriages. Research on divorcing families continues to demonstrate that marital dissolution causes severe emotional distress in children and disrupts parent-child relationships. Single parents, usually mothers, frequently reduce their parenting for several years after separation. The situation improves only gradually and with the addition of close, dependable new relationships. The relationship between the child and the noncustodial parent usually becomes attenuated. Symptoms of divorce are related to age, and range from grief, fear, and yearning for reconciliation in six-to-eight-year-olds, to anger in nine-to-twelve-year-olds, and open rebellion in adolescents. At all ages, children's behavior at home and school tends to deteriorate.[27]

The economic impact of divorce will also be felt by children in the next century. There will continue to be a direct correlation between divorce and poverty, both as a catalyst for separation and as a result of dissolution.

Recent census data of a selected two-year-period, for example, indicate that nearly twice as many poor as nonpoor families dissolved (13 versus 7 percent).[28] While this pattern is understandable, the economic effects on children will continue to take a heavy toll. Most children of divorce reside with their mothers. Since female earnings are not equal to most male incomes, children raised in single-parent households headed by women are more likely to fall into poverty.[29] Currently, fifteen million children reside with single mothers whose family incomes average $11,400, which is within $1,000 of the poverty level. In comparison, the average income of married couples with children is $34,000.[30]

The vast number of children who are economically affected by divorce is scandalous. What is more devastating, however, are their chances for future economic well-being. Research indicates that the socioeconomic status of a family highly correlates with the value and emphasis that is placed on education and achievement.[31] At a time when educational job requirements are rising, what hope will these children have to improve their circumstances? One also cannot help but contrast the marital status, income, and educational level of parents whose children attend Ivy League schools (Harvard, Yale, Princeton, Dartmouth, Cornell, Brown, Columbia, and the University of Pennsylvania). A recent study of more than 3,000 undergraduates at these schools revealed that 29 percent are from families earning $150,000 or more, compared with 2 percent of students at all four-year colleges. More than 86 percent were raised in two-parent homes and more than 4 in 10 of their mothers and 5 in 10 of their fathers had done some graduate study. These percentages were triple those at other four-year colleges.

Historically, the Ivy League has educated America's ruling class. Although 50,700 undergraduates comprise less than 1 percent of the enrollment in the nation's four-year colleges, 15 percent of the chief executives of the nation's 800 largest corporations are Ivy League graduates. One fifth of President Clinton's cabinet earned undergraduate degrees at Ivy League schools.[32] It is deeply distressing to think that approximately 15 million children who live with one parent with reduced income have almost no chance to acquire the education necessary not only for personal well-being but also to assume leadership roles in our country.

Future Family Restructuring Trends

Statistics reveal that women are less likely to remarry after they divorce. In the future, more females are expected to never marry but to bear children. Recent census data confirm this pattern. The number of unmarried American women with at least one child rose 60 percent during the past decade from 15 percent to almost 24 percent. Although these numbers are still fairly small, the largest increases were found among whites, educated women, and women in white-collar positions. For many years out-of-wedlock births were associated with low educational levels and poverty. This rationale, while accounting for much of the increase, however, will probably be an unsatisfactory explanation in the future. It now appears that an increasing number of intelligent, well-educated women will decide to become mothers without becoming wives.[33]

Choosing to divorce, to never marry, to remarry, or to have a live-in partner will make family structures more complex, especially for children. Relationships between stepparents, former in-laws, and stepsiblings are predicted to become increasingly litigious. More importantly, they can be expected to be extremely stressful to children, who will be forced to divide their loyalties and love among a mosaic of semirelations. To further complicate matters, role confusion is likely to become widespread. What will be the role and responsibility, for example, of a biological parent, as opposed to a stepparent? More arguments are expected to ensue over household responsibilities, property, inheritance, and even rivalries for affection.[34] Unfortunately, the debilitating strain on children as families dissolve or restructure is predicted to worsen in the coming decade. Sociologists estimate that more than 50 percent of all white children and 75 percent of African-American children will live some portion of their formative years with only their mother.[35]

Working Parents and Parenting Trends

Nothing in recent census data suggests that two-parent working families are a temporary phenomenon. In fact, economic and employment factors almost dictate that both parents work. The consequences of work, whether it be in a single- or two-parent family setting, strain familial relationships. Mothers are home less frequently and fathers do not fill the void.[36] A late 1980s study of high school students found that more than 50 percent had parents who did not monitor their homework, one third acknowledged that their parents were unaware of their academic progress, and 50 percent said they did not have dinner with their parents daily.[37]

For younger children, child care, rather than benign neglect, is the problem. Currently, mothers of children under three are the fastest-growing segment of the labor market. While juggling jobs and preschoolers is difficult for two-parent families, single parents find the task almost impossible to handle. Yet approximately two thirds of single mothers with preschool children work, most of them full-time. Both types of parents are engaged in finding some type of child care. This usually entails either enrolling their children in nursery schools or finding homes that will provide care.

As more mothers of preschoolers are forced by economic circumstances to work, responsibility for their children rests with strangers. In 1985, for example, only 14 percent of children less than five years old were cared for in formal preschool facilities. By 1990, half of all children of employed parents were being cared for in either child care centers or other homes. As the pattern of working parents continues, so does the phenomenon of child care by strangers or established preschool centers.[38]

CHILDREN OF THE TWENTY-FIRST CENTURY

Probably the best way to predict the social and behavioral trends of children in the next century is to analyze current research studies and surveys concerning children of the 1990s. What are their social and behavioral characteristics? How have they changed in comparison to previous generations? Does it look as though these patterns will stabilize, improve, or worsen?

Adolescent Pregnancy

One of the saddest trends concerning children of the 1990s has been the increase in teenage pregnancy, especially among girls under age fifteen.[39] The United States now has one of the highest rates of teenage pregnancy among developed countries. Adolescents account for two thirds of all out-of-wedlock births. Approximately 1.3 million children reside with teenage mothers, only about half of whom are married. Six million preschool children live with mothers who were teenagers when they gave birth. The description of "babies having babies" is accurate. What compounds this tragedy is the lack of familial and social service support for both mother and child. In the past, our society provided some forms of secure employment, albeit low-paying, and a neighborhood usually populated by family members and relatives. A support network actually existed that assisted both mother and child. This scene, however, is becoming rarer as more adolescent mothers are socially isolated in alienated neighborhoods.

As this safety net of community support sags, neglect of preschool children is increasing. At its most flagrant stage, adolescent mothers are simply abandoning their babies after birth or consigning them to relatives or foster homes to raise. Studies continue to show that adolescent mothers are often less responsive to the needs of their babies than are more mature mothers. They also tend to have more babies than older mothers without allowing time for their bodies to recover. Thus they place themselves and all of their offspring at medical and behavioral risk. Babies raised by adolescent mothers are at increased risk for learning, emotional, health, and behavioral problems as compared to children of fully adult mothers. Unfortunately, the increase in teenage pregnancy is not an emerging trend. Census data have reported the rise for the last three decades. There is also no reason to expect that this incremental pattern will cease or abate in the next century.

The Self-Care Generation

A second disturbing societal trend relates to the amount of time children spend without parental supervision. Children have traditionally been responsible for themselves for part of the day, and many even assumed household chores at an early age. Several variables in self-care, however, have negatively influenced the current quantity and quality of that time. First, supportive neighborhood life has all but vanished. Since almost everyone in a neighborhood is working, children have almost no adults to rely on for medical or household emergencies or for companionship. In many cases, they are forbidden to allow their peers into the house because parents fear injuries or some form of mischief.

The number of self-care children, or latchkey children as they are termed, is continuing to increase. In 1974, for example, 50 percent of American children found no one at home after school. That number is currently 80 percent.[40] Studies of the self-care generation also reveal a different ethnic pattern of after-school care. Census data show that a higher number of white children than black children have no adult care after school—despite the fact that African-American mothers are more likely to be employed full-time than white mothers. Also, children whose mothers are in professional and managerial positions are more likely to be unsupervised than children of families in blue-collar positions.

These data naturally generate questions about these children. For example, what do they do with their time? Are they more independent as a result of the responsibility thrust upon them? If they don't go home, where do they spend their time? Are these children at greater risk than others regarding academic achievement and social interaction? How do they feel about being left alone? While many of these questions have not been thoroughly researched, teachers, psychologists, and sociologists are beginning to note some disturbing trends.

Children as Consumers

An increasing number of children spend their time shopping. A 1991 survey reported that 34 million children in the four–to–twelve age group had a combined income of $14.4 billion, of which they spent $9 billion.[41] Weekly, this amount averages out to $8.13 per child, of which a youngster spends $4.90. The fastest-growing spending items were shoes and clothing. A September 1992 Rand Youth Poll reported that teenagers spent $58.9 billion in 1992 despite the fact that their numbers have begun to decline in America.

Children do not just spend on themselves. Increasing numbers also shop for their families. A recent survey of 2,108 teenagers revealed that 40 percent (30 percent of males and 47 percent of females) regularly grocery shop for their families. In many cases, they not only influence the products their parents buy, such as soft drinks, desserts, and cereal, but also decide themselves the items to purchase.[42] As a result, it should come as no surprise that the self-care generation has become the target of advertisers. Teen Research Unlimited, a marketing research company, refers to this young generation of consumers as skippies, "school kids with income and purchasing power."[43] This company and others like it know full well the amount of time children spend watching unsupervised television. In the past, advertising aimed at children was pitched through their parents. Now, however, savvy advertisers bypass parents and directly entice children because of their own purchasing power and abilities to obtain money via parental guilt.

Children as Viewers

The amount of time children spend watching television is truly mind-boggling. Children now spend more hours watching television than in school, more hours watching television than reading (22.4 hours a week of television compared with 5.1 hours of reading outside of school), more hours watching television than playing with friends, and more hours watching television than interacting with their parents.[44] A current theme in television viewing research is the "mean-world syndrome." This is the tendency for viewers to feel more apprehensive, less trusting of others, and unwilling to venture out after dark in their neighborhoods.[45]

The amount of television viewing is taking its toll in declining test scores and a growing illiteracy. It is ironic that in the age of information overload, children are suffering from an information underload. Daily they are assaulted by a repetitive, bite-sized, usually negative strand of information. Beautifully crafted picture books designed to stir children's imaginations and creativity are ignored in favor of formula soap operas and animated cartoons. Television always resolves issues or at most produces two sides. Children grow up with the idea that major problems can be discussed and solved within twelve-minute time spans. Their own abilities to think, reflect, and discuss issues are never tested. Neil Postman in his book *Technopoly* also suggests that television may be partly responsible for current educational difficulties by causing children to be torn by two differing modes of knowledge transmission. The printed word, still typically used in schools to convey information, relies upon logic, sequence, exposition, detachment, and history; whereas television transfers information through imagery, presentness, immediacy, and intimacy.[46]

Children as Employees

Much of the income that children spend on consumer goods is money that they earn themselves. Although the thought of children working after school rather than cruising a mall or watching television is refreshing, many students place themselves at risk because of employment. A second factor relates to their inability to delay gratification of their hard-earned gains.

A recent survey of 46,800 students in the sixth through the twelfth grade revealed that 6 percent of sixth graders were employed for pay eleven or more hours per week, followed by 13 percent of ninth graders and 52 percent of twelfth graders.[47] For these students, jobs, especially entry-level service ones, are more plentiful than ever before. As the workforce ages, openings in these fields will be greater, thus luring children to work even longer hours after school. The temptation by businesses to exploit this eager source of labor will also expand as jobs go unfilled. Evidence of this pattern was documented by the Labor Department strike force that charged thousands of businesses with violating child labor laws. Violations included children working for long hours on school days and operating hazardous machinery such as meat slicers. More children worked in violation of the Fair Labor Standards Act in 1989 than in any year since the law was signed in 1938.

Critics claim that even part-time employment, especially at younger ages, places adolescents at risk for dropping out. Also, children at these ages are unable to delay gratification and quickly purchase the latest style of clothing, shoes, or entertainment. The pattern of children as employees is also unlikely to change in the future. In neighborhoods empty of playmates and parents, many children will opt for after-school employment. With its promise of money to spend and contact with adults, working after school is one of the better alternatives.[48]

Children and AIDS, Drugs, and Violence

Probably the most shocking behavioral trends regarding children are the increasing use of drugs and alcohol, the intensifying violence, and the spread of AIDS among children. As might be expected, drugs and alcohol are connected to the latchkey phenomenon. A 1989 study of 8,000 eighth graders in southern California cities found that self-care children who spent eleven or more hours a week on their own were twice as likely to use alcohol, 2.1 times as likely to smoke cigarettes, and 1.7 times as likely to use marijuana as were children with parents meeting them at home after school.[49]

Although the absence of parental involvement in children's activities is a factor in increased substance abuse, it is not the sole cause. Unfortunately, other variables such as peer pressure, television, alienation, and depression are part of the equation. Research studies on drug use by children vary. Some reports indicate a decrease in use, while others report that it has leveled off. The most catholic study reports that in a typical high school of 1,000 students, 437 will smoke pot, 103 will experiment with cocaine, 83 will try LSD, and 13 will take heroin.[50] Alcohol, probably the substance most abused by children, remains a chronic problem. For example, more than half of high school seniors report getting drunk at least once a month. Two out of five indicate that they get drunk at least once a week.[51] Many parents still see abuse of alcohol as a minor problem or are genuinely relieved that a child has chosen to abuse alcohol rather than drugs.

Schools have also been slow to respond to the deadly AIDS epidemic. Yet recent research reveals that teenagers are more likely to have multiple sex partners than persons in other age groups. Because of their promiscuity, they are at increased risk of contracting AIDS. In an attempt to protect children from this fatal disease, schools across the country are just beginning to instruct students in AIDS prevention. The availability of sex-related information, combined with school-based birth control clinics, is effective in reducing the number of teenage pregnancies. Mechanics Arts High School (St. Paul, MN) established such a program in 1973 and reduced its teenage birthrate by almost 50 percent.[52] The availability of such information in schools frequently encounters stiff resistance from various religious and socially conservative sectors of the community. If teenagers continue to become infected at the rate many epidemiologists think they will, parents will probably finally support any alternative rather than having their children face death from AIDS.

A second epidemic afflicting children concerns violence, which is spreading from the inner cities to the suburbs.[53] Attorney General Janet Reno considers youth violence to be "the greatest single crime problem in America today." The most recent statistics confirm her statement. Department of Justice figures show that between 1987 and 1991, the number of adolescents arrested for murder in the United States increased by an alarming 85 percent. In 1991, the last year for which data are available, ten-to-seventeen-year-olds accounted for 17 percent of all violent crime arrests. Adolescents are not just the criminals. Sadly, they are also the victims. In that same year, more than 2,200 murder victims were under age eighteen. More than six teenagers are killed every day. The Justice Department estimates that nearly one million adolescents between the ages of twelve and nineteen are raped, robbed, or assaulted each year, usually by their peers.

Schools are no longer a haven for students and teachers from this violence. Daily, 100,000 children carry guns to school. Approximately 6,250 teachers are threatened and 260 attacked every day. With the same regularity, 14,000 children are attacked on school property and 160,000 children miss school because of the fear of violence.[54] The most proximate causes of increased violence are the ubiquity of drugs and guns. But underlying these reasons are a significant number of young people who have been neglected, abused, impoverished, and stunted educationally. Violence is the way they have learned or been taught to solve their problems.

A recent five-year longitudinal study of 4,000 juveniles in Denver, Pittsburgh, and Rochester found that by the age of sixteen, more than 50 percent had committed some form of violent behavior. Yet among the 4,000 adolescents studied, 15 percent accounted for three quarters of all the violent offenses. Researchers who investigated the backgrounds of these teenagers confirmed not only patterns of neglect and poverty but also the frequent presence of learning disabilities. Many of the study's violent offenders could not read above the second- or third-grade level.[55]

IMPLICATIONS FOR SCHOOL LIBRARY MEDIA CENTERS

Multiculturalism

The response of school media centers to these potentially destabilizing societal trends will probably remain a function of their geographical location. States such as New Hampshire, Vermont, and Utah that are not projected to experience large influxes of immigrants will probably be under less pressure to design ethnocentric rather than multicultural curricula. On the other hand, states such as California, New York, Illinois, and Florida will be increasingly constrained to develop ethnocentric curricula that feature the ethnic group most likely to be dominant in that area in the future.

School library media centers in the former states should find it easier to collect materials on a diverse set of cultures, provide authors and speakers who reflect a variety of perspectives and values, and introduce children to a wider selection of non-European literature. Where ethnocentric battles are being waged in the name or guise of multiculturalism, problems will occur. With dwindling resources, SLMSs in these states will find it financially challenging just to increase collections for a rising ethnic group, let alone other cultures. These media centers will probably face more Hobsonian choices. The potential for censorship in these libraries will also be omnipresent. The understandable impulse by a school board to foster self-esteem in members of traditionally downtrodden ethnic groups may regress to suppression of differing viewpoints, values, and even historical fact and truth.

Media specialists in these areas may have to educate their communities about the value of pluralism within unity. They will also need to formulate well-reasoned arguments based upon the collapse of borders, growth of multinational companies, and an increasingly integrated global economy. This type of reasoning will be more conducive to showing various sectors of a school district that their children's economic success will require knowledge of many different cultures rather than in-depth study of just one. In states not expected to experience as much ethnic growth or change, SLMSs may have to serve as motivating influences to broaden the multicultural aspects of collections and curricula. Children in these states will encounter ethnic changes in America when they leave home for college and the workplace.

Probably the most valued role SLMSs can expect to play regarding multiculturalism will be to use their collections, programs, and services to help reduce ethnic tensions. Many SLMCs will be looked upon as a source of bibliotherapeutic reading regarding ethnic divisions, stereotypes, and prejudices. Faculty and students will increasingly need to rely upon media centers as information and distribution centers for multicultural print and nonprint materials, ideas for research assignments about different cultures, and course-integrated multicultural bibliographic instruction.

In the future all SLMCs will be involved not only in overtly acknowledging America's diversity but also in promoting it in more subtle ways through programs, author visits, speakers, and book/bulletin-board displays. More than any other department within the school they will be key determinators in how multiculturalism evolves as a concept for recognizing various ethnic groups' contributions to America.

Family Changes

The changes taking place in the American family will vary in their impact on SLMCs because of socioeconomic conditions. School media centers situated in economically depressed urban areas will have more students living in single-parent situations, and more of them will be poor. The lack of learning tools such as personal computers, encyclopedias, and other reference books in these families will further their dependence upon SLMCs. Materials that normally might not be circulated will have to be loaned to students just to permit them to complete their homework.

School media centers in more affluent areas will not be immune to family changes either. Children, regardless of their socioeconomic status, will still find it difficult to cope with parents who are divorcing or parents with new live-in partners. Library media specialists in every school will probably have to deal with increasing discipline problems as students in under-standable frustration, anger, and sorrow project some of their pain onto available parent figures. As families and their future relationships become more complex, SLMSs may find themselves serving as advisors or quasi counselors to students who see them in less of a teacher/evaluator role and are thus able to confide and share their problems with them.

Unless cooperative efforts between schools, government, and private agencies and parents begin to seriously address pre- and after-school care, SLMCs by default will become sanctuaries for increasing numbers of latchkey children. While the use of media centers for pre- and postschool care is extremely feasible and educationally beneficial to children, problems will arise if the same SLMSs are expected to shoulder these additional responsibilities without increasing support staff, salary, materials, and budget. School library media specialists whose facilities are open after school hours will find it difficult at closing time to usher children out who are still awaiting parents or postponing entry to empty houses. There will also be increasing pressure upon SLMCs that are not open for any extended time before or after school to provide places for these children. By the year 2000, school media specialists will have to develop policies and procedures for dealing with a self-care generation of children.

Children of the Twenty-first Century

How children choose to spend their time in the twenty-first century will be a form of serious competition for SLMCs. Currently it looks as if the battle with television for children's minds and even perhaps their mental health is going to continue. The lure of entry-level jobs and their ability to grant temporary monetary rewards will also be a source of contention between SLMSs and children. Shopping as an extracurricular activity will probably not abate either.

School library media specialists in less affluent communities will witness a self-fulfilling prophecy as their students, who are in greater need of supplementary education, succumb to watching mindless hours of televi-sion, working at low-level food service jobs, and spending all of their salary on consumer goods rather than an education. These SLMSs will be locked in a struggle to stimulate these children's minds with books, educational videos, challenging computer programs, and instructional units. Dedicated school media specialists in these schools will be characterized by unusual creativity with respect to the ways in which they endeavor to inform children of the dangers of too much television, working too many hours and neglecting their studies, and buying unnecessary consumer items.

At the higher end of the economic spectrum, SLMCs will face similar problems. Many of their students will live in homes with workaholic parents who abandon them to the same mind-dulling entertainment, jobs, and shopping options as their less affluent peers. These students will also require programs and services that show them alternatives to television and shopping.

Most school media centers will seek a form of peaceful coexistence with children's diversions, realizing perhaps that moving images versus print materials and colorful shopping malls are impossible to defeat. As a compromise, they will begin to try to educate students regarding the best television programs to watch, local area employment opportunities, and purchasing criteria for various consumer goods. They will try to explain the importance of saving certain amounts from job earnings and, more importantly, the need for further education to obtain better positions.

Children at Risk

So often the children who are at risk of pregnancy, drugs, AIDS, and violence only appear in a media center when they are desperate for information or personal assistance. They are usually academically behind their peers, and it's almost as if rooms lined with books serve as a frustrating reminder of their school failures. School media specialists in almost every type of setting will continue to find it difficult to reach them, even though their numbers are expected to increase. Library media specialists will have to be particularly inventive in educating them. Most materials will have to be of great interest to them yet at an understandable literacy level.

Students likely to become pregnant, take drugs, or be affected by sexually transmitted diseases are usually attuned to the everyday world. Their idea of the future is unusually myopic and short-term. They need strong reasons and promises of almost instant rewards to learn. School media specialists will need a great deal of patience and dedication in working with these students. They must develop collections that provide up-to-date information regarding these critical problems.

While the connection between drug use and guns is almost certain, violence is also linked to child neglect and abuse. The latter phenomena are not the sole province of inner-city schools. Disruptive behavior, disrespect toward adults, and peer violence is becoming endemic to all aspects of society and are not likely to disappear. Library media specialists will witness more of it in the decade ahead. They need to respond by purchasing a variety of materials that show children how to protect themselves, be street smart, and avoid physical confrontation.

Instructional Trends

Information technology will profoundly affect institutionalized education, both directly, via the use of computer-based instructional techniques in the classroom, and indirectly, as a consequence of the general availability of information resources and information manipulation tools. Demands on educational institutions to prepare students for roles in an increasingly information-oriented society will steadily grow.

National Resource Council

If the preceding prediction is correct, school library media specialists of the 1950s and their counterparts in the year 2000 will have only part of their title in common. Advances in computer hardware and software are rapidly altering the instructional role of the SLMS with regard not only to equipment but also to pedagogy. Library media specialists who previously provided audiovisual instruction to faculty and students will find that their role will expand to include distance education, spreadsheets, word processing programs, interactive video, on-line databases, and virtual reality. In most schools, SLMSs will become instructional technologists.

A second change involves the pedagogical role of the SLMS concerning electronic learning and the concomitant need for extending instruction to faculty and parents as well as students. Electronic learning will also demand that school media specialists change their parochial teaching methods to encompass information literacy and retrieval that permit users to access information in any library regardless of its format. Finally, as instruction is no longer based solely upon textbooks, SLMSs will become heavily involved in resource-based learning.

SCHOOL LIBRARY MEDIA SPECIALISTS AS INSTRUCTIONAL TECHNOLOGISTS

Currently the proportions of new library materials acquired each year are approximately 85 percent traditional print materials and about 15 percent nontraditional media. By the year 2000, these ratios are expected to change to 60 percent traditional print materials and 40 percent nontraditional materials. Users are expected to be "oriented more towards information and access than to the medium in which the information is contained."[1] As a result, students and faculty will require instruction from SLMSs about how to use a variety of electronically based systems to obtain the information they need.

In many schools, instruction in the use of computers and other electronic technologies was usually the province of computer coordinators who had backgrounds in computer programming or mathematics. With sophisticated operating software systems and the ubiquity of computers in every facet of school life, many teachers are no longer as intimidated by new technologies and consider learning them part of their ongoing educational development. Some are so well versed in the use of new programs or equipment that they serve as excellent sources of assistance and information with regard to new acquisitions and equipment setup. Because of their own professional commitments, however, the advisor/coordinator roles of these specialists usually cease at the point of instruction. If the equipment is housed and distributed through the SLMC, instruction in its use is considered the responsibility of the SLMS.[2] State library certification boards are fast acknowledging this change in the instructional technology role of the school media specialist. Many are requiring that education and library science departments include knowledge of computers and other advanced technologies as part of their instructional program.[3]

For librarians already in the field, changes and advances in new technologies are occurring so rapidly that it is extremely difficult to keep abreast of them. Technical literacy demands not only knowledge but also competency with computer hardware and software and other equipment such as optical scanners, modems, videodisc players, and CD-ROM players. All of this equipment operates through intricate networks, fiber-optic cable, advanced on-line information services, or by satellite.[4] While SLMSs are justifiably overwhelmed by these instructional developments, the need for their services in this area continues to increase. As a result, questions naturally arise concerning the degree of technological mastery that should be required.

Consultant Role of the Instructional Technologist

In keeping with the instructional consultant role defined in *Information Power: Guidelines for School Library Media Programs* (1988), school media specialists can be expected to serve as consultants to schools regarding the acquisition of various technologies. They will be called upon to determine whether particular technologies are instructionally effective. They will also be responsible for determining if technologies are affordable, beneficial, long-lasting, and appropriate for necessary educational tasks.

Depending upon the size and staffing structure of a school, SLMSs will serve either as the sole instructional technology consultant or as members of educational technology planning teams or committees. They will be expected to contribute their expertise and knowledge regarding the most recent technological advances. More importantly, they will need to have a vision of where their media centers fit within any school technological change. If computers are to be joined in a school-wide network, should the library on-line catalog be available on it? If a course is to be offered by distance education, what additional library materials will be required by students? Are there sufficient playback devices for audio and video?

Consulting instructional technologists will also assist various departments and individual teachers by disseminating information about subject-specific software packages or video series. This means that they will have to be extremely knowledgeable about the sociotechnical aspects of various technologies. Software that is too intricate or hardware that is too difficult to set up quickly will probably not be used in a classroom setting where teachers have many other responsibilities. School media specialists as instructional technology consultants will be responsible for structuring technology so that it humanizes the learning environment.

Teaching Role of Instructional Technologists

The range of teaching done by a SLMS in an instructional technology role is expected to vary depending upon the level of user abilities, the presence or absence of an educational technology technician, and the expectations of the individual school. In schools where many faculty and students have computers at home or use computers and other technologies at school, teaching may only entail the preparation of user instructions pertaining to entering, exiting, and manipulating the system, or short tutorials to be executed while using the new software. For faculty, it might also involve sponsoring after-school workshops to demonstrate the application of new software or equipment to specific departments or teacher subject areas. If users are not sophisticated in the use of a new technology, school librarians can expect to design instruction that is far more individualized and requires additional time with both the equipment and the instructor. Faculty and students wishing to create their own interactive video programs, for example, will need several more hours of instruction and practice than students who want to use an SAT preparation software program.

The actual teaching that is the responsibility of the SLMS can be impeded or accelerated by the presence of an educational technology technician. When school media specialists are responsible for much of the installation and troubleshooting with advanced technologies, user instructional time is necessarily diminished. The availability of adequate telephone software support and on-site hardware maintenance support affects the quantity and quality of instructional technology teaching. In schools with declining budgets, the lack of technological assistance, especially regarding hardware, is a definite hindrance to instruction in various technologies.

The expectation of various state certification boards that SLMSs teach the use of instructional technologies is beginning to filter down to school districts and individual schools. More of them in the future will expect SLMSs to educate faculty, students, and even parents in how to use the latest technology, improve access to information, manage their time, or advance learning. As schools become computerized, the role of the computer coordinator is likely to become obsolete. Once networks and other linked systems are in place, SLMSs will be expected to assume a leadership role in instructing all members of the educational community.[5]

SCHOOL LIBRARY MEDIA SPECIALISTS AS EDUCATORS IN AN ELECTRONIC AGE

In this electronic age, the American Library Association's Presidential Committee recommends that "we all must reconsider the ways we have organized information institutionally, structured information access, and defined information's role in our lives at home, in the community, and in the workplace."[6] Indeed, many SLMS concepts concerning bibliographic instruction are antediluvian in light of the availability of remote access to other libraries and the fast-approaching presence of supercatalogs. To empower students, faculty, and parents through increased access to information, media specialists are expected to dramatically change their instructional role and methods.[7]

Student Instruction in an Electronic Environment

The advances in telecommunications, computer hardware, and software have made the development of a supercatalog a reality in many SLMCs. The Anchorage School District (AK), for example, has installed a CD-ROM-based network topology in all of its media centers, thus permitting students and faculty to access such databases as LaserCAT from Western Library Network, Microsoft Works, and Express Publisher. In all, users have more than sixty different CD-ROM titles available to them.[8]

This explosion of choices has both negative and positive aspects instructionally. The fact that students and faculty can choose from a multitude of databases requires not only a tolerance for many alternatives but also the ability to choose correctly to fulfill their information needs. Studies of consumer tolerance for choosing products indicate that "more is less," not "more is more," and that consumers faced with an overwhelming supply of competing goods tend to suffer increased anxiety.[9]

There are similarities between the problems of choice consumers encounter in a shopping mall and the problems of increasing choice that are beginning to confront students in electronic library environments. As SLMCs acquire the latest CD-ROM databases or videodiscs, access patterns to information change. The evolutionary process is toward the development of a supercatalog. This catalog is characterized as (1) distant-independent, (2) maintaining multiple collections resident to one computer or available through a network, and (3) accessible via different bibliographic record points.[10] The concept of a supercatalog is an excellent one in terms of bibliographic control and user efficiency. From a single workstation, students can access their local on-line catalog, switch to other remote library collections, or tap the resources of perhaps fifty additional specialized CD-ROM on-line databases.

This supercatalog, while providing unlimited opportunities for improving the quality of student work, presents a number of instructional challenges. School library media specialists must not only assist students to choose correctly from among a plethora of electronic resources, but also teach students how to access the extraordinary amount of information available in this new on-line environment. To achieve these goals, SLMSs will have to make major changes in bibliographic education.

Recent research conducted at the college level confirms this conclusion. Initial studies of the presence of just an on-line public access catalog show that they frequently create a false sense of confidence regarding "the understanding of its content and the knowledge to use it effectively."[11] Frequent and even infrequent library users, whether they are successful in their searching or not, characterize it as an improvement over the card catalog.

Further studies reveal that students are unable to match even basic subject needs with the appropriate information retrieval database. When eighty-two undergraduates at the University of Illinois (Champaign-Urbana) were given a subject and asked to choose a database from among sixteen, only 22 percent of the searchers chose appropriate ones. Furthermore, almost 20 percent of the students selected databases not even remotely connected to their topic. Nine percent of InfoTrac users interviewed at the University of North Carolina were attempting to use this business-oriented database to locate information on Graham Greene, the Spanish Civil War, and Kierkegaard.[12]

In general, information-user studies indicate that users do not fully comprehend the large array of available search options and rarely apply the correct ones even when they are cognizant of them. Moreover, students are often frustrated when confronted with too many search options and have difficulty deciding when to employ them. For example, choosing to use a Boolean search might yield more information than choosing to use a keyword search. Studies also reveal that many students do not know how to search a subject by employing controlled vocabulary terms. Set building by use of Boolean operators is only performed by skilled searchers. Lastly, students frequently make errors in groups, thus building mistakes internally into the search so that no information matches result.[13]

There is also a direct correlation between library use and remaining in college. Approximately 43 percent of the students at California State Polytechnic College who did not use the library dropped out, compared to 26 percent of library users.[14] In an age when every student will have to acquire more education beyond high school, it will become imperative that SLMSs prepare them adequately for an electronic educational environment.

Questions generated by the preceding findings naturally occur. What, for example, should be taught? Should electronic instruction be integrated with course work or retained as a separate learning experience? What methods achieve the best results? Most library researchers no longer recommend a specific teaching method in the provision of electronic education. Future on-line instruction will be based upon concepts that are universally transferable to a variety of information storage and retrieval systems. Concepts will focus upon the most common student difficulties, such as defining their information needs, choosing appropriate databases and terminology, and designing search strategies that can capture the information in any system.[15] Specifically, end users will have to (1) comprehend the function and purpose of an on-line catalog, (2) define the scope of the catalog, (3) understand specific concepts of information retrieval systems, (4) create an on-line search by selecting, entering, and manipulating search commands, and (5) interpret search findings in relation to a specific topic.[16]

Use of Symbolic-Analytic Skills

The preceding skills will demand a high degree of symbolic-analytic thinking by students. Skills such as abstraction, system thinking, experimentation, and collaboration will constantly be required if students are to successfully cope with an increasingly complex electronic environment. Students will have to be taught to find patterns and meaning in the information they acquire from diverse databases. They will have to discern and assess the relationships between various pieces of information and a problem or subject. They will have to experiment in their search for information by selecting different databases, creating several search strategies, and varying their search options. Finally, students will have to engage in several forms of collaboration by interacting with librarians, teachers, and their peers in different course-integrated on-line instruction units.[17]

Faculty Instruction in an Electronic Environment

The use of electronic technologies in SLMCs has changed the mode of bibliographic instruction not only for students but also for faculty. As SLMCs become computerized, faculty will need as much instruction as their students.[18] While many students bring a helpful level of computer literacy to on-line education, a substantial number of faculty may not even be keyboard-literate. They will require more individualized instruction and perhaps even private sessions with media specialists. With the exception of faculty who are engaged in continuing education courses or working toward advanced degrees, most teachers will not feel motivated to learn how to search in an on-line environment by themselves. Unlike students, who frequently use the library for recreational reading or research, faculty members can continue to exist with textbooks and assigned reserve materials in their classrooms. As a result, faculty will require more sensitive instructional approaches. Whenever possible, instruction should be geared to their specific subject areas and, more importantly, to demonstrating how the SLMC can assist them to facilitate student learning. On-line aspects that save time, print materials, and create bibliographies will help faculty to appreciate the benefits of an electronic environment.

Parent Instruction in an Electronic Environment

Once SLMCs are no longer bound by time or space, their on-line catalogs will be searchable via modem or television monitor twenty-four hours a day, 365 days a year. Students will be able to search their school's supercatalog not only from various classrooms but also from home. Because these supercatalogs will access the collections of remote public and academic libraries, parents who wish to further their education or simply acquire information will require on-line instruction.[19] At Columbine High School (Jefferson County, CO), for example, a pilot program connecting the Library of Congress American Memory Project to the library's computer is already under way. A cable TV and computer modem connection permit users of the school library's computer to access LC's multimedia collection housed at the cable company's facilities on laser disc and CD-ROM.[20] Once similar connections are in homes via fiber-optic cable, interested parents will be able to search this database as well. They will be able to access homework hotlines and arrange for homework assignments to be delivered via electronic mail. Parents may even wish to partake of career and vocational information that will be available in various on-line databases and networks.[21]

Providing on-line instruction to parents is probably the most efficacious strategy that school media specialists could adopt. They will have the opportunity to demonstrate to parents their teaching skills and the need for SLMC instructional programs. Although parent on-line instruction will probably have to be offered in the evening and on weekends, because of parent employment, it will be the most valuable investment that SLMCs can make to ensure their future existence. Computer-literate parents will become valuable allies when SLMSs ask for additional funds or initiate new programs or services.

SCHOOL LIBRARY MEDIA SPECIALISTS AND INFORMATION LITERACY

As depressing literacy statistics are regularly issued by various testing services, foundations, and think tanks, it is no wonder that schools are responding with information literacy curricula. Because the word *literacy* has been associated with the word *reading* and reading has always been related to libraries, our profession has finally arrived at center stage in the battle to reform education. School library media specialists are being presented with an unprecedented opportunity to fulfill their instructional role within the school community.

In light of the technological, economic, and employment trends previously discussed, information literacy will be an essential survival skill in the twenty-first century.[22] To achieve a higher degree of information literacy than previously reported, our children will need to improve their abilities to (1) acquire appropriate information, (2) organize and apply it at relevant times, and (3) use information effectively with others. The ability to acquire appropriate information involves reading, study skills, reference, and information-search proficiencies and an understanding of on-line information concepts. Being able to organize and apply information on relevant occasions entails thinking skills that necessitate classifying, interpreting, analyzing, summarizing, synthesizing, and evaluating information. Using the information to adopt a well-reasoned strategy is also essential. Developing competency in employing information effectively with others requires fostering of cooperative skills in group settings. The abilities to persuade, debate, contribute to and negotiate with others by using facts, logical arguments, and information is considered critical to the furtherance of a democratic society.[23]

In view of the current economic situation, it is unlikely that funds will be forthcoming for schools to develop and adopt information studies curricula. Instead, schools will probably restructure the learning process so that information literacy skills are integrated throughout the various disciplines.[24] Faculty will be primarily responsible for accomplishing information literacy goals with their students as they integrate the necessary skills into their individual subject areas. The majority of teachers will try to incorporate information skills by use of a single textbook and perhaps through some assigned reserve reading material. Unless something extremely untoward occurs, they will expect to produce information-literate students by never using the school library.

Educational and technological changes, however, are combining to close the chapter of the single teacher, textbook, and classroom approach to learning. The demand for a literate population has not been initiated by self-serving SLMSs. Its impetus was derived from a battery of declining test scores and the realization that America's workforce is educationally underequipped. School media specialists and their professional associations have merely responded to these data by declaring their support for integrating information skills into the curriculum. Therefore, the mandate for change rests not only with SLMSs but also with educators. In that sense, it is twice blessed. Faculty will be under pressure from administrators as well as SLMSs to reform their teaching styles.[25]

With the proliferation of on-line databases, supercatalogs, and interactive media, students will be exposed to vast quantities of information in differing formats in their various courses. Many will initially be drawn to the supercatalog under the belief that it will enable them to shortcut an assignment. Whether they succeed or not, their impatience for the traditional style of teaching will increase. Consequently, SLMSs will be in a prime instructional position to assist faculty and students with a new approach.

RESOURCE-BASED LEARNING

The most disturbing indictment of the text/lecture/reserve materials syndrome is provided by a retention study that employed this instructional method. Forgetting course content usually occurs at the 50 percent level within a few months. Yet when students in a study were informed that they were to be evaluated immediately following the lecture, were allowed to use their notes, and were given a prepared lecture summary, they retained less than 42 percent of the lecture content. A follow-up test a week later, without the use of notes, yielded a dismal 17 percent retention rate.[26] The implications of this study suggest that it is time to amend our reliance on this pedagogical method as the sole vehicle for conveying information to students. The complexity of the on-line environment, requiring symbolic-analytic skills, will not accommodate students who are unable to reason this way and cannot apply these concepts in an electronic environment. Future educational methodologies must foster these skills.

One of the most promising approaches to improve student symbolic-analytic abilities is called resource-based learning. Essentially it translates to structuring learning activities to enable students to assume primary responsibility for the information transfer process. Instead of faculty furnishing nearly all of the course content through lectures, instructors provide students with opportunities and activities to find, retrieve, use, and evaluate information.[27] Since classrooms cannot serve as the repositories of all the information students will need to successfully complete their assignments, a natural instructional partnership between faculty and SLMSs is likely to develop. In some areas of the country, the educational benefits to be gained from this association are already being extolled. At Littleton High School (Littleton, CO), a faculty project entitled Direction 2000 restructured their entire curriculum to reflect a resource-based one. Hundreds of students used the media center daily to access such technologies as the Colorado Alliance of Research Libraries (CARL) on-line system, University Microfilm's ProQuest (CD-ROM index to 450 abstracted periodicals), and Information Access' Newsbank (CD-ROM-based newspaper index).[28] Assignments were also designed that crossed disciplines. One curriculum publication, entitled, "A Coordinated Approach to Writing and Library Usage," involved the instructional expertise of not only SLMSs but also members of the English and Social Studies departments. The document contains suggestions for a variety of library- and curriculum-oriented writing assignments.

The School Library Media Specialist's Instructional Role

The advent of resource-based learning on a significant scale has the potential to finally enable SLMSs to become an "integral, essential part of the instructional program [and] an integral part of the system of schooling."[29] Perhaps school media specialists will finally fulfill their role advocated in *Information Power: Guidelines for School Media Programs* (1988) as instructional designers. Certainly the opportunities with resource-based learning are self-evident. Most faculty, already burdened with large classes, piles of paperwork, and discipline problems, will find it difficult to find the time to design resource-based learning activities and lessons without the assistance of an SLMS. They will need media specialists to confirm that sufficient materials exist and to develop lessons based upon their intimate knowledge of library resources.

Many teachers, however, may not readily recognize the instructional expertise that can be provided by their SLMS. In 1992, a disappointing study conducted with 458 elementary classroom teachers revealed that a statistically significant number of faculty who sought assistance with hypothetical instructional problems did not consult their school media specialists.[30] They instead chose to seek assistance from peers who had reputations as good teachers. Library media specialists were only consulted in academically successful elementary schools where intellectual sharing and collegial work arrangements were thought to be more prevalent. A strategy suggested in the study would consist of targeting teachers with strong instructional reputations for cooperative resource units. By clearly demonstrating to them the positive learning aspects of a library-based learning resource unit, SLMSs would be able to count upon their support for future units and cooperation with other teachers.

IMPLICATIONS FOR SCHOOL LIBRARY MEDIA CENTERS

Never before have economic, educational, and technological events conspired to provide SLMSs with both unparalleled, successful instructional opportunities and the potential for possible extinction. The electronic age that previously bypassed SLMCs is now a reality. As more SLMCs obtain the funding to access remote databases, purchase videodisc equipment, or install on-line catalogs, the instructional role of SLMSs will be permanently changed.

Instructional Technology

Whether school media specialists like it or not, they will probably find themselves in charge of acquiring, installing, and maintaining not only library-based software and hardware but also equipment that circulates or connects the media center to other classrooms. Instructing faculty and students to use these technologies will probably be an administrative priority, as it was for simpler audiovisual materials. School media specialists who have an aversion to new electronic technologies will have to rely upon technically expert assistants or face serious questions from their immediate supervisors. Depending upon the electronic sophistication level of individual faculty members and students, instructional materials may consist of short handouts, brief tutorials, or longer, private sessions. The aversion to advanced technologies that may affect SLMSs will definitely afflict some faculty members and students. Age will not be a determining function of on-line use. In the future, SLMSs may be characterized by greater patience and understanding of various client fears, as they provide technology instruction.

Rapid change will continue to be the watchword of the electronic age as various pieces of software and hardware become obsolete, modified, or enhanced. In their new capacity as instructional technology consultants, SLMSs will probably maintain current awareness services pertaining to new educational products and equipment. It will be their responsibility to arrange for previews of potential electronic acquisitions.

Instruction in an Electronic Age

One of the most important factors affecting the instructional role of SLMSs is the supercatalog. The presence of multiple databases, access to other libraries, and increased searching capabilities will render school-centered bibliographic instruction obsolete. School library media specialists whose library skills curriculum consisted of location skills and learning circulation procedures will find their instructional materials and methods archaic. In their place, students will need an overall information-seeking framework that stimulates symbolic-analytic skills. By nature instruction will become more active, because students will need to manipulate information in the computer to understand the result of various search strategies and commands.

Inventive school media specialists will create simulations designed to teach students the advantages of Boolean logic, keyword searching, and controlled vocabularies. Unlike most former library skills classes, students will probably respond favorably to on-line instruction. They will be impressed with the increased information-processing speed and the variety of search options.

Instructional services for faculty will become paramount. If faculty are intimidated by the media center's electronic environment, they will be unlikely to bring their classes for instruction lest they appear uninformed. Library media specialists will need all of their interpersonal skills to persuade reluctant faculty members to visit the media center for on-line instruction. In the end, SLMSs may have to accept an instructional rate of less than 100 percent.

Parent involvement with the SLMC may hold the real key to its future technological development. Most parents are fully aware that their children's future employment will, in some manner, require computer use. If not, seeing the capabilities in an on-line environment will certainly convince them. School media specialists will find it politically advantageous to instruct parents. It may be the most inexpensive insurance they will have in difficult economic times.

Information Literacy and Resource-based Learning

The influences of information literacy and resource-based learning could not have occurred at a more propitious time for SLMSs. If ever the expression *carpe diem* was applicable, it is now. Library media specialists are perfectly poised to assume the role of instructional designer as schools throughout the country begin to embrace the concepts underlying information literacy and resource-based learning.

The opportunities for an equal instructional partnership between SLMSs and teachers have never been truly advocated by educational associations until now. Yet research shows that change may not occur that quickly. School media specialists are not necessarily the first choice of faculty members for the fulfillment of their information needs. These results suggest that SLMSs will be in danger of losing these instructional opportunities if they passively sit and wait for them to happen. School media specialists will instead be wise if they employ a more evangelistic approach to resource-based learning and information literacy. It may not be prudent to wait for cooperating faculty to appear in the media center with their own ideas for lessons and activities. Rather, SLMSs may wish to initiate contact themselves and, when necessary, design most of the lessons, leaving final emendations to the cooperating faculty member.

Organizational and Managerial Trends

7

The future will belong to those who take bold steps necessary to redesign our institutions and methods of operating.

W. David Penniman

In the years to come, school library media centers will be in a transitory phase, precipitated to a large extent by advances in technology, stagnation of the economy, and restructuring of the family. These forces will also affect their organizational and managerial functions. School media centers will evolve from time-and edifice-bound buildings into boundaryless, modem-accessible electronic environments. In better economic times, this transformation would have entailed purchasing new hardware, software, and books. In light of rising costs and relatively stable or declining budgets, decisions concerning access versus ownership and purchasing either the print or electronic version of an item will be required. As school library media specialists struggle with these challenges and difficult decisions, many will be opening their doors earlier and closing them later because their parent institutions will have decided to serve the self-care generation.

SOCIETAL FORCES

Despite increasing problems with substance abuse, adolescent pregnancy, peer violence, and the growing number of latchkey children, most schools still close their doors at three o'clock. While the family has been transformed, the majority of schools have failed to meet their desperate need for child care and community support. Sociologists refer to this phenomenon as a cultural lag.[1]

The failure of schools to adapt, however, appears to be changing. In publications such as *Education for the New Century* (1993), principals are calling for schools to end their isolation and develop cooperative and coordinated relationships with other societal agencies.[2] In Denver, for example, a different kind of recreational system designed expressly to match new school hours is in effect. All of the schools, parks, and recreation departments have agreed to cooperate in providing child care, both before and after school—year round—from 6:30 in the morning until six-thirty in the evening. Although some children remain as long as twelve hours, supervised care is still considered better than a latchkey life.

This view is partially confirmed by another school program that is strictly volitional on the part of children. When a grade school in Liberty City (Miami, FL) opened the school on Saturday for one hour of uninter-rupted reading, one hour of writing, and one hour of math, they planned for fifty children, but two hundred arrived. The children are still attending, are being taught by teachers paid hourly, and are supplied with snacks financed by the PTA. Although the ulterior motive with respect to many of these after-school programs is clearly safety, most SLMSs would prefer to see their media centers used on Saturdays by children for recreational reading than remain closed to those in need.[3]

The use of the SLMC for various forms of child care is also expected to become more prevalent as a result of the recently passed 1990 budget reconciliation bill. The government has appropriated more than $22.5 billion to states covering the next five years for provision of child care services, and tax credits for parents of preschoolers. Most importantly, the monies permit state school agencies to develop and support preschool programs within the public schools. Already twenty-eight of fifty states are funding prekindergarten programs.

CHILD CARE ORGANIZATIONAL CONSIDERATIONS

School media specialists will face a number of organizational problems when their media centers are used during pre- and post-school hours. Even if SLMSs are absent from their libraries during these times, they will need to ensure that the environment is safe for intended activities. Al-though preschoolers will probably have scheduled times to visit the SLMC, the room itself will have to be safely accessible by children three to four feet tall. Library media specialists will have to childproof either rooms or areas of the media center perhaps more rigorously than they do for elementary schoolers.[4] Similar procedures will have to be followed in SLMCs where older children will be supervised. If the media center is to be used as a homework assistance center, furniture, textbooks, and core reference books will have to be organized and arranged to suit their information needs.

As collection managers, SLMSs will probably seek extra funding to purchase preschool books, videos, and educational toys. For older students media specialists will probably acquire recreational paperbacks, videos, and tutorial and work processing software. When preschoolers are cared for during the school day, SLMSs will usually incorporate these children into their regular class schedules. The problems will occur when the media center is scheduled to open at 6:30 in the morning and close at 6:30 in the evening. Questions naturally arise concerning who will be responsible for the children in the SLMC during these hours. If it is not the SLMS, will it be someone responsible to the school media specialists if vandalism or loss of equipment occurs? Will the SLMC's entire collection be totally available to pre- and after-school children or only a designated part such as periodicals and specially purchased paperbacks? If the after-school supervisor is late or absent, should the children be permitted to enter or remain in the SLMC unattended? These potential problems will require substantial administrative tact and skill on the part of SLMSs to achieve successful programs.

PARENT INVOLVEMENT

By the year 2000, many SLMSs, regardless of the socioeconomic status of their schools, will have to grapple with these organizational and managerial problems. In addition to hosting children during nonschool hours, their media centers will also be used for parent activities. Programs are already under way in many schools that attempt to decrease parent isolation and foster better relations with the schools. Administrators are finally accommodating parents by offering programs during the majority of parent nonworking times. For example, at East High School in rural Excelsior Springs (MO), the school sponsors regular breakfast seminars designed to acquaint parents with new programs, curriculum information, faculty, and community events. Breakfast is followed by a tour of classrooms, computer labs, and other areas.[5]

Research confirms that visits by parents to schools are likely to improve student grades. Psychiatrist James Comer, director of the Yale Child Study Center, has developed parent involvement programs in more than fifty schools nationwide. Comer's schools not only encourage parent involvement, by urging frequent visits, they also employ parents as teacher aides, carpenters, and painters. Results of parent involvement have been extremely positive. In one New Haven school, the dropout rate declined from

42 to 15.5 percent and the percentage of children choosing some form of post–high school education rose from 45 to 73 percent.

The underlying concept of these programs is to substitute the school for the loss of neighborhoods, extended families, and churches that formerly assumed some responsibility when schools closed at three o'clock. Schools are now attempting to become that community by providing children and their parents with positive adult interaction and a sense of belonging. At Hoover High in San Diego (CA), for example, administrators are developing a hub school with weekend sports and classes for children and adults in Spanish, French, computers, and martial arts.

As schools become part of the child care network, their media centers will be seen as attractive, learning-conducive environments enabling children to engage in reading, study, and viewing educational nonprint materials such as videos and computer games. Organizing the SLMC for this increased use will involve parents as aides, storytellers, booktalkers, or readers. Entrepreneurial SLMSs, faced with extended media center use but no additional funds to purchase books and other items, will probably ask parents to assist them with fund-raising.[6]

MANAGING TECHNOLOGIES

Technological advances will affect not only the organization of SLMCs but also how they are managed. Because most SLMCs are operated by only one SLMS with little or no clerical assistance, administrative functions have usually been constrained by time. School library media specialists are constantly juggling their administrative duties alongside those of bibliographic instruction and curriculum development. Despite these effective counterbalancing techniques, a recent study found that while most SLMSs would like to devote 25 percent of their time to media center management, they actually spend 32 percent of their time doing administrative work.[7] Unfortunately, in sole practitioner SLMCs this administrative portion of time will probably not decline. While administrative tasks will no longer be as bibliographic-centered, managing an electronic database and coordinating resource sharing is expected to occupy a similar amount of time.

By the year 2000, most SLMSs will have moved beyond their established role as custodians of printed and audiovisual materials and will be engaged in integrating new methods of information storage, retrieval, and transmission into existing collections and services. Unlike many businesses that can replace their older information formats with computers, SLMCs must continue their traditional mission as keepers of books while simultaneously adapting their media centers to electronic environments. It is no wonder that there will be some administrative ambivalence as SLMSs try to cope with many of their previous responsibilities and shoulder new and different ones caused by such technologies as distance learning, on-line catalogs, interactive media, and resource sharing.[8]

REFERENCE AND INFORMATION SERVICES MANAGEMENT

Managing and organizing reference and information services in electronic environments is going to require additional knowledge, planning, and skills on the part of SLMSs. While some may receive assistance from computer coordinators, others will have to learn either on-the-job or from continuing education courses to administrate in an on-line setting. In the case of sole practitioners with no technologists to help them, SLMSs will probably construct a database of experts at companies and in the community who can assist them when they have to make important purchasing decisions or wish to develop their media centers in a certain direction.[9]

Most technologies are tending to merge and the element of connectivity is increasingly present. School library media specialists will realize that administrative tasks tend to escalate when elements of connectivity are added to either established information systems or stand-alone equipment. Most technologists, for example, agree that networking equipment and databases, be they CD-ROM or computerized OPACs (on-line public access catalogs), add a substantial organizational and managerial dimension to administering the technology. This trend is best illustrated by a creative distance learning project that originated at Medford High School (MA). Using local electronic bulletin boards and the nationwide network of FidoNets to communicate between schools, students at twelve separate schools participated in a simulated constitutional convention. Prior to their telecommunicated convention, students used various databases, such as the full-text Massachusetts State House Reporter, ERIC, and the Bureau of Labor Statistics databank, to locate information and to synthesize and formulate their arguments as "state representatives" to the convention.[10]

When one identifies the administrative tasks involved in setting up such a project, they can appear quite daunting from several perspectives. First, the technological aspects entail (1) arranging for the installation of a telecommunications network that features electronic mail, (2) connecting other school libraries and classrooms, (3) providing dial-up access to various on-line databases, and (4) arranging for the use of in-house CD-ROM databases. Second, the project requires scheduling and coordinating time for participants at all schools not only to communicate with each other but also to receive instruction in the use of various reference databases. Third, and most importantly, it necessitates securing the agreement of SLMSs, faculty members, and administrators at various schools to participate.

As organizers and managers of reference and information services, SLMSs will also be responsible for providing continuous access to information on a round-the-clock basis. For example, students in Washington and Pennsylvania already have access to school, public, and academic library catalogs via home terminals and can search or request interlibrary loans at any hour.[11] As administrators of this technology, SLMSs regularly disseminate modem access protocol information to students and faculty with home terminals, arrange for appropriate off hours to schedule regular maintenance, and serve as troubleshooters when users experience problems accessing the network.

School library media specialists will also have to develop new acquisitions criteria and decision-making systems that permit them to make cost-effective choices of new information databases or software packages. Rural SLMCs, for example, may wish to search for and acquire full-text databases, so that most of the information retrieved by students is readily available.

MANAGEMENT OF THE COLLECTION

Organizing and managing the collection will be a demanding part of SLMSs' professional activities in the future. The impact of new technologies such as hypermedia, interactive video, and supercatalogs is going to redefine the nature and composition of a collection and alter its direction. In the past, SLMSs defined their collections as those materials that were physically accessible within one or several buildings. With access to remote databases or the presence of substantial in-house commercial reference databases and school-created hypermedia databases, the concept of a collection will change almost daily. It will also challenge the concept of ownership. If, for example, a library subscribes to a serials full-text database such as TOM (Information Access, Inc.) and users can obtain the full text of a periodical article, does the library own the item or merely have yearly access to it by subscription? Now, consider the problem even further removed. If a librarian can access a particular book from a network or remote on-line library, can this item be considered part of the media center's collection? This dilemma, termed access versus ownership, will be a major administrative problem for collection managers in the years ahead. They will constantly be trying to strike a balance between locally owned materials and information accessible only through electronic sources.

A critical factor SLMSs will have to consider when managing their collections will involve the weighing of access against availability. Geographical location, the information needs of the SLMC's population, and user ability to delay information gratification will all be relevant when deciding whether to own or acquire access. In geographically isolated schools or ones where items are needed within twenty-four hours, media specialists may decide to purchase items. In schools near other libraries and under budget constraints, the decision may be to purchase access through networks or on-line services.

A second fast-developing trend concerns the changing composition of the collection. Studies already indicate that users will be less concerned with informational format than they will be about access. Yet what constitutes a collection and how to package and coordinate it will be an increasing source of uncertainty for collection managers. Will SLMSs include bibliographic or cataloged descriptions of faculty or student-designed multimedia databases in their on-line or supercatalogs? Will commercial prepackaged software information be at least identifiable through an on-line catalog? For example, should students in succeeding English classes have access to a hypermedia project called "Grapevine" created by a student and media specialist?[12] Based upon Steinbeck's *Grapes of Wrath* and the 1930s, Grapevine consists of a multimedia adventure of linked stories, images, and sound associated with the book. Should next year's students decide to add or eliminate information, the very nature of the cataloged item will change. How will SLMSs indicate and reflect content changes in various electronic materials? How will they ensure that these materials are accessible to everyone, not just those students who are in a specific English class? School library media specialists as organizers and managers of the collection will have to account for these changes in information contents and will have to develop new cataloging procedures for ensuring continuing access to new types of materials.

The third trend affecting collection management relates to the general direction or philosophy behind collection management. The availability of new techniques such as distance learning permits schools to transmit and receive information globally. In Massachusetts, for example, schools, higher education, and business collaborated to produce Kids Interactive Telecommunications Project by Satellite (KITES). The project permitted students in several Massachusetts schools to discuss a variety of international issues with West German students. As more schools engage in this form of instruction, SLMSs as collection managers are going to acquire a variety of materials in different formats that reflect a transnational approach to problems and decision making. More importantly, they will be administratively responsible for introducing their students and teachers to the various technologies that make such programs possible.[13]

COLLECTION AVAILABILITY AND DELIVERY

In addition to changes in the nature, composition, and direction of collections, issues concerning material availability and document delivery will arise. For years, academic and large public libraries have struggled with these performance measures that affect service. Once SLMCs become part of the electronic age, they will also be actively participating in discussing similar matters. The idea of an item being readily available has usually been linked to user satisfaction. For SLMCs, the term *availability* usually meant that students used the card catalog, wrote down the correct call number, and retrieved the item from the shelf. If the item was not there, the student informed the SLMS, who either placed a reserve on it, if it was circulating, or, if not, initiated a search. The use of supercatalogs, on-line services and dial-up access from outside the media center will render the concept of availability subject to many interpretations. Is a book considered available if it is identified in a remote library's collection? How available is that item to a student who needs it and does not have a driver's license or access to a car? If a library is using a courier system with seventy-two-hour delivery capability, is the book still considered available to a student who needs it by the following day?

Although fax machines are fast solving availability and document problems with regard to serials, books will remain a problem. As more SLMCs begin to access remote databases or even ones that supply lists of citations, SLMSs will need to organize efficient systems to satisfy requests for these materials. Once students comprehend the world of information that is quasi-available to them, they will make their information needs known much more forcefully than they have done in the past.[14]

ECONOMIC FORCES

Unfortunately, in the majority of SLMCs many of the changes driven by society and technology may have to be achieved at the expense of other media programs and services. The combination of rising materials costs and declining or stationary budgets will force SLMSs to make hard choices to enable their students and faculty to enter the electronic age. School media specialists will have to be extremely able financial managers, always on the watch for applicable grants, in-kind equipment donations, and parent contributions in addition to their normal budgetary allocations. This same combination of factors will persuade many SLMSs to share resources and to network. While many SLMCs are already engaged in various cooperative ventures, this number will grow appreciably in the next few years. As funds diminish and educational reform continues, there will also be increased attention to accountability and productivity. Parents and administrators, to justify increased expenditures, are going to demand that SLMCs quantitatively evaluate their investment by linking it to increased student achievement, satisfaction, or some other measures. School library media specialists will have to contemplate using some type of output or performance measures to account for their services instead of just listing circulation and acquisition statistics in their annual reports.[15]

BUDGET MANAGEMENT

In a recent study of SLMCs, Millbrook Press, Inc., recommended that SLMSs become more actively involved in the development of their budgets. The survey also noted feelings of powerlessness by SLMSs when it came to financial allocations. Most seemed to accept what was allocated to them, because governments and in turn local administrators were in charge of this area, not media specialists. Many, when questioned concerning the sources of their allocations, were unsure or ignorant.[16] These shocking data reveal an unacceptable level of passivity and acquiescence on the part of many SLMSs regarding the very lifeblood of their libraries.

Budgeting is really all about priorities and there should be no doubt as to which department should be ranked first. A SLMC represents the core of an educational institution from which students, faculty, administrators, and parents use materials and equipment that facilitates learning. Students, especially, acquire the skills to be lifelong learners in a media center. An adequate budget will determine not only student access to reading materials and information but also access to the technologies that they will be expected to comprehend and manipulate in the workforce.

As monies become more difficult to obtain, it will be essential that SLMSs maintain expenditure records that particularly account for curriculum development and instruction. These records can also be used to establish productivity and be tied to requests for additional monies. Relating expenditures to the educational needs of the school and community actually helps to build a budget for the future. It tends to focus community and administrative support on student performance rather than the cost of technologies or instructional supplies. School library media specialists who practice this type of fund management already know that no budget is really set in stone. Allocations are really reflections of the educational philosophy of an institution. It is based on priorities, which many SLMSs need to redirect, if they are going to provide the programs, services, and equipment that their students need.[17]

RESOURCE SHARING AND NETWORKING

Libraries have engaged in formal cooperative ventures or contractual agreements with other institutions to expand the availability of materials and services since World War II. For years, however, the majority of resource-sharing activities took place between various academic and public libraries.[18] School library media centers have been notoriously slow to join networks for a variety of psychological, political, legal, fiscal, and administrative reasons. Only within the last six years have SLMCs begun participating significantly in such networks. In 1987, a national survey reported

257 networks and more than 18,000 participating SLMCs, and another survey conducted in 1988 provided further evidence of SLMC networking in Alaska, Illinois, Minnesota, New York, Pennsylvania, and Wisconsin.[19]

The most recent research performed in this area confirmed that the majority of building level SLMSs in networks such as Access Pennsylvania, AMIGOS, OCLC, and WLN (Western Library Network) were enjoying substantial economic benefits from resource sharing and network participation. When asked to list some of the benefits of networking, the most frequently cited one was "greater access to resources."[20] One SLMS even noted that "the collections of 586 libraries are now a keyboard away." From an economic standpoint, networking also proved to be extremely cost-beneficial. Networking furnished opportunities for joint purchase of audiovisual materials and supplies, serials, and equipment. A significant number of SLMCs had access through networks to material-previewing centers. Schools were also involved in resource sharing. Almost all engaged in interlibrary loan. Delivery systems ran the gamut, with the majority of SLMCs using school system couriers, followed by the post office, multitype network couriers, United Parcel, telefacsimile, satellite, cable, and one SLMS's personal automobile.

In general, faculty and student responses to networking were extremely positive. Some schools began revising their curricula as they realized the resources available through the network. Teacher expectations of media center services increased as they comprehended what expanded access could supply in the way of materials. Library media specialists reported "fantastic use" and general appreciation for the additional resources by students. One SLMS wisely observed that networking had removed the media center walls and enabled the provision of better services to the college bound. Finally, a rural SLMS found that networking had removed isolation and increased resources.[21]

From an economic standpoint, this study demonstrates the savings to be gained when SLMCs engage in resource sharing and networking. Networking not only provides access to more resources, without media centers having to purchase them, but also eliminates the need for acquiring peripheral materials. School library media centers can also save money by sharing the costs of cataloging and processing services among network members.[22]

COORDINATED COLLECTION MANAGEMENT

Once SLMCs become members of networks, they will comprehend the wisdom of agreeing to develop and maintain their collections to their mutual benefit. Each SLMC will purposefully acquire materials in designated subject areas with the understanding that other media centers will balance those purchases by developing their respective collections in other needed areas. The result will be a composite collection that has been achieved at considerable savings for all of the networked SLMCs.

Usually coordinated collection management begins in networks after an on-line union catalog has been created. The electronic environment tends to speed up searching and verification procedures that are necessary to determine if a designated subject-collecting library has a particular title on order or already cataloged in the system. At this point in time, there is only scant reporting of SLMCs participating in systematic cooperative collection management. The most recent survey, conducted in 1989, indicated that only seven of forty-five responding districts had coordinated collection management programs. An ongoing study of forty-six school systems in New York revealed that many SLMSs found coordinated collection management "extremely time consuming and difficult."[23] In response to these complaints, system directors emphasized coordinating only in new curriculum areas and called for SLMCs to voluntarily collect in various ethnic group fields and health sciences.[24]

It is obvious from these surveys that coordinated collection development with regard to SLMCs will happen more slowly than it has with academic and public libraries. Perhaps SLMCs equipped with on-line catalogs are not experiencing the economic pressure that has forced their academic and public library counterparts to engage in this cost-savings collection management approach. As SLMCs are forced to spend more of their budget on various technologies and become fully automated members of networks, coordinated collection management will probably become a standard resource-sharing process.

SCHOOL LIBRARY PERFORMANCE MEASURES

It is hard to estimate if performance measures for SLMCs will become the norm in the next century or will only be proposed in the library literature. Yet there are a number of trends in SLMCs that encourage the development of performance measurement for specific programs and services. With the increasing need to expand media center services, there is little doubt that objective data will be required in many schools to justify such expenditures. There is also increased school-based pressure for standards. Resource-based and site-based management are currently the administrative terms for the 1990s.

Counterbalancing the trend toward performance measures are the amount of time and training these techniques would require. In addition, many services such as instructional design and course-integrated on-line instruction are difficult to measure. Most SLMSs would be distressed if information retrieval skills were evaluated by another standardized test which really only measured the acquisition of facts rather than symbolic-analytic skills. Also present is a generalized fear of something different and a general trend toward maintaining the status quo.

In the future, advances in both technology and evaluative software will reduce the time involved in data collection and analysis.[25] The computer will gather and manipulate all of the acquisitions and circulation statistics, thus freeing SLMSs to evaluate subjective areas of the program. It is these areas of the program, however, that will be so difficult to assess. In light of recent research studies that have demonstrated ineffective use of on-line searching by students, it will be necessary to design pre- and postevaluative instruments that measure student on-line learning. Pre- and posttests should evaluate student abilities to (1) select appropriate information resources, (2) design appropriate search strategies to obtain the information, (3) demonstrate an understanding of the concepts underlying information retrieval systems, (4) perform satisfactory on-line searches by selecting and manipulating search commands, and (5) interpret search results in relation to the specified information need. As more SLMCs purchase these technologies, parents and administrators will require these kinds of objective measures to justify their investment. School library media specialists will be concentrating their evaluation efforts on objectively measuring student performance with regard to information literacy and symbolic-analytic skills. Demonstrating improved student performance in the acquisition of information and symbolic-analytic skills will help propel SLMCs into the forefront of the educational process.

SCHOOL LIBRARY MEDIA CENTER IMPLICATIONS

Societal Influences

Organizing and managing SLMCs to facilitate instruction by faculty and learning by students is going to tax the administrative creativity of every SLMS in the years ahead. Working parents will want them to assume more responsibility for care of their children before and after work. While many SLMSs will welcome the opportunity to see children safely ensconced in their media centers during nonschool hours, others may perceive it as an unnecessary intrusion. Those who envision SLMCs as places for quiet study, research, and reading may find it difficult to witness activities that result in additional noise, perhaps the provision of snacks, or even playing of games.

Since most faculty members are usually associated with their subject specialties and assigned classrooms, SLMSs will be the most likely people to be asked if they will serve as child care supervisors. If they choose not to, they will probably be asked to organize their facilities so that others can use them safely and effectively. For some media specialists this additional administrative task will not be a problem, but others will see it as an additional administrative chore.

Technological Factors

New technologies are going to permanently alter the organizational and managerial roles of SLMSs. In many cases they are going to become by default database managers, network supervisors, and general electronic-age troubleshooters. For most, the benefits of distance learning, on-line systems, and reference databases for faculty and students will far outweigh the increased administrative work engendered by technologies. School library media specialists will see use of the SLMC expanding, students being excited by learning, and faculty requests for curriculum assistance increasing. On the other hand, librarians who have not kept current with regard to new technologies will be under increasing administrative pressure to initiate some form of computerization even if it means acquiring a computer, modem, and a fax machine. If they are sole practitioners, there will be no "separate peace" for them. Technology is advancing so rapidly that it is not going to bypass their SLMCs. Their only recourse will be to seek assistance from in-house computer coordinators or hire additional staff to assume these new managerial tasks.

As managers of technologies, SLMSs can expect to feel anxious about the rapidity of change. Equipment in this field becomes obsolete shortly after purchase. Just maintaining technology awareness programs for faculty and administrators will be stressful. Providing purchasing guidance will be a serious administrative responsibility, since so much technology is not only expensive but also rarely universally compatible.

Collection management will also entail new responsibilities and administrative choices. For all SLMCs, the expanded access for students and faculty will easily balance the increased administrative work involved. The opportunity to have millions of volumes searchable and available at the touch of a computer will be irresistible to most SLMSs. Think of the joy of almost always being able to fulfill teacher and student requests for information. Imagine being able to design course-related instruction units on almost any topic because suddenly a wealth of materials is available at your fingertips.

While the advantages of increased access clearly outdistance the disadvantages, SLMSs will be forced to make decisions and redefine their concept of collections. The issue of access versus ownership will be disconcerting. At times it will be hard to estimate the use of particular titles. Should they be purchased or not? When acquiring CD-ROM reference databases, should the hard copy versions be canceled?

With any collection the idea of availability is customarily assumed by the user. School library media specialists, in organizing expanded access for students and faculty via remote databases or on-line services, will have to keep this patron confidence uppermost. Deciding to increase access with new technologies will achieve little if users cannot have prompt physical access to the item they want. Nothing will be more tantalizing or frustrating to users than to print a citation list of materials accessible only through laborious interlibrary-loan procedures.

Economic Factors

Extending the opening and closing times of SLMCs and acquiring new technologies will strain the resources of most media centers' budgets. In light of the present economic situation, most public SLMCs will find it difficult to obtain additional funds to make these necessary social and technological improvements. As more SLMSs are forced to choose between their collections and technologies, resource sharing and networking will no longer be options. They will become economic necessities. As easier collection management procedures are described in school library literature and disseminated broadly, coordinated collection management will be a requirement of network membership and participation.

In addition to combining and coordinating resources, many SLMSs will have to become innovative fund managers. It will be unacceptable for many to acquiesce to shrinking allocations in the face of rising material costs and increasing electronic needs. Media specialists of this type will become more assertive concerning their basic budget allocations and in seeking additional local, national, and federal funding sources. School media specialists who are threatened by new technologies and sharing their collections, on the other hand, may have the perfect justification for maintaining their status quo SLMCs. They will simply announce a lack of funds to achieve these changes.

Although most school communities will readily comprehend how expanded access, resource sharing, and collection management has improved SLMC programs and services, most will require supporting data and test results to warrant their investment. In response, SLMCs will develop evaluative performance measures to demonstrate increased student learning. Parents and administrators, while interested in media center use, circulation, and acquisitions statistics, will be especially concerned about student improvement with regard to symbolic-analytic skills. Sole practitioner SLMSs, whose administrative time is divided among many other responsibilities, will concentrate their instructional measurement and evaluation time in this area.

Challenges

8

Librarians must be more willing not just to accept change, but to become its agents.

Frederick G. Kilgour

School library media centers are at a crossroads. Over the next decade, our institutions will face fundamental technological, economic, societal, instructional, and administrative changes. School library media centers of the twenty-first century will be very different from today's media centers not only in their physical appearance but also in their approaches to information, society, and education.

The opportunities before SLMCs are exciting, but to take advantage of them will require many changes. New strategies must be developed if SLMSs are to succeed in meeting the challenges in the years ahead. For the first time we are truly at the brink of an electronic revolution. Our parent institutions will naturally turn to us for short-term and long-range planning in this area. Unfortunately, many will do so with diminishing resources, making it more difficult for us to provide them with the equipment and materials they need to change. Many parents are just beginning to realize that secure employment and economic well-being will only be achieved if their offspring obtain education beyond high school.

Never before have SLMCs been so essential to their parent institutions. Our media center programs and services are educationally imperative if schools are to supply students with the skills, training, and knowledge they must have to prosper in America. My vision for school library media centers is not without hope. Despite the changes occurring with technology, the economy, education, and society, I believe that we have been given an unprecedented opportunity to shape our future. Our organizational mission is to position SLMCs as central to the goals and objectives of educational institutions. We must become the centers for information access, storage, dissemination, and instruction. Our educational responsibility is to design programs and services that assist faculty to teach and help students to learn.

With rapid change occurring in all these areas, it is urgent that SLMSs take bold steps to redesign their organizations to meet the challenges of the twenty-first century. School media specialists who do not take action to shape their future will have it shaped for them by frustrated administrators, anxious parents, and demanding students. If SLMSs do not accept this unique mandate to change their SLMCs, they will become professionally obsolete.

CHALLENGE 1

School library media centers must acquire sufficient information technologies to enable students to learn the concepts and skills required to function successfully in electronic environments.

In an increasingly competitive global economy, it will border on negligence if SLMCs fail to provide information technologies. With improvements in telecommunications, access to multitype networks, declining costs in computers, and availability of fax machines, SLMSs in even small school media centers should be able to provide students with some form of expanded access and document delivery of at least serials. Determining a level of sufficiency should be based upon factors such as (1) size of the school population, (2) current technological development stage, (3) level of funding, (4) geographical location, (5) collection size, (6) student research needs, (7) document delivery capabilities, (8) technological maintenance, and (9) software support. There are currently no formal school library media standards defining the appropriate level of information technologies; thus, SLMSs must develop their own. Given the increasing trend toward digitalization and interconnectivity of various technologies, SLMSs should evaluate any technology for its current and future potential for interactivity and networking.

Expanding both on-site and off-site electronic access to materials should be the primary goal of all SLMCs within the next decade. Increased resource sharing and networking are the means to achieve this goal. Using interactivity and interconnectivity as overall criteria, SLMSs should develop their own acquisition guidelines for in-house electronic technologies based upon the preceding factors. Off-site expanded access should be based upon librarian-defined levels of acceptable availability and document delivery.

Acquiring sufficient technologies on a continual basis requires the development of long-range plans based upon research and current/future economic, educational, and employment data. It also involves obtaining the support of administrators, faculty, and parents. In an age of accountability, members of the educational community will need supporting documentation before releasing funds for the purchase of expensive new technologies. Library media specialists are going to have to furnish statistics that reinforce the need for students to acquire these skills. They will have to present research findings showing America's academic position compared to other developed countries. Administrators and parents will want employment data concerning the types of jobs that are likely to be available in the future and the skills that will be required to secure those positions.

School media specialists must develop plans to gain administrative and parental approval. Once this stage is reached, SLMSs should be prepared to make formal presentations of their plans at building and board of education levels. In school districts with media supervisors, this proposal phase may become the responsibility of district library personnel. In smaller districts, it could be a group of SLMSs. Knowledgeable parents should be invited to attend and, if necessary, to speak in favor of the proposals. Parent newsletters and local newspapers should feature information about the current status of the plans.

CHALLENGE 2

School library media specialists must assume a leadership role in the promotion and application of various technologies that facilitate teaching and foster the symbolic-analytic skills of students.

The increasing digitalization of all information, regardless of format, and the improved capacity to electronically connect various technologies mean that SLMSs must play an active role in alerting faculty, administrators, parents, and students to evolving technologies that are relevant to their educational needs. School library media specialists can no longer afford the luxury of assuming that new technologies are the responsibility of a computer coordinator or technology committee. If they do relinquish this function, many new technologies will be available, stored and distributed outside the library. As technology encroaches further into the educational life of the school, the media center will be viewed as an unnecessary artifact of times past.

School library media specialists must first develop technology current-awareness programs. Merely disseminating written evaluations or literature about new technologies will not be sufficient. With emerging technologies, much more is needed. School media specialists must demonstrate the usefulness of new technologies in staff development programs, in after-school workshops, and at faculty meetings. Examples of particular software programs or equipment must apply to specific subjects so that teachers can readily understand their utility in their course areas. When a technology does not lend itself to an on-site demonstration, SLMSs should identify other institutions that are successfully using it and schedule field trips for interested administrators and faculty. Demonstrating new technologies with a supportive faculty member is a beneficial part of technological current awareness.

School media specialists must also acquire the technical knowledge and skills necessary to operate electronic technologies, to provide instruction to faculty and students, and to manage and maintain media center–related ones. They must begin by reading technology-related journals like *PC World* and *MACWORLD* as well as library periodicals. While the latter include some technological information, they are not as current regarding emerging technologies. School media specialists needing consumer information about new products will find these serials more helpful.

Continuing education is essential if SLMSs are to assume leadership roles that foster the use of various technologies. Attending workshops, taking library-school extension courses, and participating in conference presentations at various local, state, and national meetings are crucial to learning and upgrading skills in this rapidly changing field.

A third way to acquire necessary technical skills will, by necessity, occur on the job. Many technologies such as the new multimedia packages are so complicated that they require intermediary technical assistance to streamline access by relatively novice users. School media specialists will have to work with various technologies to develop electronic shortcuts that minimize the initial learning process. Teachers and students can easily become discouraged by software packages with information structures that are so complex they require days to master simple concepts.

Assuming leadership roles with respect to the application of electronic technologies to various learning situations will also involve SLMSs as instructors. All current-awareness activities and technological proficiencies of SLMSs will be wasted if they do not design course-integrated on-line units that incorporate the new electronic advancements. Most faculty will have neither the time nor the inclination to change their traditional textbook approach to learning. It will be up to SLMSs to discover specific points in courses where on-line instruction, use of CD-ROM references, accessing remote libraries and databases, and so forth will be pedagogically helpful. School media specialists, especially with new technologies, will have to proselytize with many faculty. Their instructional role will have to be more proactive than in previous decades. Although students can be expected to readily adapt to the incorporation of information technologies into their courses, many faculty members will only improve in this area if SLMSs do most of the initial instructional design.

CHALLENGE 3

School library media specialists must develop performance-based models of programs and services that will enable them to justify investment by a variety of government, corporate, and nonprofit institutions.

Future economic trends do not indicate that there will be a favorable resolution of the fiscal problems facing most SLMCs. Increasing indebtedness, ranging from individual to corporate and national, make it unlikely that SLMCs will receive adequate funding in the near future. To satisfy increasing demands for information technologies and current print and nonprint materials, it will be incumbent upon SLMSs to seek funding from traditional and alternative sources. Enlisting financial support from alternative sources, such as corporations, local businesses, and foundations, will require media specialists to take a product-oriented approach to expenditures. They will have to design and implement performance-based objectives that are linked to increased information literacy, improved symbolic-analytic skills, and increased learning through resource-based instruction. Unlike individual subjects such as mathematics and English that readily lend themselves to standardized test evaluation, school media specialists will have to devise their own measures of progress to justify funding. In the face of declining test scores and an overall educational malaise, SLMSs must concentrate their measurement and evaluation of programs and services on those that facilitate learning. They must endeavor to demonstrate improved student abilities to (1) identify correct information needs, (2) select appropriate print and electronic sources, (3) integrate and synthesize information into a coherent form, and (4) present their findings in an organized and logical format.

When resource-based learning activities are employed, SLMSs cannot assume that this form of instruction is superior to textbook-lecture-classroom methods. They must discern support for the former by comparing use of both methods in similar content-research designs. Most corporate investors will not accept measures based upon student, teacher, and SLMS testimonials of increased use of materials. Their idea of productivity translates to increased performance or learning. School library media specialists will have to design valid pre- and post-performance measures that schools and alternative funding sources can rely upon to justify further expenditures for programs and services.

CHALLENGE 4

School library media specialists must use their collections and information technologies to ensure that students and their parents are cognizant of changing employment opportunities and the need for lifelong retraining and education.

The employment outlook for many students in the next century is not promising. Even college graduates are expected to experience further occupational insecurities, as other countries compete to perform their jobs for less pay. While the situation is expected to be tenuous for those with higher education, it will be utterly bleak for those without it. High school graduates and dropouts will become members of the working poor, because the jobs they obtain will be so unremunerative and unreliable.

School library media specialists at all levels must develop programs and services that link learning with future employment. Many students whose parents are not college graduates will question these trends or deem them irrelevant to their situations. School media specialists must use all of their resources to demonstrate the realities of today's employment picture. Current career materials are needed that indicate the educational requirements for particular occupations. Sources that supply the long-range outlook for various professions should be recent to help students make wise educational and career decisions.

Materials that assist students to prepare for entrance exams such as the SAT (scholastic aptitude test) should be available in print and electronic form. College selection materials should also be available in both formats. Most colleges send free videos to schools describing their curricula, entrance requirements, costs, and the like. These should be accessible from SLMCs. Library media specialists should periodically sponsor speakers willing to discuss the positive and negative aspects of their careers to enable students to question them personally concerning occupational qualifications and opportunities.

For students whose aspirations do not include education beyond high school, SLMSs must employ all of their information skills to make them aware of this self-defeating choice. Showing comparative data reflecting the relationship between education and potential earnings and displaying help wanted advertisements to demonstrate how little is available for high school graduates are all means SLMSs can use to motivate students with low educational aspirations.

CHALLENGE 5

School library media centers must offer a range of programs and services that are competitive with those in local district and private schools.

As parents realize the extent of illiteracy and the implications of declining test scores, their demands for educational reforms will increase. Given the state of the economy, however, most will be unable or unwilling to allocate additional funds to pay for improvements. As a relatively inexpensive solution to cries for reform, many school districts will engage in restructuring various schools to give parents and their children more choices while simultaneously forcing schools to become more competitive.

Educators reason that if schools are placed in a position of vying for students then those schools will become more effective. Restructuring may involve the creation of (1) magnet schools, (2) school/college partnerships, (3) high-tech schools, (4) open enrollment schools, and (5) self-governing schools. All would be characterized by some form of parental/student choice. Within these schools, each department will be under pressure to design and present to prospective students their curricula and special programs. School library media centers must be an integral part of these program descriptions. To ensure that their programs are academically rigorous, SLMCs will need to offer many of the following information services: (1) students should receive a series of course-integrated instruction units that teach them basic information search and retrieval skills in an electronic environment; (2) there should be sequential programs of reading guidance available in elementary and secondary schools, augmented with frequent booktalks and, if affordable, author visits; (3) reference and information services should be readily available, with secondary SLMCs offering term paper counseling at appropriate times of the year; (4) the SLMC should offer students electronic access to other library collections accompanied by timely delivery systems; and (5) the SLMC should exude an ambience where students can relax with books, ask any questions, and receive assistance without bureaucratic impediments.

CHALLENGE 6

School library media specialists must develop programs, services, and collections that are responsive to students' cultural, social, and behavioral needs.

Although technology is playing a major role in the evolution of SLMCs and will continue to affect them in the years to come, these media centers are also social systems. Within a specified set of hours, SLMSs serve *in loco parentis* as do all faculty and staff within the school. Social and behavioral trends concerning families and children indicate that incidences of divorce, latchkey children, drug abuse, adolescent pregnancy, AIDS, and violence are unlikely to lessen by the year 2000. Educational institutions have long been aware of the connection between students' social and behavioral problems and academic achievement in school. They are finally beginning to respond to children's familial, societal, and physical concerns with special life skills classes, programs, and services. School library media specialists need to do likewise.

The fact that America is fast becoming a multicultural society needs to be reflected in the collections of all SLMCs, regardless of the ethnic composition of individual schools. All subject areas, including religion, mathematics, science, and literature should be infused with the creative contributions of various ethnic groups. As our economy becomes inextricably linked with those of other nations, it will be imperative for SLMSs to expose students through special speakers, author visits, booktalks and course-integrated instruction to the social customs of other cultures. Developing collections responsive to student cultural needs can also be used to diffuse ethnic tensions. For cultures that have been and still are the victims of discrimination, using media center collections to display and acknowledge this history can help relieve some of the pain and suffering caused by society's blindness to it.

School library media specialists must also develop collections that can assist students to deal with serious social problems. So many of the subjects that adults wish to shield students from threaten their lives. Young people have the right to information concerning these matters, and SLMSs must provide it. Materials about divorce, stepfamilies, gay families, live-in partners, and single-parent families should be available. So should materials about child abuse, homosexuality, teenage pregnancy, AIDS, and other sexually transmitted diseases. Members of the new self-care generation also need more how-to materials. For example, videos and books that demonstrate how to be street smart and how to prepare simple nutritional meals should be acquired.

CHALLENGE 7

School library media specialists must design resource-based learning units for all subject areas that require students to use symbolic-analytic skills in electronic environments.

The instructional role of the SLMS is being influenced not only by advances in technology but also by changes in education. Faced with expanded access and increased storage and retrieval capabilities in an electronic environment, SLMSs are fast discovering how obsolete their former methods of bibliographic instruction have become. Educators, confronted with a similar explosion in information, are realizing how limiting the textbook-lecture-classroom method is in this new electronic age. Both groups are publicly espousing resource-based learning as a means to provide students with opportunities to locate, evaluate, and use information. Faculty also realize that resource-based learning lends itself to individualizing instruction.

The use of SLMCs for resource-based learning units is especially appropriate because of the presence in their collections of print and nonprint materials and the increasing availability of CD-ROM references, on-line catalogs, and electronic access to other library collections. Designing resource-based lessons and activities that merely require students to locate correct information in electronic environments will not improve their higher-order thinking skills. School media specialists must design resource-based learning units that require students to use symbolic-analytic skills.

These skills encompass abstraction, system thinking, experimentation, and collaboration.

The second hurdle SLMSs must overcome when designing symbolic-analytic resource-based learning units is to use technologies in pedagogically sound ways. Overarching these units should be on-line concepts that enable students to readily transfer from one technology to another. If students are not to be overwhelmed with access to sixty CD-ROM databases locally mounted in a supercatalog, they must receive instruction in (1) the purpose and function of on-line catalogs, (2) the range and nature of their contents, (3) information retrieval techniques, (4) formulation of appropriate search strategies, (5) manipulating selected search commands, and (6) interpreting their results in relation to their assignments.

CHALLENGE 8

School library media specialists must organize and manage their media centers to meet the changing social and information needs of their users.

Out of concern for the academic welfare of students, educational institutions will begin to provide pre- and after-school care. Library media specialists in elementary and secondary schools will have to organize and manage their SLMCs to accommodate the possible establishment of (1) scheduled preschool classes, (2) homework assistance centers, and (3) recreational reading and viewing programs. School library media specialists will need to restructure their management systems to assist pre- and after-school supervisors to access materials and equipment during their absence. Depending upon the type of non–school hour usage, SLMSs must acquire additional materials to satisfy the information and social needs of students who are no longer in formal classes.

With the availability of new technologies, the information needs of students, faculty and even parents will change. Users with computers and modems will be able to access library collections, CD-ROM databases, and remote databases round-the-clock. School media specialists must become managers of information by (1) establishing electronic access protocols, (2) troubleshooting technical problems, (3) ensuring information transfers, and (4) scheduling and arranging for information delivery.

Managing the collection will be further complicated by its changing nature. The collection will no longer consist of the holdings of the SLMC, but also the contents of on-site CD-ROM and remote library databases. As SLMSs expand access to other information networks, deciding to own particular items versus accessing them through on-line catalogs will have to be based upon a new set of acquisition criteria that must include collection-centric versus peripheral concepts.

By far the greatest administrative challenge to SLMSs will be to restructure their SLMCs while simultaneously managing stationary or declining budgets. Obtaining funds for new technologies, materials, and equipment will test the innovative and entrepreneurial skills of every librarian. To successfully usher SLMCs into the next century, media specialists must (1) lobby local, state, and federal funding sources for mandated, categorical SLMC funding, (2) renegotiate local allocations if they are deemed unsatisfactory, and (3) seek additional funding at local, state, and national levels. The latter source must include local companies, corporations, and nonprofit foundations and trusts.

Increased resource sharing and networking will be an essential part of future budgetary management. School media centers that participate in these arrangements will receive expanded collection access and can reduce costs by collectively purchasing materials and equipment and cooperatively cataloging and processing materials. Once networked, SLMCs must develop union catalogs, and institute coordinated collection development to enable them to avoid needless duplication of materials.

Notes

INTRODUCTION

1. Milo Nelson, "Crunching Knowledge: The Coming Environment for the Information Specialist," paper presented at the 4th Annual Conference on Computers in Libraries, March 14–16, 1989 (Oakland, CA), ERIC Document ED 322 913, 1–8.

2. Alvin Toffler, *Previews and Premises* (New York: William Morrow, 1983), 10–16.

3. John Naisbett, *Megatrends: Ten New Directions Transforming Our Lives* (New York: Warner, 1982), 18.

4. *Leadership for the 90's*, Final Report of the State Superintendent's Task Force on School Library Media Issues, Bulletin 91095 (Madison, WI: Wisconsin State Department of Public Instruction Division for Library Services, 1990), ERIC Document ED 329 279, 3.

5. Robert E. Rubenstein, "Changing Schools from Within," *The World & I* 8 (February 1993): 102.

6. Patricia Glass Schuman, "Reclaiming Our Technological Future," *Library Journal* 115 (March 1, 1990): 36.

7. *Leadership for the 90's*, 3.

8. William E. Halal, "The Information Technology Revolution," *The Futurist* 26 (July–August 1992): 10–12.

9. David W. Penniman, "Shaping the Future," *Library Journal* 117 (October 15, 1992): 40.

10. Eldred Smith, *The Librarian, the Scholar and the Future of the Research Library* (Westport, CT: Greenwood Press, 1990), 1.

11. Frances Laverne Carroll, *Recent Advances in School Librarianship* (Oxford, England: Pergamon Press, 1981), 249.

12. John M. DeBroske, "Electronic Reference—The School Library Revolution," *The Bookmark* 50 (Fall 1991): 19.

13. Marilyn Miller, "The Birth of the Electronically Smart Media Center," *Media Methods* 17 (November/December 1991): 77.

14. Rubenstein, "Changing Schools from Within," 105.

15. Schuman, "Reclaiming Our Technological Future," 35.

16. Ibid., 37.

17. Nelson, "Crunching Knowledge: The Coming Environment for the Information Specialist," 2.

18. *Leadership for the 90's*, 28.

19. Mary Ellen Roberts, "CD ROM Usage—Taking the Cues From Students," *Media & Methods* 26 (May/June 1990): 53.

20. Theodore Sizer, *Horace's School: Redesigning the American High School* (Boston: Houghton Mifflin, 1992); and Lewis J. Perelman, *School's Out: Hyperlearning, the New Technology, and the End of Education* (New York: William Morrow, 1992).

21. Barbara Wilson and Abigail Hubbard, "Redefining the Role of School Media Specialists . . . Bridging the Gap," *Online* 11 (November 1987): 53.

22. John C. Swan, "Rehumanizing Information: An Alternative Future," *Library Journal* 115 (September 1, 1990): 178–182.

23. Nelson, "Crunching Knowledge: The Coming Environment for the Information Specialist," 6.

24. Swan, "Rehumanizing Information: An Alternative Future," 181.

CHAPTER ONE

1. Kathleen W. Craver, "The Future of School Library Media Centers," *School Library Media Quarterly* 12 (Summer 1984): 266–284.

2. John S. Mayo, "R & D in the Third Millennium," *Vital Speeches of the Day* 59 (October 15, 1992): 26–29.

3. Lauren H. Seilor, "The Concept of Book in the Age of the Digital Electronic Medium," *Library Software Review* 11 (January–February 1992): 19–29.

4. Jerry M. Rosenberg, *Dictionary of Computers, Data Processing, and Telecommunications* (New York: Wiley, 1984), 531.

5. Robert Swisher, Kathleen L. Spitzer, Barbara Spriestersbach, Tim Markus, and Jerry M. Burris, "Telecommunications for School Library Media Centers," *School Library Media Quarterly* 19 (Spring 1991): 153–160.

6. Michael Eisenberg and Keith Williams, "Microcomputers-based Telecommunications for Management and Decision-Making," in *Microcomputers for Library Decision Making: Issues, Trends, and Applications*, edited by Peter Hernon and Charles R. McClure (Norwood, NJ: Ablex, 1986), 130–131.

7. Stewart Brand, *The Media Lab* (New York: Viking, 1987), 67–68.

8. Brand, *The Media Lab*, 18, 19, 68.

9. Philip Elmer-Dewitt, "Take a Step into the Future on the Electronic Superhighway," *Time* 141 (April 12, 1993): 53.

10. Ibid., 54.

11. Savan W. Wilson, "Television Is for Learning a New Agenda," in *School Library Media Annual*, Vol. 8, edited by Jane Bandy Smith (Englewood, CO: Libraries Unlimited, 1990), 92–111.

12. Scott S. Schiller, "Educational Applications of Instructional Television and Cabling Programming," *Media & Methods* 27 (March/April 1991): 20–21, 52.

13. Wilson, "Television Is for Learning a New Agenda," 104–105.

14. Elmer-DeWitt, "Take a Trip into the Future on the Electronic Superhighway," 52.

15. Richard Loglin, "When the Revolution Comes What Will Happen to . . .," *Time* 141 (April 12, 1993): 56–58.

16. Swisher, "Telecommunications for School Library Media Centers," 154.

17. Mayo, "R & D in the Third Millennium," 26.

18. Seilor, "The Concept of Book in the Age of the Digital Electronic Medium," 20.

19. William E. Halal, "The Information Technology Revolution," *The Futurist* 26 (July–August 1992): 10.

20. "A Chip with Zip," *Time* 141 (April 3, 1993): 18.

21. Halal, "The Information Technology Revolution," 11.

22. Ruth V. Curtis, "The Contributions of Technology to Instruction and Learning," in *School Library Media Annual*, Vol. 8, edited by Jane Bandy Smith (Englewood, CO: Libraries Unlimited, 1990), 59–66.

23. Richard J. Newman, "Your Digital Future," *U.S. News & World Report* 114 (April 5, 1993): 55.

24. Peter H. Lewis, "Computer-to-Go Generation," *New York Times* Education Life Section A (April 4, 1993): 12–13.

25. Curtis, "The Contribution of Technology to Instruction and Learning," 61.

26. Lewis J. Perelman, *School's Out: Hyperlearning, the New Technology and the End of Education* (New York: William Morrow, 1992), 35.

27. James A. Martin, "All about Scanners," *MACWORLD* 9 (October 1992): 150–155.

28. "How Optical Character Recognition Works," *PC-Computing* 6 (February 1993): 299–300.

29. James A. Martin, "All about Scanners," 154–155.

30. Caroline Arms, ed., *Campus Strategies for Libraries and Electronic Information* (Rockport, MA: Digital Press, 1990), 360.

31. Brand, *The Media Lab*, 22.

32. Arms, *Campus Strategies for Libraries and Electronic Information*, 360.

33. Roxanne Baxter Mendrinos, "CD-ROM Technology for Reference in Secondary School Library Media Centers," in *School Library Media Annual*, Vol. 10, edited by Jane Bandy Smith and J. Gordon Coleman, Jr. (Englewood, CO: Libraries Unlimited, 1992), 159–163.

34. Michael Rogers, "CD-ROM Is Still Shining Brightly at UMI," *Library Journal* 118 (March 15, 1993): 20.

35. Roxanne Baxter Mendrinos, "CD-ROM and At-Risk Students," *School Library Journal* 38 (October 1992): 31.

36. Kimberlie Pelsma, "CD ROM and Information Literacy across the Curriculum," *Media & Methods* 26 (May/June, 1990): 10.

37. Carol Tenopir, "Electronic Access to Periodicals," *Library Journal* 118 (March 1, 1993): 54.

38. Mendrinos, "CD-ROM Technology for Reference in Secondary School Library Media Centers," 160.

39. Brand, *The Media Lab*, 23.

40. William J. Cook, "The New Rockefeller," *U.S. News & World Report* 114 (February 15, 1993): 65.

41. Mayo, "R & D in the Third Millennium," 26.

42. Halal, "The Information Technology Revolution," 11.

43. Cook, "The New Rockefeller," 72.

44. Mayo, "R & D in the Third Millennium," 26.

45. William J. Cook, "The Next Test for Bill Gates," *U.S. News & World Report* 114 (February 15, 1993): 70–72.

46. Cook, "The New Rockefeller," 67.

47. Pat Molholt, "Libraries and the New Technologies: Courting the Cheshire Cat," *Library Journal* 113 (November 15, 1988): 39.

48. Arms, *Campus Strategies for Libraries and Electronic Information*, 321–322.

49. "Grammar Checkers," *PC World* 11 (April 1993): 103.

50. Perelman, *School's Out*, 43.

51. Arms, *Campus Strategies for Libraries and Electronic Information*, 363.

52. Molholt, "Libraries and the New Technologies: Courting the Cheshire Cat," 38.

53. Judy Guthrie and Beverley Crane, "Online Retrieval Adds Realism to Science Projects," *The Computing Teacher* 19 (February 1992): 32.

54. Gary Marchionini, "Tomorrow's Media Center: A Look into the Future," *Media & Methods* 28 (November/December 1991): 10–12.

55. Arms, *Campus Strategies for Libraries and Electronic Information*, 319–321.

56. Gary Marchionini, "Technological Trends and Implications toward the New Millennium," in *School Library Media Annual*, Vol. 9, edited by Jane Bandy Smith and J. Gordon Coleman (Englewood, CO: Libraries Unlimited, 1991), 183.

57. Diane Gayeski and David Williams, *Interactive Media* (Englewood Cliffs, NJ: Prentice Hall, 1985): 226.

58. Ibid., 7, 227.

59. Ibid., 120–121.

60. Mary Ellen McDonnell, "San Francisco GTV," *The Computing Teacher* 19 (February 1992): 37–38.

61. Gary J. Anglin, ed., *Instructional Technology Past, Present, and Future* (Englewood, CO: Libraries Unlimited, 1991): 45.

62. McDonnell, "San Francisco GTV," 38.

63. Daniel T. Lake, "Art: Technologies in the Curriculum," *The Computing Teacher* 19 (March 1992): 44–45.

64. Wilbur Schramm, *Big Media, Little Media* (Beverly Hills, CA: Sage Publications, 1977): 27–36.

65. Seilor, "The Concept of Book in the Age of the Digital Electronic Medium," 24–25.

66. Judy Mallory, "Electronic Storytelling in the 21st Century," in *Visions of the Future*, edited by Clifford A. Pickover (New York: St. Martin's Press, 1992): 137.

67. Whiteley Sandy, "Trends in Reference and Electronic Publishing," *Booklist* 88 (May 1, 1992): 1626.

68. Charles Anderson, "The Multimedia Encyclopedia of Mammalian Biology," *Booklist* 89 (March 1, 1993): 1266.

69. Mallory, "Electronic Storytelling in the 21st Century," 140.

70. Daniel D. Barron, "Distance Education and School Library Media Specialists," in *School Library Media Annual*, Vol. 9, edited by Jane Bandy Smith and J. Gordon Coleman (Englewood, CO: Libraries Unlimited, 1991): 20–22.

71. Schiller, "Educational Applications of Instructional Television and Cable Programming," 20.

72. Perelman, *School's Out*, 56.

73. Lee Monk, "Distance Education: Learning from the Stars," *Media & Methods* 26 (January/February 1990): 8, 54.

74. Perelman, *School's Out*, 56.

75. Catherine Barr, ed., *The 1992 Bowker Annual Library and Book Trade Almanac* (New Providence, NJ: R. R. Bowker, 1992): 430, 440.

76. Patricia A. Hooten, "Online Catalogs: Will They Improve Children's Access?" *Journal of Youth Services in Libraries* 2 (Spring 1989): 267–272.

77. George S. Machovec and Dennis R. Brunning, "Decision 2000: Moving beyond Boundaries," paper presented at the Joint Conference of the Arizona State Library Association and the Arizona Educational Media Association (Phoenix, AZ: Arizona State Library Association, November 13–17, 1990) ERIC Document ED 332 705, 12–23.

78. Machovec and Browning, "Decision 2000," 19.

79. Arms, *Campus Strategies for Libraries and Electronic Information*, 312–316.

80. Arms, *Campus Strategies for Libraries and Electronic Information*, 350–352; Machovec and Brunning, "Decision 2000," 14–16; Jean Armour Polly, "NREN for ALL: Insurmountable Opportunity," *Library Journal* 118 (February 1, 1993): 38–41; and Charles R. McClure and others, "Toward a Virtual Library: Internet and the National Research and Education Network," in *The 1992 Bowker Annual Library and Book Trade Almanac*, 39th edition, edited by Catherine Barr (New Providence, NJ: R. R. Bowker, 1993): 39.

81. Polly, "NREN for All: Insurmountable Opportunity," 39.

82. Machovec and Brunning, "Decision 2000," 16; and Marchionini, "Tomorrow's Media Center: A Look into the Future," 12.

83. Susan Hess, "Beyond Juan Morel Campos: Telecommunications Links for Learning," *The Bookmark* 50 (Fall 1991): 27–29.

84. M. D. Roblyer, "Electronic Hands across the Ocean: The Florida-England Connection," *The Computing Teacher* 19 (February 1992): 16–19.

85. Raymond Kurzweil, "The Virtual Book Revisited," *Library Journal* 118 (February 15, 1993): 145.

86. Perelman, *School's Out*, 29.

87. Robert A. Benfer, Edward E. Brent, Jr., and Louanna Furbee, *Expert Systems* (Newbury Park, CA: Sage Publications 1991): 1.

88. Arms, *Campus Strategies for Libraries and Electronic Information*, 323.

89. Gary G. Bitter, "Artificial Intelligence: The Expert Way," *Media & Methods* 25 (May/June 1989): 22.

90. Ibid., 24–25.

91. Halal, "The Information Technology Revolution," 11–12.

92. Perelman, *School's Out*, 32–33.

93. Halal, "The Information Technology Revolution," 12.

94. George Philip, "Applications of Automatic Speech Recognition and Synthesis in Libraries and Information Services: A Future Scenario," *Library Hi Tech* 9 (March 1991): 89–92.

95. Keith Wetzel, "Speech Technology II: Future Software and Hardware Predictions," *The Computing Teacher* 19 (October 1991): 19–21.

96. Perelman, *School's Out*, 34.

97. Philip, "Applications of Automatic Speech Recognition and Synthesis in Libraries and Information Services: A Future Scenario," 90–92.

98. Wetzel, "Speech Technology II: Future Software and Hardware Predictions," 19–20.

99. Myron W. Krueger, "Artificial Reality: Past and Future," in *Virtual Reality: Theory, Practice, and Promise*, edited by Sandra K. Helsel and Judith Paris Roth (Westport, CT: Meckler, 1991): 25.

100. Gary Ferrington and Kenneth Loge, "Virtual Reality: A New Learning Environment," *The Computing Teacher* 19 (April 1992): 16.

101. Scott S. Fisher, "Virtual Environments: Personal Simulations & Telepresence," in *Virtual Reality: Theory Practice, and Promise*, 101–109; and Gary Ferrington and Kenneth Loge, "Virtual Reality: A New Learning Environment," 16.

102. Perelman, *School's Out*, 40–43.

103. Ferrington and Loge, "Virtual Reality: A New Learning Environment," 16.

CHAPTER TWO

1. Paul M. Kennedy, *Preparing for the Twenty-first Century* (New York: Random House, 1993), 291.

2. Ratu Kamiani and Katherine Mihok, "How the World Will Look in 50 Years," *Time* 140 (Fall 1992, "The Century Ahead," special issue): 36–38; and Marc Levinson, "The Trashing of Free Trade," *Newsweek* 122 (July 12, 1993): 42–45.

3. Kennedy, *Preparing for the Twenty-first Century*, 297.

4. James Dale Davidson, "Boom or Bust: Two Views of One Future," *The Futurist* 26 (September–October 1992): 10–14.

5. Lewis J. Perelman, *School's Out: Hyperlearning, The New Technology, and the End of Education* (New York: William Morrow, 1992), 105.

6. "State and Local Taxes Grew 4.7 Percent in 1991; Smallest Increase since 1952," *Census and You* 28 (May 1993): 7.

7. Kennedy, *Preparing for the Twenty-first Century*, 297–298.

8. "Nation's Population Projected to Grow by 50 Percent over Next 60 Years," *Census and You* 28 (January 1993): 1–2.

9. Robert B. Croneberger, "External Influences on Public Library Management in the 21st Century," *Journal of Library Administration* 11 (No. 1, 1989): 209–220; and Kennedy, *Preparing for the Twenty-first Century*, 311–312.

10. Dory Adams, ed., "Did You Know That . . .? Have You Thought of . . .?" *NAIS/EMSC Noteboard* (Spring 1993) N. Pag.; and "School Population Explosion Predicted for Early 21st Century," *School Library Journal* 39 (April 1993): 14.

11. Charles S. Clark, "Hard Times for Libraries," *CQ Researcher* 2 (June 26, 1992): 551–567.

12. "The Elementary and Secondary School Library Media Act: Excerpts from the Congressional Record," (Washington, DC: ALA Washington Office, October 1992), 1.

13. Marilyn L. Miller and Marilyn Shontz, "Expenditures for Resources in School Library Media Centers FY 1991–92," *School Library Journal* 39 (October 1993): 26–36.

14. Denis P. Doyle and others, "Education Ideas & Strategies for the 1990s," *American Enterprise* 4 (March/April 1991): 25-33.

15. Clark, "Hard Times for Libraries," 551.

16. Marilyn L. Miller and Marilyn Shontz, "Expenditures for Resources in School Library Media Centers FY 1989–90," *School Library Journal* 37 (August 1991): 33.

17. Clark, "Hard Times for Libraries," 551–552.

18. Miller and Shontz, "Expenditures for Resources in School Library Media Centers FY 1989–1990," 32–40; Lillian N. Gerhardt, "Average Book Prices '93," *School Library Journal* 39 (March 1993): 94; and Adrian W. Alexander and Kathryn Hammel Carpenter, "Periodical Price Index for 1993," *American Libraries* 24 (May 1993): 438.

19. Miller and Shontz, "Expenditures for Resources in School Library Media Centers FY 1991–92," 29–30.

20. "The Elementary and Secondary School Library Media Act," 4–5.

21. Miller and Shontz, "Expenditures for Resources in School Library Media Centers FY 1991–92," 28–29.

22. Ibid., 29.

23. "The Elementary and Secondary School Library Media Act," 5.

24. Grace Anne A. DeCandido and Alan P. Mahony, "Overworked and Under-budgeted," *School Library Journal* 38 (June 1992): 25-29.

25. Keith Curry Lance, Lynda Welborn, and Christine Hamilton-Pennell, *The Impact of School Library Media Centers on Academic Achievement* (Castle Rock, CO: Hi Willow Research and Publishing, 1993), 96.

26. David V. Loertscher, "Objective: Achievement Solution: School Libraries," *School Library Journal* 39 (May 1993): 30–33; "The Elementary and Secondary School Media Act," 4; and Stephen Krashen, *The Power of Reading* (Englewood, CO: Libraries Unlimited, 1993).

27. Pat Molholt, "Libraries and the New Technologies: Courting the Cheshire Cat," *Library Journal* 113 (November 15, 1988): 37–41.

28. "The Elementary and Secondary School Library Media Act," 1; and Senator Paul Simon, "A Call for Progress," *School Library Journal* 39 (April 1993): 26–29.

29. Joan V. Rogers, "Real Information Power," *School Library Journal* 39 (March 1993): 113–117.

30. Eleanor Branch, "Can Businesses Save Our Schools?" *Black Enterprise* 4 (March 1991): 40; and Doyle and others, "Educational Ideas & Strategies for the 1990s," *American Enterprise* 4 (March/April 1991): 25-34.

31. Perelman, *School's Out*, 110–111.

32. Ibid., 253.

33. Branch, "Can Business Save Our Schools?," 25-34.

34. Lillian N. Gerhardt, Grace Anne A. DeCandido, and Alan P. Mahony, "SLJ News: 1991 Unfinished Business," *School Library Journal* 37 (December 1991): 41–44; and Kris Kurtenback, "Library Power and Local Education Funds: An Ideal Partnership," *Library Power Newsletter* 1 (Spring 1993): 2–5.

35. J. Ingrid Lesley, "Library Services for Special User Groups," in *The 1992 Bowker Annual Library and Book Trade Almanac*, edited by Catherine Barr (New Providence, NJ: R. R. Bowker, 1992), 34–35.

36. "Five Budget Stretching Ideas," *School Librarian's Workshop* 13 (June 1993): 1.

37. Kennedy, *Preparing for the Twenty-first Century*, 305-307.

38. Robert Heinich, "Restructuring Technology, and Instructional Productivity," in *Instructional Technology Past, Present, and Future*, edited by Gary J. Anglin (Englewood, CO: Libraries Unlimited, 1991), 237.

39. Ibid., 237.

40. Doyle, "Educational Ideas & Strategies for the 1990s," 30.

41. Ibid., 25-33.

42. Perelman, *School's Out*, 320–321.

43. Gerhardt, "SLJ News: 1991 Unfinished Business," 44.

44. JoAnn V. Rogers, "Real Information Power," *School Library Journal* 39 (March 1993): 113–117.

45. Rogers, "Real Information Power," 113–117; and DeCandido and Mahony, "Overworked and Underbudgeted," 25-29.

CHAPTER THREE

1. Lewis J. Perelman, *School's Out: Hyperlearning, the New Technology and the End of Education* (New York: William Morrow, 1992), 67.

2. Jerry Borrell, "America's Shame: How We've Abandoned Our Children's Future," *MACWORLD* 9 (September 1992): 25-30.

3. William B. Johnson and Arnold E. Packer, *Workforce 2000* (Indianapolis, IN: Hudson Institute, 1987), 1–2.

4. Robert B. Reich, *The Work of Nations* (New York: Alfred A. Knopf, 1991), 210–211.

5. Perelman, *School's Out*, 68–69.

6. Johnson and Packer, *Workforce 2000*, 21–22.

7. Reich, *The Work of Nations*, 173–203.

8. Perelman, *School's Out*, 191.

9. Cass G. Genry and Josephine Csete, "Educational Technology in the 1990s," in *Instructional Technology Past, Present, and Future*, edited by Gary J. Anglin (Englewood, CO: Libraries Unlimited, 1991), 25.

10. Borrell, "America's Shame: How We've Abandoned Our Children's Future," 25.

11. Morton Kondracke, "The Official Word How Our Government Views the Use of Computers in Schools," *MACWORLD* 9 (September 1992), 232–236.

12. Charles Piller, "Separate Realities," *MACWORLD* 9 (September 1992), 221–223.

13. Johnson and Packer, *Workforce 2000*, 48.

14. Ibid., 48–96.

15. Ibid., 97.

16. "Participants in Assistance Programs: A Profile," *Census and You* 28 (January 1993): 1–12; and "Education Is the Ticket to Higher Earnings," *Census and You* 28 (April 1993): 1–16.

17. Richard J. Murnane and Frank Levy, "Why Today's High School–Educated Males Earn Less Than Their Fathers Did: The Problem and Assessment of Responses," *Harvard Educational Review* 63 (Spring 1993), 1–19; and Reich, *The Work of Nations*, 205-207. (The absence of women in the Murnane-Levy study was due to the difficulty in interpreting earnings of women over a period of time (1973–1987) because of differences in Census Bureau reporting of full-time and part-time employment.)

18. Murnane, "Why Today's High School–Educated Males Earn Less Than Their Fathers Did: The Problem and Assessment of Responses," 1–19.

19. Ibid., 8.

20. Johnson and Packer, *Workforce 2000*, 98–99.

21. Reich, *The Work of Nations*, 227.

22. Ibid., 227–229.

23. Johnson and Packer, *Workforce 2000*, 96–98.

24. Paul M. Kennedy, *Preparing for the Twenty-first Century* (New York: Random House, 1993), 315.

25. Arthur G. Wirth, *Education and Work for the Year 2000* (San Francisco: Jossey-Bass Publishers, 1992), 54.

26. Ibid., 54–58.

CHAPTER FOUR

1. "School Population Explosion Predicted for Early 21st Century," *School Library Journal* 39 (April 1993): 14.

2. Michael V. McGill, "Humanity and Technology in the School of the Future," *The Bookmark* 50 (Fall 1991): 6–11.

3. Robert B. Reich, *The Work of Nations* (New York: Alfred A. Knopf, 1991), 226.

4. Patricia Senn Breivik, "A Signal for the Need to Restructure the Learning Process," *NASSP Bulletin* 75 (May 1991): 1–7.

5. Paul M. Kennedy, *Preparing for the Twenty-first Century* (New York: Random House, 1993), 306. (The 1980 Census Bureau relied on people reporting that they could not write a simple message.)

6. "America's F for Effort," *The Sunday Times*, Wordpower Section (March 14, 1993): 22–27.

7. Breivik, "A Signal for the Need to Restructure the Learning Process," 2; and Thomas Sowell, *Inside American Education* (New York: Free Press, 1993), 3.

8. Breivik, "A Signal for the Need to Restructure the Learning Process," 1–7.

9. Sowell, *Inside American Education*, 1–9.

10. Jonathan Kozol, *Savage Inequalities* (New York: Crown Publishers, 1991), 27; and Jill Zuckman, "The Next Education Crisis: Equalizing School Funds," *Congressional Quarterly* 51 (March 27, 1993): 749–754.

11. Zuckman, "The Next Education Crisis: Equalizing School Funds," 749–754.

12. Reich, *The Work of Nations*, 227–228.

13. Christopher Lasch, "Is Progress Obsolete?" *Time* 140 (Fall 1992, "The Century Ahead," special issue): 71.

14. Arthur G. Wirth, *Education and Work for the Year 2000* (San Francisco: Jossey-Bass Publishers, 1992), 198–199.

15. Lewis J. Perelman, *School's Out: Hyperlearning, the New Technology and the End of Education* (New York: William Morrow, 1992), 107–108.

16. Robert E. Rubenstein, "Changing Schools from Within," *The World & I* 8 (February 1993), 103.

17. Perelman, *School's Out*, 193.

18. Richard J. Murnane and Frank Levy, "Why Today's High School–Educated Males Earn Less Than Their Fathers Did: The Problem and an Assessment of Responses," *Harvard Educational Review* 63 (Spring 1993): 10.

19. Perelman, *School's Out*, 194.

20. Theodore R. Sizer, *Horace's School: Redesigning the American High School* (Boston: Houghton Mifflin, 1992), 207–208. (Information on the Coalition of Essential Schools is available at the Coalition of Essential Skills, Box 1969, Brown University, Providence, Rhode Island 02912. The first major documentation of the coalition in its first years was published in 1993.)

21. George H. Wood, *Schools That Work: America's Most Innovative Public School Education Programs* (New York: Dutton, 1992), 246.

22. Thomas Toch, *In the Name of Excellence* (New York: Oxford University Press, 1991), 268–270.

23. Thomas Toch, "The Perfect School," *U.S. News & World Report* 114 (January 11, 1993): 46–61.

24. Toch, *In the Name of Excellence*, 253–257.

25. Todd Barrett, "Be Careful What You Ask For," *Newsweek* 121 (February 15, 1993): 43.

26. Toch, "The Perfect School," *U.S. News & World Report*, 59–60.

27. Denis P. Doyle and others, "Education Ideas & Strategies for the 1990s," *American Enterprise* 4 (March/April 1991): 25-34; and Perelman, *School's Out*, 208–210.

28. Toch, "The Perfect School," *U.S. News & World Report*, 58–59.

29. Bruce Keegan and Tim Westerberg, "Restructuring and the School Library: Partners in an Information Age," *NASSP Bulletin* 75 (May 1991): 9–22.

30. Stewart Brand, *The Media Lab: Inventing the Future at MIT* (New York: Viking, 1987), 119–130.

31. Perelman, *School's Out*, 253; and Toch, "The Perfect School," 58–59.

32. Sowell, *Inside American Education*, 11–12; and Toch, "The Perfect School," 50.

33. Doyle and others, "Education Ideas & Strategies for the 1990s," 28–33.

34. Sowell, *Inside American Education*, 70–99.

35. Wirth, *Education and Work for the Year 2000*, 197–199.

36. Joan Boykoff Baron and Robert J. Sternberg, *Teaching Thinking Skills: Theory and Practice* (New York: W. H. Freeman, 1987), 95-105, 156.

37. Reich, *The Work of Nations*, 225-233; and Toch, "The Perfect School," 53–54.

CHAPTER FIVE

1. Nathan Gardels, "The Education We Deserve," *New Perspectives Quarterly* 7 (Fall 1990): 2–3.

2. Donald D. Gainey, *Education for the New Century* (Reston, VA: National Association of Secondary School Principals, 1993), 12.

3. Ibid., 12.

4. "One in Four of Nation's Foreign Born Arrived since 1985," *Census and You* 28 (February 1993): 1–16. ("Foreign born" includes foreign-born naturalized citizens and foreign-born noncitizens. It also includes those born abroad to American parents and those born in Puerto Rico or the outlying areas.)

5. Tom Morganthau, "America: Still a Melting Pot?" *Newsweek* 122 (August 9, 1993): 16–23.

6. "Latinos on the Rise," *The Futurist* 27 (January–February 1993): 48–49; and "U.S. Hispanics: Challenges for the 1990s," *The Futurist* 23 (July–August 1989): 53.

7. David A. Hamburg, "The American Family Transformed," *Society* 30 (January/February 1993): 60–69.

8. Paul Kennedy, *Preparing for the Twenty-first Century* (New York: Random House, 1993), 313; and Morganthau, "America: Still a Melting Pot?" 22.

9. Leonard Wertheimer, "Library Services to Ethnocultural Minorities: Philosophical and Social Bases and Professional Implications," *Public Libraries* 26 (Fall 1987): 99.

10. Stryker McGuire, "Immigrant Schools: The Wrong Lessons," *Newsweek* 122 (August 9, 1993): 23.

11. Oscar Handlin, *The Uprooted* (Boston: Little, Brown, 1951), 4.

12. Thomas C. Wheeler, ed., *The Immigrant Experience: The Anguish of Becoming American* (New York: Dial Press, 1977), 3–11.

13. Kathleen W. Craver, "Bridging the Gap: Library Services for Immigrant Populations," *Journal of Youth Services in Libraries* 4 (Winter 1991): 123–130.

14. McGuire, "Immigrant Schools: The Wrong Lessons," 23.

15. Ruth Jacobs Wertheimer and Kathleen M. Foy, "Children of Immigrants and Multiethnic Heritage: Australia, Canada, and the United States," *Library Trends* 28 (Fall 1980): 339.

16. Ibid., 335.

17. Lynn H. Colwell, "School Library's Heritage Center: A Program You Can Make Your Own," *American Libraries* 19 (February 1988): 136–137.

18. David Reiff, "Multiculturalism's Silent Partner," *Harper's* 287 (August 1993), 69–70.

19. Ibid., 70.

20. Hamburg, "The American Family Transformed," 68; and Morganthau, "America: Still a Melting Pot?" 20.

21. Amitai Etzioni, "Social Science as a Multicultural Canon," *Society* 29 (November/December 1991): 14–18.

22. Arthur M. Schlesinger, Jr., *The Disuniting of America* (Knoxville, TN: Whittle Direct Books, 1991), 74.

23. Ibid., 68.

24. Ibid., 69–70.

25. Claudia Wallis, "The Nuclear Family Goes Boom!" *Time* 140 (Fall 1992, "The Century Ahead," special issue): 42–44.

26. Hamburg, "The American Family Transformed," 60–61.

27. Ibid., 63.

28. "When Families Break Up," *Census and You* 28 (February 1993): 1–16.

29. Hamburg, "The American Family Transformed," 63.

30. Arthur G. Wirth, *Education and Work for the Year 2000* (San Francisco: Jossey-Bass, 1992), 118.

31. Donald B. Childs, "Changing the School Environment to Increase Parent Involvement," *NASSP Bulletin* 75 (May 1991): 84–90.

32. Thomas Toch, "Inside the Ivy League," *U.S. News & World Report* 114 (April 12, 1993): 55–63.

33. Jean Seligman and Kendall Hamilton, "Husbands No, Babies Yes," *Newsweek* 122 (July 26, 1993): 53.

34. Wallis, "The Nuclear Family Goes Boom!" 43.

35. Arthur G. Wirth, *Education and Work for the Year 2000*, 18.

36. Hamburg, "The American Family Transformed," 62.

37. Laura Mansnerus, "Kids of the 90's: A Bolder Breed," *New York Times* Section 4A (April 4, 1993): 14–15.

38. Hamburg, "The American Family Transformed," 61–62.

39. Ibid., 60–63.

40. David Gelman, "The Violence in Our Heads," *Newsweek* 122 (August 2, 1993): 48; and Richard Louv, *Childhood's Future* (Boston: Houghton Mifflin, 1990), 84–88.

41. Susan Antilla, "'I Want' Now Gets," *New York Times* Section 4A (April 4, 1993): 1.

42. "Teenage Shoppers," *The Futurist* 27 (January–February 1993): 46.

43. Louv, *Childhood's Future*, 90.

44. Ibid., 138.

45. Ibid., 138–139.

46. Neil Postan, *Technopoly: The Surrender of Culture to Technology*, (New York: Knopf, 1992).

47. Mansnerus, "Kids of the 90's: A Bolder Breed," 15.

48. Louv, *Childhood's Future*, 91–92.

49. J. L. Richardson and others, "Substance Use among Eighth Graders Who Take Care of Themselves after School," *Pediatrics* 84 (September 1989): 556.

50. Gainey, *Education for the New Century*, 22.

51. William Kilpatrick, *Why Johnny Can't Tell Right from Wrong* (New York: Simon & Schuster, 1992), 46.

52. Louv, *Childhood's Future*, 154–157.

53. Barbara Kantrowitz, "Wild in the Streets," *Newsweek* 122 (August 2, 1993): 40–46.

54. Felicia R. Lee, "Disrespect Rules," *New York Times* Section 4A (April 4, 1993): 16.

55. Kantrowitz, "Wild in the Streets," 45–46.

CHAPTER SIX

1. Patricia Senn Breivik and E. Gordon Gee, *Information Literacy Revolution in the Library* (New York: Macmillan, 1989), 110–111.

2. Doris Ray, "Educational Technology Leadership for the Age of Restructuring," *The Computing Teacher* 19 (March 1992): 8–14.

3. Patsy H. Perritt, "School Library Media Certification Requirements 1992 Update," *School Library Journal* 38 (June 1992): 30–49.

4. Cynthia F. Bonn, "Critical Issues for Instructional Technology in Business and Industry in the 1990s," in *Instructional Technology Past, Present, and Future,* edited by Gary J. Anglin (Englewood, CO: Libraries Unlimited, 1991), 286–289; Michael A. Burke, "Distance Education and the Changing Role of the Library Media Specialist" (Syracuse, NY: ERIC Clearinghouse on Information Resources, 1989), ED 321 775; and Ray, "Educational Technology Leadership for the Age of Restructuring," 9–14.

5. Ray, "Educational Technology Leadership for the Age of Restructuring," 8–14.

6. *American Library Association Presidential Committee on Information Literacy Final Report* (Chicago: American Library Association, 1989), 11.

7. Bruce Keegan and Tim Westerburg, "Restructuring and the School Library: Partners in an Information Age," *NASSP Bulletin* 75 (May 1991): 9–14.

8. "Technically Speaking on Information Navigation," *Connections* 1 (May 1993): 5–6.

9. Cerise Oberman, "Avoiding the Cereal Syndrome, or Critical Thinking in the Electronic Environment," *Library Trends* 39 (Winter 1991): 189.

10. Ward Shaw, "Technology and Transformation in Academic Libraries," in *Libraries and the Search for Academic Excellence,* edited by Patricia Senn Breivik and Robert Wedgeworth (Metuchen, NJ: Scarecrow Press, 1988), 137–144.

11. Betsy Baker, "A New Direction for Online Catalog Instruction," *Information Technology and Libraries* 5 (March 1986): 36.

12. Oberman, "Avoiding the Cereal Syndrome, or Critical Thinking in the Electronic Environment," 191–192.

13. Betsy Baker, Mary M. Huston, and Maureen Pastine, "Making Connections: Teaching Information Retrieval," *Library Trends* 39 (Winter 1991): 210–222.

14. Breivik, *Information Literacy Revolution in the Library,* 105.

15. Baker, Huston, and Pastine, "Making Connections: Teaching Information Retrieval," 213–214.

16. Betsy Baker, "A Conceptual Framework for Teaching Online Catalog Use," *The Journal of Academic Librarianship* 12 (May 1986): 90–96.

17. Robert B. Reich, *The Work of Nations* (New York: Alfred A. Knopf, 1991), 228–230.

18. Sandra Whiteley, "Librarian's Library," *American Libraries* 24 (July/August 1993): 657.

19. Daniel Callison, "The Impact of New Technologies on School Library Media Center Facilities and Instruction," *Journal of Youth Services in Libraries* 6 (Summer 1993): 414–416.

20. "Cable TV Links Library of Congress with Colorado High School," *School Library Journal* 39 (July 1993): 14.

21. Callison, "The Impact of New Technologies on School Library Media Center Facilities and Instruction," 416.

22. *American Library Association Presidential Committee on Information Literacy Final Report,* 6.

23. "In Search of Scope and Sequence for Social Studies," *Social Education* 53 (October 1989): 386–387.

24. *American Library Association Presidential Committee on Information Literacy Final Report,* 7.

25. Patricia Senn Breivik, "Education for the Information Age," *New Directions for Higher Education* 78 (Summer 1992): 5–13.

26. K. Patricia Cross, "A Proposal to Improve Teaching or What 'Taking Teaching Seriously' Should Mean," *AAHE Bulletin* 39 (September 1986): 10–11.

27. Robert Burnheim and Anne Floyd, *Resource-based Teaching and Learning: A Workshop* (Queensland, Australia: Technical and Further Education-TEQ, 1992), ERIC Document ED 353 975, 5–7.

28. Keegan and Westerburg, "Restructuring and the School Library: Partners in an Information Age," 9–14.

29. Carol-Ann Haycock, "The Changing Role from Theory to Reality," in *School Library Media Annual*, Vol. 9, edited by Jane Bandy Smith and J. Gordon Coleman (Englewood, CO: Libraries Unlimited, 1991), 65.

30. Michael Bell and Herman L. Totten, "Cooperation in Instruction between Classroom Teachers and School Library Media Specialists," *School Library Media Quarterly* 20 (Winter 1992): 79–85.

CHAPTER SEVEN

1. David Gelman, "The Violence in Our Heads," *Newsweek* 122 (August 2, 1993): 48.

2. Donald D. Gainey, *Education for the New Century* (Reston, VA: National Association of Secondary School Principals, 1993), 13.

3. Richard Louv, *Childhood's Future* (Boston: Houghton Mifflin, 1990), 347–349.

4. James L. Thomas, "Prekindergarten Students in the Library Media Center," in *School Library Media Annual*, Vol. 9, edited by Jane Bandy Smith and J. Gordon Coleman (Englewood, CO: Libraries Unlimited, 1991), 3–12.

5. Larry Kopp, "Involving Parents in Small Schools," *NASSP Bulletin* 75 (May 1991): 89.

6. Louv, *Childhood's Future*, 333–369.

7. "Changing Role of the School Librarian," in *School Library Media Annual 1991*, Vol. 9, edited by Jane Bandy Smith and J. Gordon Coleman (Englewood, CO: Libraries Unlimited, 1991), 147–151.

8. Peggy Johnson, "Technological Change in Libraries," in *Encyclopedia of Library and Information Science*, Vol. 48, Supplement 11, edited by Allen Kent (New York: Marcel Dekker, 1991), 327–332.

9. Doris Ray, "Educational Technology Leadership for the Age of Restructuring," *The Computing Teacher* 19 (March 1992): 8–14.

10. Calvin L. Carpenter, "Plugging In to the Information Age," *The Computing Teacher* 19 (April 1992): 38–39.

11. Daniel Callison, "The Impact of New Technologies on School Library Media Center Facilities and Instruction," *Journal of Youth Services in Libraries* 6 (Summer 1993): 414–419.

12. Shirley L. Aaron, "The Collection Developer's Link to Global Education," *School Library Media Quarterly* 19 (Fall 1990): 40.

13. Ibid., 35–43.

14. Don H. Revill, "Performance Measures for Academic Libraries," in *Encyclopedia of Library and Information Science*, Vol. 45, Supplement 10, edited by Allen Kent (New York: Marcel Dekker, 1990), 306–312.

15. Gary Marchionini, "Technological Trends and Implications toward the New Millennium," in *School Library Media Annual*, Vol. 9, edited by Jane Bandy Smith and J. Gordon Coleman (Englewood, CO: Libraries Unlimited, 1991), 184.

16. "Changing Role of the School Library," 149.

17. John T. Gillespie and Diana L. Spirt, *Administering the School Library Media Center* (New York: R. R. Bowker, 1983), 68–79.

18. Ibid., 322.

19. Eleanor R. Kulleseid, "Cooperative Collection Development in the School Library Revolution," *The Bookmark* 50 (Fall 1991): 21.

20. Phyllis J. Van Orden and Adeline W. Wilkes, "School Library Media Centers and Networks," *Library Resources & Technical Services* 37 (January 1993): 7–10.

21. Ibid., 7–16.

22. Gillespie and Spirt, *Administering the School Library Media Center*, 323.

23. Kulleseid, "Cooperative Collection Development in the School Library Revolution," 21–23.

24. Ibid., 22.

25. Johnson, "Technological Change in Libraries," 334–336.

Selected Bibliography

Aaron, Shirley. "The Collection Developer's Link to Global Education." *School Library Media Quarterly* 19 (Fall 1990): 35-43.

Adams, Dory. Ed. "Did You Know That . . .? Have You Thought of . . .? *NAIS/EMSC Noteboard* (Spring 1993): N. Pag.

Alexander, Adrian W. and Carpenter, Kathryn Hammel. "Periodical Price Index for 1993." *American Libraries* 24 (May 1993): 390ff.

American Library Association Presidential Committee on Information Literacy Final Report. Chicago: American Library Association, 1989.

"America's F for Effort." *The Sunday Times* (March 14, 1993): 22–27.

Anderson, Charles. "The Multimedia Encyclopedia of Mammalian Biology." *Booklist* 89 (March 1, 1993): 1266.

Anglin, Gary J. Ed. *Instructional Technology Past, Present and Future.* Englewood, CO: Libraries Unlimited, 1991.

Antilla, Susan. "'I Want' Now Gets." *New York Times* Section 4A (April 4, 1993): 1.

Arms, Caroline. *Campus Strategies for Libraries and Electronic Information.* Rockport, MA: Digital Press, 1990.

Baker, Betsy. "A New Direction for Online Catalog Instruction." *Information Technology and Libraries* 5 (March 1986): 35–41.

———. "A Conceptual Framework for Teaching Online Catalog Use." *The Journal of Academic Librarianship* 12 (May 1986): 90–96.

Baker, Betsy; Huston, Mary M.; and Pastine, Maureen. "Making Connections: Teaching Information Retrieval." *Library Trends* 39 (Winter 1991): 210–222.

Baron, Joan Boykoff and Sternberg, Robert J. *Teaching Thinking Skills: Theory and Practice.* New York: W. H. Freeman, 1987.

Barr, Catherine. Ed. *The 1992 Bowker Annual Library and Book Trade Almanac.* 39th ed. New Providence, NJ: R. R. Bowker, 1992.

Barrett, Todd. "Be Careful What You Ask For." *Newsweek* 121 (February 15, 1993): 43.

Bell, Michael and Totten, Herman L. "Cooperation in Instruction between Classroom Teachers and School Library Media Specialists." *School Library Media Quarterly* 20 (Winter 1992): 79–85.

Benfer, Robert A.; Brent, Edward E., Jr.; and Furbee, Louanna. *Expert Systems*. Newbury Park, CA: Sage Publications, 1991.

Bitter, Gary G. "Artificial Intelligence: The Expert Way." *Media & Methods* 25 (May/June 1989): 22–25.

Borrell, Jerry. "America's Shame: How We've Abandoned Our Children's Future." *MACWORLD* 9 (September 1992): 25-30.

Branch, Eleanor. "Can Business Save Our Schools?" *Black Enterprise* 4 (March 1991): 39–50.

Brand, Stewart. *The Media Lab*. New York: Viking, 1987.

Breivik, Patricia Senn. "A Signal for the Need to Restructure the Learning Process." *NAASP Bulletin* 75 (May 1991): 1–7.

Breivik, Patricia Senn and Gee, E. Gordon. *Information Literacy Revolution in the Library*. New York: Macmillan, 1989.

Breivik, Patricia Senn and Wedgeworth, Robert. Eds. *Libraries and the Search for Academic Excellence*. Metuchen, NJ: Scarecrow Press, 1988.

Burke, Michael A. "Distance Education and the Changing Role of the Library Media Specialist." Syracuse, NY: ERIC Clearinghouse on Information Resources, 1989. ERIC Document ED 321 775.

Burnheim, Robert and Floyd, Anne. *Resource-based Teaching and Learning: A Workshop*. Queensland, Australia: Technical and Further Education, 1992. ERIC Document ED 353 957.

"Cable TV Links Library of Congress with Colorado High School." *School Library Journal* 39 (July 1993): 14.

Callison, Daniel. "The Impact of New Technologies on School Library Media Center Facilities and Instruction." *Journal of Youth Services in Libraries* 6 (Summer 1993): 414–416.

Carpenter, Calvin L. "Plugging In to the Information Age." *The Computing Teacher* 19 (April 1992): 38–39.

Carroll, Frances Laverne. *Recent Advances in School Librarianship*. Oxford, England: Pergamon Press, 1981.

Childs, Donald B. "Changing the School Environment to Increase Parent Involvement." *NASSP Bulletin* 75 (May 1991): 84–90.

"A Chip with Zip." *Time* 141 (April 5, 1993): 18.

Clark, Charles S. "Hard Times for Libraries." *CQ Researcher* 2 (June 26, 1993): 551–567.

Colwell, Lynn H. "School Library's Heritage Center: A Program You Can Make Your Own." *American Libraries* 19 (February 1988): 136–137.

Cook, William J. "The New Rockefeller." *U.S. News & World Report* 114 (February 15, 1993): 64–67.

———. "The Next Test for Bill Gates." *U.S. News & World Report* 114 (February 15, 1993): 70–72.

Craver, Kathleen W. "The Future of School Library Media Centers." *School Library Media Quarterly* 12 (Summer 1984): 266–284.

———. "Bridging the Gap: Library Services for Immigrant Populations." *Journal of Youth Services in Libraries* 4 (Winter 1991): 123–130.

Croneberger, Robert B. "External Influences on Public Library Management in the 21st Century." *Journal of Library Administration* 11 (No. 1) 1989: 209–220.

Cross, K. Patricia. "A Proposal to Improve Teaching or What 'Taking Teaching Seriously' Should Mean." *AAHE Bulletin* 39 (September 1986): 10–11.

Davidson, James Dale. "Boom or Bust: Two Views of Our Future." *The Futurist* 26 (September–October 1992): 10–14.

DeBroske, John M. "Electronic Reference—The School Library Revolution." *The Bookmark* 50 (Fall 1991): 19–20.

DeCandido, Grace Anne A. and Mahony, Alan P. "Overworked and Under-budgeted." *School Library Journal* 38 (June 1992): 25-29.

Doyle, Denis P. and others. "Educational Ideas & Strategies for the 1990s." *American Enterprise* 4 (March/April 1991): 25-33.

"Education Is the Ticket to Higher Earnings." *Census and You* 28 (April 1993): 1–16.

"The Elementary and Secondary School Library Media Act: Excerpts from the Congressional Record." Washington, DC. ALA Washington Office (October 1992): 1–5.

Elmer-DeWitt, Philip. "Take a Trip into the Future on the Electronic Superhighway." *Time* 141 (April 12, 1993): 50–55.

Etzioni, Amitai. "Social Science as a Multicultural Canon." *Society* 29 (November/December 1991): 14–18.

Ferrington, Gary and Loge, Kenneth. "Virtual Reality: A New Learning Environment." *The Computing Teacher* 19 (April 1992): 16–19.

"Five Budget Stretching Ideas." *The School Librarian's Workshop* 13 (June 1993): 1–16.

Gainey, Donald D. *Education for the New Century*. Reston, VA: National Association of Secondary School Principals, 1993.

Gardels, Nathan. "The Education We Deserve." *New Perspectives Quarterly* 7 (Fall 1990): 1–4.

Gayeski, Diane and Williams, David. *Interactive Media*. Englewood Cliffs, NJ: Prentice Hall, 1985.

Gelman, David. "The Violence in Our Heads." *Newsweek* 122 (August 2, 1993): 48.

Gerhardt, Lillian N. "Average Book Prices '93." *School Library Journal* 39 (March 1993): 94.

Gerhardt, Lillian N.; DeCandido, Grace Anne A.; and Mahony, Alan P. "SLJ News: 1991 Unfinished Business." *School Library Journal* (December 1991): 41–44.

Gillespie, John T. and Spirt, Diana L. *Administering the School Library Media Center*. New York: R. R. Bowker, 1983.

"Grammar Checkers." *PCWorld* 11 (April 1993): 103.

Guthrie, Judy and Crane, Beverly. "Online Retrieval Adds Realism to Science Projects." *The Computing Teacher* 19 (February 1992): 32.

Halal, William E. "The Information Technology Revolution." *The Futurist* 26 (July/August 1992): 10–15.

Hamburg, David A. "The American Family Transformed." *Society* 30 (January/February 1993): 60–69.

Handlin, Oscar. *The Uprooted*. Boston: Little, Brown, 1951.

Helsel, Sandra K. and Roth, Judith Paris. *Virtual Reality: Theory, Practice, and Promise*. Westport, CT: Meckler, 1991.

Hernon, Peter and McClure, Charles R. *Microcomputers for Library Decision Making: Issues, Trends and Applications*. Norwood, NJ: Ablex, 1986.

Hess, Susan. "Beyond Juan Morel Campus: Telecommunications Links for Learning." *The Bookmark* 50 (Fall 1991): 27–29.

Hooten, Patricia A. "Online Catalogs: Will They Improve Children's Access?" *Journal of Youth Services in Libraries* 2 (Spring 1989): 267–272.

"How Optical Character Recognition Works." *PC Computing* 6 (February 1993): 299–300.

"In Search of a Scope and Sequences for Social Studies." *Social Education* 53 (October 1989): 376–387.

Johnson, William B. and Packer, Arnold E. *Workforce 2000*. Indianapolis, IN: Hudson Institute, 1987.

Kamiani, Ratu and Mihok, Katherine. "How the World Will Look in 50 Years." *Time* 140 (Fall 1992, "The Century Ahead," special issue): 36–38.

Kantrowitz, Barbara. "Wild in the Streets." *Newsweek* 122 (August 2, 1993): 40–46.

Keegan, Bruce and Westerberg, Tim. "Restructuring and the School Library: Partners in an Information Age." *NASSP Bulletin* 75 (May 1991): 9–22.

Kennedy, Paul M. *Preparing for the Twenty-first Century*. New York: Random House, 1993.

Kent, Allen. Ed. *Encyclopedia of Library and Information Science*. Vol. 45. Supplement 10. New York: Marcel Dekker, 1990.

_____. Ed. *Encyclopedia of Library and Information Science*. Vol. 48. Supplement 11. New York: Marcel Dekker, 1991.

Kilpatrick, William. *Why Johnny Can't Tell Right from Wrong*. New York: Simon & Schuster, 1992.

Kondracke, Morton. "The Official Word How Our Government Views the Use of Computers in Schools." *MACWORLD* 9 (September 1992): 232–236.

Kopp, Larry. "Involving Parents in Small Schools." *NASSP Bulletin* 75 (May 1991): 89.

Kozol, Jonathan. *Savage Inequalities*. New York: Crown Publishers, 1991.

Krashen, Stephen. *The Power of Reading*. Englewood, CO: Libraries Unlimited, 1993.

Kulleseid, Eleanor R. "Cooperative Collection Development in the School Library Revolution." *The Bookmark* 50 (Fall 1991): 21–23.

Kurtenbach, Kris. "Library Power and Local Education Funds: An Ideal Partnership." *Library Power Newsletter* 1 (Spring 1993): 1–5.

Kurzweil, Raymond. "The Virtual Book Revisited." *Library Journal* 118 (February 15, 1993): 145.

Lance, Keith Curry; Welborn, Lynda; and Pennell, Christine Hamilton. *The Impact of School Library Media Centers on Academic Achievement*. Castle Rock, CO: Hi Willow Research and Publishing, 1993.

Lake, Donald T. "Art: Technologies in the Curriculum." *The Computing Teacher* 19 (March 1992): 44–45.

Lasch, Christopher. "Is Progress Obsolete?" *Time* 140 (Fall 1992, "The Century Ahead," special issue): 71.

"Latinos on the Rise." *The Futurist* 27 (January–February 1993): 48–49.

Leadership for the 90's. Final Report of the State Superintendent's Task Force on School Library Media Issues. Bulletin 91095. Madison, WI: Wisconsin

State Department of Public Instruction Division for Library Services, 1990. ERIC Document ED 329 279.

Lee, Felicia. "Disrespect Rules." *New York Times* Section 4A (April 4, 1993): 16.

Levinson, Marc. "The Trashing of Free Trade." *Newsweek* 122 (July 12, 1993): 42–45.

Lewis, Peter H. "Computer-to-Go Generation." *New York Times* Education Life Section A (April 4, 1993): 12–13.

Loertscher, David V. "Objective: Achievement Solution: School Libraries." *School Library Journal* 39 (May 1993): 30–33.

Louv, Richard. *Childhood's Future*. Boston: Houghton Mifflin, 1990.

McDonnell, Mary Ellen. "San Francisco GTV." *The Computing Teacher* 19 (February 1992): 37–38.

McGill, Michael V. "Humanity and Technology in the School of the Future." *The Bookmark* 50 (Fall 1991): 6–11.

McGuire, Stryker. "Immigrant Schools: The Wrong Lessons." *Newsweek* 122 (August 9, 1993): 23.

Machovec, George and Brunning, Dennis R. "Decision 2000: Moving beyond Boundaries." Paper presented at the Joint Conference of the Arizona State Library Association and the Arizona Educational Media Association. Phoenix, AZ: Arizona State Library Association, November 13–17, 1990. ERIC Document ED 332 705, 12–23.

Mansnerus, Laura. "Kids of the 90's: A Bolder Breed." *New York Times* Section 4A (April 4, 1993): 14–15.

Marchionini, Gary. "Tomorrow's Media Center: A Look into the Future." *Media & Methods* 28 (November/December 1991): 10–17, 77.

Martin, James A. "All about Scanners." *MACWORLD* 9 (October 1992): 150–155.

Mayo, John S. "R & D in the Third Millennium." *Vital Speeches of the Day* 59 (October 15, 1992): 26–29.

Mendrinos, Roxanne Baxter. "CD-ROM and At-Risk Students." *School Library Journal* 38 (October 1992): 29–31.

Miller, Marilyn. "The Birth of the Electronically Smart Media Center." *Media & Methods* 17 (November/December 1991): 77.

Miller, Marilyn L. and Shontz, Marilyn. "Expenditures for Resources in School Library Media Centers FY 1989–90." *School Library Journal* 37 (August 1991): 31–40.

———. "Expenditures for Resources in School Library Media Centers FY 1991–92." *School Library Journal* 39 (October 1993): 26–36.

Molholdt, Pat. "Libraries and the New Technologies." *Library Journal* 113 (November 15, 1988): 37–41.

Monk, Lee. "Distance Education: Learning from the Stars." *Media & Methods* 26 (January/February 1990): 8, 54.

Morganthau, Tom. "America: Still a Melting Pot?" *Newsweek* 122 (August 9, 1993): 16–23.

Murnane, Richard J. and Levy, Frank. "Why Today's High School–Educated Males Earn Less Than Their Fathers Did: The Problem and an Assessment of Responses." *Harvard Educational Review* 63 (Spring 1993): 1–19.

Naisbett, John. *Megatrends: Ten New Directions Transforming Our Lives*. New York: Warner, 1982.

"Nation's Population Projected to Grow by 50 Percent over Next 60 Years." *Census and You* 28 (January 1993): 1–17.

Nelson, Milo. "Crunching Knowledge: The Coming Environment for the Information Specialist." Paper presented at the 4th Annual Conference on Computers in Libraries. Oakland, CA: March 14–16, 1989. ERIC Document ED 322 913.

Newman, Richard J. "Your Digital Future." *U.S. News & World Report* 114 (April 5, 1993): 55.

Oberman, Cerise. "Avoiding the Cereal Syndrome, or Critical Thinking in the Electronic Environment." *Library Trends* 39 (Winter 1991): 189–202.

"One in Four of Nation's Foreign Born Arrived since 1985." *Census and You* 28 (February 1993): 1–16.

"Participants in Assistance Programs: A Profile." *Census and You* 28 (January 1993): 1–16.

Pelsma, Kimberlie. "CD-ROM and Information Literacy across the Curriculum." *Media & Methods* 26 (May/June 1990): 10, 52.

Penniman, David W. "Shaping the Future." *Library Journal* 117 (October 15, 1992): 40–44.

Perelman, Lewis J. *School's Out: Hyperlearning, the New Technology, and the End of Education.* New York: William Morrow, 1992.

Perritt, Patsy H. "School Library Media Certification Requirements for 1992 Update." *School Library Journal* 38 (June 1992): 30–49.

Philip, George. "Applications of Automatic Speech Recognition and Synthesis in Libraries and Information Services: A Future Scenario." *Library Hi Tech* 9 (March 1991): 89–92.

Pickover, Clifford A. Ed. *Visions of the Future.* New York: St. Martin's Press, 1992.

Piller, Charles. "Separate Realities." *MACWORLD* 9 (September 1992): 218–230.

Polly, Jean Armour. "NREN for All: Insurmountable Opportunity." *Library Journal* 118 (February 1, 1993): 38–41.

Postman, Neil. *Technopoly: The Surrender of Culture to Technology.* New York: Knopf, 1992.

Ray, Doris. "Educational Technology Leadership for the Age of Restructuring." *The Computing Teacher* 19 (March 1992): 8–14.

Reich, Robert. *The Work of Nations.* New York: Alfred A. Knopf, 1991.

Reiff, David. "Multiculturalism's Silent Partner." *Harper's* 287 (August 1993): 62–72.

Richardson, Jean L. and others. "Substance Use among Eighth Graders Who Take Care of Themselves after School." *Pediatrics* 84 (September 1989): 556–566.

Roberts, Mary Ellen. "CD-ROM Usage—Taking the Cues from Students." *Media & Methods* 26 (May/June 1990): 53.

Roblyer, M. D. "Electronic Hands across the Ocean: The Florida-England Connection." *The Computing Teacher* 19 (February 1992): 16–19.

Rogers, JoAnn V. "Real Information Power." *School Library Journal* 39 (March 1993): 113–117.

Rogers, Michael. "CD-ROM Is Still Shining Brightly at UMI." *Library Journal* 118 (March 15, 1993): 20.

Rosenberg, Jerry M. *Dictionary of Computers, Data Processing, and Telecommunications.* New York: Wiley, 1984.

Rubenstein, Robert E. "Changing Schools from Within." *The World & I* 8 (February 1993): 100–107.

Schiller, Scott S. "Educational Applications of Instructional Television and Cabling Programming." *Media & Methods* 2 (March/April 1991): 20–21, 52.

Schlesinger, Arthur M., Jr. *The Disuniting of America.* Knoxville, TN: Whittle Direct Books, 1991.

"School Population Explosion Predicted for Early 21st Century." *School Library Journal* 39 (April 1993): 14.

Schramm, Wilbur. *Big Media Little Media.* Beverly Hills, CA: Sage Publications, 1977.

Schuman, Patricia Glass. "Reclaiming Our Technological Future." *Library Journal* 115 (March 1, 1990): 34–38.

Seilor, Lauren H. "The Concept of Book in the Age of the Digital Electronic Medium." *Library Software Review* 11 (January-February 1992): 19–29.

Seligman, Jean and Hamilton, Kendall. "Husbands No, Babies Yes." *Newsweek* 122 (July 26, 1993): 53.

Simon, Senator Paul. "A Call for Progress." *School Library Journal* 39 (April 1993): 26–29.

Sizer, Theodore. *Horace's School: Redesigning the American High School.* Boston: Houghton Mifflin, 1992.

Smith, Eldred. *The Librarian, the Scholar and the Future of the Research Library.* Westport, CT: Greenwood Press, 1990.

Smith, Jane Bandy. Ed. *School Library Media Annual 1990.* Vol. 8. Englewood, CO: Libraries Unlimited, 1990.

Smith, Jane Bandy and Coleman, J. Gordon, Jr. Eds. *School Library Media Annual 1991.* Vol. 9. Englewood, CO: Libraries Unlimited, 1991.

———. Eds. *School Library Media Annual 1992.* Vol. 10. Englewood, CO: Libraries Unlimited, 1992.

Sowell, Thomas. *Inside American Education.* New York: Free Press, 1993.

"State and Local Taxes Grew 4.7 Percent in 1991; Smallest Increase since 1952." *Census and You* 28 (May 1993): 1–16.

Swan, John C. "Rehumanizing Information: An Alternative Future." *Library Journal* 115 (September 1, 1990): 178–182.

Swisher, Robert and others. "Telecommunications for School Library Media Centers." *School Library Media Quarterly* 19 (Spring 1991): 153–160.

"Technically Speaking on Information Navigation." *Connections* 1 (May 1993): 1–6.

"Teenage Shoppers." *The Futurist* 27 (January/February 1993): 46.

Tenopir, Carol. "Electronic Access to Periodicals." *Library Journal* 118 (March 1, 1993): 54.

Toch, Thomas. *In the Name of Excellence.* New York: Oxford University Press, 1991.

———. "The Perfect School." *U.S. News & World Report* 114 (January 11, 1993): 46–61.

———. "Inside the Ivy League." *U.S. News & World Report* 114 (April 12, 1993): 55–63.

Toffler, Alvin. *Previews and Premises.* New York: William Morrow, 1983.

"U.S. Hispanics: Challenges for the 1990s." *The Futurist* 23 (July–August 1989): 53.

Van Orden, Phyllis J. and Wilkes, Adeline W. "School Library Media Centers and Networks." *Library Resources & Technical Services* 37 (January 1993): 7–10.

Wallis, Claudia. "The Nuclear Family Goes Boom!" *Time* 140 (Fall 1992, "The Century Ahead, special issue): 42–44.

Wertheimer, Leonard. "Library Services to Ethnocultural Minorities: Philosophical and Social Bases and Professional Implications." *Public Libraries* 26 (Fall 1987): 98–102.

Wertheimer, Ruth Jacobs and Foy, Kathleen M. "Children of Immigrants and Multiethnic Heritage: Australia, Canada and the United States." *Library Trends* 28 (Fall 1980): 335–351.

Wetzel, Keith. "Speech Technology II: Future Software and Hardware Predictions." *The Computing Teacher* 19 (October 1991): 19–21.

Wheeler, Thomas C. Ed. *The Immigrant Experience: The Anguish of Becoming American.* New York: Dial Press, 1977.

"When Families Break Up." *Census and You* 28 (February 1993): 1–16.

Whiteley, Sandra. "Trends in Reference and Electronic Publishing." *Booklist* 88 (May 1, 1992): 1626.

_____. "Librarian's Library." *American Libraries* 24 (July/August 1993): 657.

Wilson, Barbara and Hubbard, Abigail. "Redefining the Role of School Media Specialists . . . Bridging the Gap." *Online* 53 (November 1987): 50–54.

Wirth, Arthur G. *Education and Work for the Year 2000.* San Francisco: Jossey-Bass Publishers, 1992.

Wood, George H. *Schools That Work: America's Most Innovative Public School Education Programs.* New York: Dutton, 1992.

Zoglin, Richard. "When the Revolution Comes What Will Happen to . . . " *Time* 141 (April 12, 1993): 56–58.

Zuckman, Jill. "The Next Education Crisis: Equalizing School Funds." *Congressional Quarterly* 51 (March 27, 1993): 749–754.

Index

About the Author

KATHLEEN W. CRAVER has been Head Librarian at the National Cathedral School in Washington, D.C., since 1987. Prior to that time, she was Associate Professor of Library Administration, University High School, University of Illinois at Urbana-Champaign. She received her Ph.D. in Library and Information Science from the University of Illinois in 1987, her M.L.S. from the University of California at Berkeley in 1974, her M.A. in Guidance and Counseling from the University of Michigan in 1971, and a B.S. from Ithaca College in 1967. Dr. Craver has been a school librarian in both public and private institutions for the past eighteen years. She is the author of numerous publications on school librarianship.